THE PROSPERING PARACHURCH

THE PROSPERING PARACHURCH

Enlarging the Boundaries of God's Kingdom

Wesley K. Willmer

J. David Schmidt

with Martyn Smith

Jossey-Bass Publishers
San Francisco

Scripture quotations are from the New Revised Standard Version of the Bible, copyright © 1989 by the Division of Christian Education of the National Council of the Churches of Christ in the United States of America.

Jossey-Bass books and products are available through most bookstores. To contact Jossey-Bass directly, call (888) 378-2537, fax to (800) 605-2665, or visit our website at www.josseybass.com.

Substantial discounts on bulk quantities of Jossey-Bass books are available to corporations, professional associations, and other organizations. For details and discount information, contact the special sales department at Jossey-Bass.

TCF Manufactured in the United States of America on Lyons Falls Turin Book. This paper is acid-free and 100 percent totally chlorine-free.

Library of Congress Cataloging-in-Publication Data

Willmer, Wesley Kenneth.
  The prospering parachurch: enlarging the boundaries of
  god's kingdom/Wesley K. Willmer and J. David Schmidt
  with Martyn Smith.—1st ed.
    p. cm.
  Includes bibliographical references and index.
  ISBN 0-7879-4198-0
  1. Religious institutions. 2. Church.   I. Schmidt,
  J. David (John David)   II. Smith, Martyn.   III. Title.
  BV900.W55   1998
  250—ddc21   98-25331

FIRST EDITION
HB Printing   10 9 8 7 6 5 4 3 2 1

CONTENTS

95683

PART FOUR
Where Is the Parachurch Headed?

LIST OF FIGURES

PREFACE

AT 11:15 P.M. ON SATURDAY evening, Rick Rood receives a call from a
Dallas hospital telling him that a family's elderly mother has just died and
the family would like a chaplain to pray and be with them during their
time of loss. So instead of crawling into bed, Rick drives in his five-year-
old car twenty minutes across town to spend time ministering to the spiritual needs of this family. Rick has a seminary degree; in addition he is an
ordained minister, and one of more than one hundred such people who
minister in hospitals around the country under the direction of a parachurch organization called Hospital Chaplains' Ministry of America
(HCMA). These chaplains raise their personal support and are more motivated by ministry as an expression of their Christian faith than by a career
of moves up a corporate ladder. Rick Rood and many others like him are
shaping a new parachurch paradigm that is enlarging the boundaries of
God's work well beyond the traditional church.

Our image of Christianity in the United States has long been that of a
small white church with a steeple in a New England town, surrounded by
fall colors, or a Gothic cathedral with altars and stained glass windows.
If you see this image on television or in a movie, you probably also hear
the hymn "Amazing Grace" wafting out through the door. The reality is
much larger and more complex. Increasingly, ministries are carried on
beyond church walls by people like Rick Rood who are part of parachurch organizations. Although the traditional or local church continues
to be a focus of many Christian activities, the parachurch is a growing
and significant force in God's kingdom.

Parachurch organizations such as camps, foreign missions, social services, prison ministries, and rescue missions and groups devoted to discipleship, relief and development, evangelism, literature, media, education,
outreach, and the like are not just playing an increasing role in U.S. religion; they have become an essential part of its definition. Studies now suggest that almost half of the giving to religion is going to parachurch
organizations, not to the traditional local churches or denominations.
Although many Christians have not noticed it, and many theologians

refuse to acknowledge it, there has been a paradigm shift of God's work, from church centered to kingdom centered.

Dozens of parachurch ministries, such as the American Bible Society, Navigators, Campus Crusade for Christ, Habitat for Humanity, Focus on the Family, World Vision, and the Billy Graham Evangelistic Association, hold prominent places on the *Chronicle of Philanthropy*'s list of the largest nonprofit organizations. Tens of thousands of smaller parachurch organizations, such as Turning Point, Olive Crest, Paxton Ministries, and Home Free Ministries, quietly carry out similar missions.

In the early 1980s, Jerry White wrote in *The Church and the Parachurch: An Uneasy Marriage,* "The proliferation of para-local church movements and organizations will be one of the distinguishing hallmarks of the last half of the twentieth century" (1983, p. 35). Similarly, Robert Wuthnow wrote that these organizations "have grown to such large proportions that they now appear to cast their imprint heavily on the character of American religion" (1988, p. 121).

It is estimated that parachurch organizations have grown more than a hundredfold in this century. This proliferation is viewed with alarm by some and guarded delight by others. Some panic as they view the dwindling influence of the traditional local church in our society and the growing strength of nontraditional institutions. Others see parachurch influence simply as a passing fad. Both miss the more significant reality that parachurch groups are religion gone entrepreneurial, as God expands his work by enlarging the boundaries of Christian ministry.

The parachurch (the term means *beside* or *beyond the church*) is a movement that has mushroomed, particularly since the end of World War II. Some estimate that organizations of the parachurch today could number up to 100,000. Although the parachurch has grown by leaps and bounds in size and influence, little has been done to describe, categorize, analyze, or understand it and its growth.

In 1992, we started to study the financing of the parachurch. The Lilly Endowment funded a grant for the study of "the financing of selected American Protestant parachurch religious organizations," and this exploratory study, initiated and directed by Wes Willmer, required extensive research with over 1,500 different parachurch organizations and resulted in eight books that described the financing of the parachurch for eight different parachurch constituent groups. This study also exposed the tremendous lack of information available on the entire parachurch and the need for a publication that gives people an understanding of the burgeoning and prospering parachurch.

To further confirm this need, seminaries across the country that were members of the Association of Theological Schools (ATS) were written to and asked, "Are you aware of any classes being taught, research such as dissertations being conducted, or other material available on the parachurch?" Most responded with no suggestions. The typical answer was, "I'm sorry. I know of no classes or research on the parachurch. I wish you well in pursuing this much-needed study." One seminary said it offers a class for managers in the parachurch, but the class does not describe or discuss the parachurch movement. Literature searches also confirmed that little information is available.

As a subset of the larger nonprofit sector, parachurch organizations form a vast, faith-based but largely hidden safety net in society today. They are not hidden because they are clandestine. They operate within the law, and are typically organized under IRS section 501(c)3 to accomplish their mission. Yet because their financial reports seldom show up in the *Wall Street Journal* or other publications, the organizational realities of the parachurch are largely unknown.

Moreover, for all of these organizations' numbers and impact on society, most people know very little about the day-to-day operations of typical parachurch organizations. Their information is like the information they have about the milk on their morning cereal. They have some vague idea that a cow, a farmer, and a milk truck have something to do with it, but they have given little thought to the strategic linkage, sequence, or organization that results in the milk-soaked cornflakes in front of them.

Where can you find a definition of the parachurch? Where is a taxonomy, a list of types, of parachurch organizations? Who has written a history explaining parachurch roots or growth? Where can you find a practical description of how the parachurch operates? Where can you find a discussion of where it is going and what the future holds? Our exploration turned up no definite answers to these questions. Therefore we concluded there is a tremendous need for this book and its explanation of the dramatic paradigm shift in God's work. A capstone to our research effort, this book tries to supply the information people need to understand the parachurch.

The Audience for This Book

The Prospering Parachurch will help the reader understand the enlarging nature, context, people, operations, and future of the growing parachurch. Presidents, board members, employees, laypeople, and scholars with an interest in religion should find its insights helpful. Those involved in both traditional churches and parachurch ministries should find it instructive in helping them be more effective. Practical-minded scholars, theologians, and researchers interested in bridging theory and practice, and also seminary students and faculty, can use it to better understand the significant place of the parachurch movement. Social scientists can find fresh clues for understanding the influence of the parachurch and the shifting religious paradigm. Similarly, many laypeople will identify with the ways God is working through the people of the parachurch to address the deepest needs of the human condition.

Overview of the Contents

Although there are many books on managing nonprofit organizations— how to run them, how to raise money for them, how to define the roles of their boards, and how to lead them—to our knowledge, *The Prospering Parachurch* is the only book to look at the parachurch movement as a whole and describe what it is, where it came from, how it operates, who supports it, and what its future is likely to be. This book looks at the unique challenges and role of the parachurch, made up of faith-based organizations operating from a Christian worldview and transforming Christianity in the new century.

To address all these issues, this book is divided into four parts. Part One (Chapters One through Four) deals with the nature and context of the parachurch by describing the depth and breadth of the parachurch, defining the parameters within which it operates, explaining the roots of its growth, and demonstrating the role it plays in bridging faith and culture. Part Two (Chapters Five through Eight) explores the people of the parachurch. Who are those who care about the parachurch (the stakeholders)? What are the responsibilities of the board, the leaders, and finally, the donors—all those who keep the parachurch operating? The third section (Chapters Nine through Twelve) turns a corner and explores how to enlarge parachurch impact by knowing strategically where you want to go, understanding where you are, and finding the way to reach the goals. In the final section some of the future issues that will face the parachurch are tackled, starting in Chapter Thirteen with how the parachurch should approach financial issues. The two remaining chapters (Fourteen and Fifteen) then look at the potential partnership of the church and parachurch and the future challenges to further parachurch proliferation.

Acknowledgments

Any undertaking like this book is the result of the work of a team of people, each of whom has uniquely provided his or her gifts, expertise, and encouragement to see the project completed. The embers that started the fire of this effort began with a request for a grant from the Lilly Endowment. Fred L. Hofheinz, program director, religion, and Craig Dykstra, vice president for religion, had the foresight to recommend that the Lilly Endowment fund exploratory research on the financing of selected American Protestant parachurch religious organizations. Without this grant and encouragement, our effort would not have moved forward.

The Lilly grant was made to the Christian Stewardship Association (CSA), and several CSA officers at the time were instrumental in the early stages of the effort. Norman Edwards (then president) and Stanley Thompson (then board chair) approved of the project. More recently, CSA president Brian Kluth and the full board supported the project.

From an early stage of the research, Jossey-Bass Religion-in-Practice Series editor Sara Polster expressed an interest and followed through with encouragement and advice about the final product, even while on leave from her job. Jossey-Bass editorial assistants Darren Hall and Jennifer Morley assisted the process as well.

Many parachurch personnel or former personnel were interviewed, observed, or consulted. They include Cliff Barrows of the Billy Graham Evangelistic Association; Mark Noll of Wheaton College; Jim Truxton, former president of the Mission Aviation Fellowship; Clyde Cook, president of Biola University; John Gration, former chair of the Department of Missions and Intercultural Studies at Wheaton College; and Doug McConnell, associate professor at Wheaton College and current chair of the Department of Missions and Intercultural Studies. Each contributed wisdom to this book.

Numerous people assisted with clerical and research help; they include Anne Creamer, Mickie Fisher, and Jennifer Cannon.

And lastly we acknowledge our families and co-workers, whose patient support allowed ideas to become sentences and sentences books.

August 1998

WESLEY K. WILLMER
La Mirada, California

J. DAVID SCHMIDT
Wheaton, Illinois

MARTYN SMITH
Pasadena, California

THE AUTHORS

WESLEY K. WILLMER AND J. David Schmidt have spent their entire collective professional careers of almost fifty years working with parachurch organizations around the world. They have been parachurch consultants, parachurch volunteers and professional staff, and recipients of parachurch services.

Wesley K. Willmer is vice president of university advancement and professor at Biola University, in La Mirada, California, with responsibility for enrollment management, alumni and university relations, marketing, development, and intercollegiate athletics. Previously he held professional positions at Seattle Pacific University, Roberts Wesleyan College, the Billy Graham Center, and Wheaton College.

In 1987, Willmer chaired the national conference *Funding the Christian Challenge,* which attracted nationwide media attention in such publications as *Christianity Today, U. S. News and World Report, Fund Raising Management,* and the *Washington Post.* In the last few years, he has initiated and obtained grants of more than $1 million to study and improve parachurch management practices. From 1992 to 1996, he served as chair of the board of the Christian Stewardship Association.

In addition to addressing various conferences and consulting to parachurch organizations in the field of resource development, Willmer has been author, editor, or editor-in-chief of sixteen books and many professional journal articles. In 1986, the Council for Advancement and Support of Education selected Willmer from among its 14,000 individual members at more than 2,800 institutions to receive its annual award for significant contributions in research and writing. In 1993, he was chosen from the same membership to serve on the National Commission on Philanthropy. *Fund Raising Management* magazine selected him to write its twenty-fifth anniversary issue on the future of funding religion.

Willmer earned a B.A. degree in psychology and an M.Ed. degree in counseling and guidance at Seattle Pacific University. His Ph.D. degree in higher education was granted by the State University of New York in

Buffalo. He resides in Fullerton, California, with his wife, Sharon, and three children, Brian, Kristell, and Stephen.

J. David Schmidt was born and raised in Pennsylvania, the son of a minister. He holds a B.A. degree from Nyack College and an M.A. degree in marketing and communications from Wheaton College in Illinois. He now resides in Wheaton, Illinois, with his wife, Melinda, and children, Kelly and Kevin.

In 1977, he founded the Wheaton-based management consulting firm J. David Schmidt and Associates. This agency provides organizational development counsel to Christian parachurch organizations, denominations, and churches. Schmidt has worked with scores of parachurch organizations and denominations, including many of the best known, such as the Billy Graham Evangelistic Association, Salvation Army, Southern Baptist Convention, and Willow Creek Association, and also many lesser known.

Schmidt is a regular speaker at conferences around the country and was recently recognized as one of the top ten speakers by the Christian Stewardship Association. He has written five devotional books, with 260,000 copies presently in print, and has published numerous articles and book chapters. His most recent book is *Choosing to Live: Financing the Future of Religious Body Headquarters* (1996).

Martyn Smith, of Pasadena, California, is a graduate of Prairie Bible College, an independent Christian college in Alberta, Canada, with strong ties to various parachurch missions and service organizations. Smith holds an M.A. degree in theology from Fuller Theological Seminary. He is a freelance writer and frequent presenter of seminars on religious and literary topics.

THE PROSPERING PARACHURCH

PART ONE

WHAT IS THE PARACHURCH AND WHY IS IT THRIVING?

THIS SECTION DEALS with the breadth and depth of the parachurch by defining its parameters and then explaining its historical roots and the part it continues to play in bridging faith and culture. The following questions are answered in the next four chapters:

- Where can you find the parachurch?
- How can it be defined and described?
- Where did the parachurch come from?
- How does the parachurch meet cultural needs?

GOD'S WORK ENLARGED

AN AVERAGE DAY for an average Christian family often begins with the sudden blare of a radio. Only it is not the latest pop hit that awakens the sleeping couple but a gentle Christian song. The station playing this song is one of hundreds in the United States devoted to Christian programming—enough to make Christian music and talk shows available to most Americans. James Dobson's popular radio program *Focus on the Family* is heard by over two million listeners every weekday and heads an ever-changing list of popular Christian programs.

As it is for many couples who both work, one of the first challenges of the day is to get the children ready and off to school. In this case the children cannot simply go to the corner and wait for a bus nor can they walk to the public school up the street. Their parents have decided to send them to an independent Christian school, which is a few miles from the house, and this means that every day the children must be driven to school. Our couple are not alone in their choice of an independent Christian school, about nineteen thousand church-affiliated schools exist in the United States.

After leaving the children at the Christian school, the mother drives to the office where she works. During her lunch hour she reads a chapter of her book—on this day it is *The God You're Looking For,* by Bill Hybels (1997), pastor of the Willow Creek Community Church. In a different week it could be a book by Charles Colson or Philip Yancey. Our working mother bought her book at the local Christian bookstore, one of the eight to nine thousand Christian bookstores that now exist in the United States. Each year the web of Christian publishers and bookstores grows stronger.

At the end of her day, as she walks out to her car, our mother spots something white under the windshield wiper. She expects an advertisement but is surprised to find a Christian tract that explains in simple terms the way to salvation. Looking around, she sees the same white tract on the windshields of the surrounding cars. Once again the parachurch has made its presence felt in her life. Parachurch organizations such as Campus Crusade for Christ or Jews for Jesus have been so effective in their efforts that it is hard for the average person not to come across a presentation of the Gospel regularly.

Later that evening, after dinner and as the children play with friends, our average couple watch the evening news. Again it is not long before parachurch organizations are brought to their attention. Perhaps it is local coverage of a house being built by Habitat for Humanity, or maybe it is a brief human interest spot about a humanitarian organization such as Heifer Project International, which provides livestock to needy people all over the world, or maybe it is a follow-up on what is happening with Promise Keepers; whichever the particular organization, the parachurch is in the news—and often.

Now at the end of the day but also the end of the month, the father decides to work through some of the family's bills. After the gas and electric and credit card bills, he writes a customary check to the local rescue mission and to a missionary couple in Latvia who serve with Greater Europe Mission. The parachurch has come to have an important place in the financial life of Christians. The couple give generously to their church, but they feel there are other Christian organizations whose work they also want to support.

Modern Christians, like this average couple, have grown as used to the parachurch as they have to telephones, televisions, and computers. The parachurch has become embedded in our daily Christian lives, and we would feel lost if the services and ministries of these independent organizations disappeared all of a sudden. For example, reflecting on their upbringing in Columbia, North Carolina, Nathan Hatch and Michael Hamilton recalled the strength of the religious life and the many churches that lined the streets. They wrote that, nevertheless, this "religious life had a one dimensional quality, being confined largely to church programs and activities. The broader culture was mildly supportive of Christian belief, but churches had a virtual monopoly on winning the lost and sustaining the faithful" (Hatch and Hamilton, 1992, p. 21). We have become so used to the parachurch that we forget how new it is. The local church still provides the rhythm of Christian life with its weekly worship and fellowship opportunities, but parachurch organizations have added new options for every Christian.

The Many Ministries of the Parachurch

Many Christians have not reflected on the way the parachurch has radically transformed Christian life and do not realize the degree to which the parachurch has entered their own lives. But the parachurch is much broader than any one individual's life. The variety of parachurch ministries is astounding, and most individuals catch only a small glimpse of their breadth. There are big-name organizations such as Campus Crusade for Christ, World Vision, American Bible Society, Gideons International, or Youth for Christ that a large percentage of Christians recognize, but there is also a universe of smaller organizations whose combined impact is tremendous.

Many organizations go unnoticed because they address a highly specialized need. People who are not connected to the large deaf community, for example, will probably not know that Deaf Missions, based in Corona, California, is translating the Bible into American Sign Language. The translation will be recorded on a series of videotapes, whose total running time will be over two hundred hours. It is a project that will provide the scripture to many thousands of the deaf and hearing impaired in their primary language.

Other parachurch organizations take as their task upbuilding those already working in Christian ministry. John Maxwell recognized in the mid-eighties that there were few available resources for pastors and other Christian leaders. In response to this need, he began to hold seminars for these leaders. The mission statement for his organization, INJOY Ministries, expresses his purpose of "developing leaders of excellence and integrity by providing the finest resources and training for personal and professional growth" (Rabey, 1997, p. 6). Maxwell's organization now has about ninety employees and reaches over fourteen thousand Christian leaders each month.

The Jericho Road Cooperative Computer Ministry in Memphis, Tennessee, illustrates another way that some parachurch organizations serve as support ministries. This small organization is headed by Rich Cook and Nathan Hill, who refurbish used computers and donate them to faith-based organizations such as schools, children's homes, and food pantries. In addition to making the gifts of hardware, Jericho Road performs free setup and installation. In a recent project a homeless women's shelter received a computer network for five users.

A host of parachurch organizations have taken up the calling of evangelism. The thousands of organizations that actively engage in evangelism use diverse methods. Athletes in Action, among other ministries, sponsors an exhibition basketball team made up of former professional and college players. This team plays against such big-name universities as Indiana, Kentucky, and the University of California at Los Angeles. During pre-game meals members of the team have an opportunity to present the Gospel to the opposing team. Another organization, Re-enactors Missions for Jesus Christ, has taken a very different approach to the same task of evangelism. Its focus is unique: it reprints religious tracts from the Civil War era and hands them out to participants in reenactments of Civil War battles. To date its members have distributed more than 750,000 tracts and recorded seven hundred professions of faith.

Evangelism is a major concern for parachurch organizations, but a large number are also involved in social concerns. Buses International turns old yellow school buses into traveling medical and dental clinics. These refurbished buses are then sent to places like Mexico, Honduras, and El Salvador, and missionaries recruit volunteer doctors and dentists to take medical tours through destitute areas.

Parachurch organizations are also supporting environmental efforts. The Eden Conservancy, founded by Roy Goble, buys acres of tropical rain forest to protect them from development and destruction. Recently the conservancy purchased more than three thousand acres in Belize.

The social work being done by the parachurch comes in almost as many varieties as evangelistic work. A huge parachurch organization such as World Vision International serves annually somewhere around fifty million people in one hundred different countries. Fundraising for World Vision brings in about $300 million annually, and these funds are disbursed to numerous small programs. World Vision is a parachurch giant, but for every large organization, there are hundreds that work on the local level. One such organization is Marriage Savers in Bethesda, Maryland, which helps cities reduce their divorce rates through clergy networking and encouragement of premarital counseling.

Finally, there are the parachurch organizations that fit into no single category. FCA Golf Ministry in Florida, for example, holds junior golf camps during the summer, and teens are challenged to improve their spiritual health as well as hone their golf skills. The parachurch has a knack for breaking out of molds.

There is no easy way to categorize many of the ministry opportunities that spiritually motivated leaders have discovered, and the examples here are only the barest tip of the iceberg. On and on we could go with examples of small parachurch organizations that are run independently of any traditional church or denomination, each working in its own ministry niche. Browsing through the taxonomy in the Resource will reveal still more varieties of parachurch ministries. The opportunities for parachurch organizations are endless, and they blow the lid off any attempt to limit God's work to the traditional church setting.

Moreover, these organizations are reaching great numbers of people. Campus Crusade for Christ estimates that in one year, 7.1 million viewers saw the film *Jesus*. In one year Gideon International distributed thirty-eight million Bibles in seventy languages to 158 countries. Over a half century, Billy Graham crusades have reached one hundred million people in person and two billion people on television. In one year Good News Mission of Richmond, Virginia, saw 16,039 prison inmates make a first-time commitment to Christ. And daily, the Los Angeles Union Rescue Mission provides 3,200 meals to the needy.

The Parachurch Meets Individual Needs

Such statistics prove that the parachurch is prospering, but they do nothing to explain its growth. The reason for the growth becomes clear only as we examine the lives of individuals who have been changed by the parachurch.

Finding a Navigator

Dr. Chris Grace grew up in a family that was nominally Roman Catholic. High moral standards were kept, but there was little emotional commitment to the faith. The large family Bible was used more as a prop to hold up the other books on the shelf than as a source for spiritual guidance. His experience was like that of the many other nominal Christians—Roman Catholic or Protestant—who grow up with only a hazy connection to a church and a faith.

Once in college Chris looked for something more in life. Brief experimentation with alcohol and drugs brought no satisfaction, and he remembers feeling lonely and lacking purpose. He prayed to the vague God remembered from drowsy Sunday mornings that he would make himself known. Chris had deep spiritual needs but had no idea where to find answers, or whom to ask for help, or what words to pray.

The answers came from an unexpected source: the registration line at the University of Northern Colorado. The school's various clubs and services had set up booths to attract new students. Among them was a booth for the Navigators, a parachurch organization that ministers primarily to young people in college and the military. At this unassuming booth, Chris was handed a simple survey asking four questions about his ideas on spiritual issues. From the questions, Chris realized how little he knew about Christianity. He checked the box at the end of the survey to indicate he would like to know more about God.

A short time later a Navigator showed up at Chris's dorm room. He could answer the questions Chris had, and give him the big picture of what it meant to have faith in Christ. Chris learned that every person was separated from God by sin and that Christ was the bridge by which men and women could return to God. It was a standard Evangelical presentation of the Gospel. Chris responded enthusiastically. He not only accepted Christ into his heart but gathered a number of dorm friends for a Bible study. Within a few months, Chris found himself part of a large Christian community. Once a week he attended a small Bible study, once a week he met for one-on-one discipling, and once a week he went to a large gathering for all the Christian groups on campus.

Chris's spiritual conversion is different in one important way from the typical experience of past Christians: nowhere is there mention of a church. Chris remembers that the Navigators encouraged him to attend church, and he went on occasion. But because he was involved with the tight-knit college groups, he never felt the need to be a member of a church. When he became engaged to a Christian woman, the couple were counseled and married by a Navigator—not by a local minister. It was not until five or six years had passed and Chris had found a teaching position at Biola University, a Christian university in California, that he became actively involved with a local church.

Chris's story tells us that the prospering parachurch has a human face. The parachurch has grown because it meets the spiritual needs of thousands and thousands of individuals who, like Chris, have a hunger for spiritual reality. Chris felt an emptiness inside and wanted to know God. It was not a traditional church that met this need and showed him the way to faith; it was a parachurch organization.

Finding Old-Time Religion

Luetta Hensley was born and raised in West Virginia, back in the first decade of the twentieth century. She does not recall that the church she attended was part of any denomination. Visiting pastors preached to the congregation, and an occasional evangelist came through the area. But these itinerant speakers conveyed a common message of sin and redemption and took the Bible seriously. Old-time Gospel music surrounded Luetta. Her father taught music and led the choir, and still today she loves to sing the old favorites "Just as I Am" and "Amazing Grace."

In the Depression years, Luetta and her husband moved to Pittsburgh, where there was work. Here they began to attend a Presbyterian church. In contrast to the message Luetta was accustomed to, the sermons at this church were apt to be entitled "How to Be Happy." For Luetta the "basics" were not right. There was no serious talk about living the Christian life.

What was missing from her new church, Luetta found on the radio. Each Sunday, Luetta, her husband, and two children gathered around their small radio and listened to the Bible message of Charles Fuller on the *Old Time Revival Hour.* She also got her weekly dose of gospel music from Fuller's broadcast. At a time when those around her did not share her faith, Luetta was able to find spiritual nourishment in these programs. Fuller's parachurch ministry, based in Southern California, extended its touch to Pittsburgh, Pennsylvania, to encourage and teach a family hungry to hear the old-time Gospel.

After a few years Luetta and her family moved to California and joined a conservative Baptist church. Even after they were once again part of a Bible-teaching church, the radio's impact did not diminish for them. Billy Graham's *Hour of Decision* and J. Vernon McGee's *Talk Thru the Bible* became favorite broadcasts. "You need good Bible study on Monday as well as Sunday" is Luetta's reason why the radio remained an important part of her life. Millions of other Christians would agree with her. No church is able to provide all the resources needed to sustain a Christian in this postmodern age. The parachurch reaches into the lives of Christians seven days a week, fulfilling special needs that the traditional church lacks the resources to meet.

The parachurch thrives because it meets the needs of people like Chris Grace and Luetta Hensley. Both found their spiritual thirst slaked by the ministry of parachurch organizations. The vast array of parachurch organizations is a direct result of the diversity of spiritual needs that can be found in the United States and all over the world. Parachurch organizations love to throw around huge numbers: Ten million people reached! One hundred thousand New Testaments distributed! Five thousand graduates on the mission field! These are valuable numbers, but they often obscure the true reason for success: the fact that the parachurch has been able to change the lives of countless individuals.

The Parachurch Enlarges the Tent of God's Work

For centuries Christians have been comfortable with an understanding that God works in this world through the traditional church, through denominations. But in the last fifty years, the strength of the independent parachurch has grown by leaps and bounds. The phenomenon of the para-church no longer fits into the easy ideas of the past. Church growth expert David Barrett estimates that monetary giving to the parachurch has now surpassed giving to traditional churches. Although there are no exact fig-ures, Barrett (1997, p. 24) believes that worldwide $100 billion is being given to parachurch organizations, whereas traditional churches receive a little less than $94 billion. According to Barrett, this monetary gap be-tween the church and parachurch will grow more pronounced in the next century.

The human tendency is to make God small, to fit God into an easy con-tainer, one that everyone understands and accepts. Theologians fall into this trap when they tightly define each step to salvation, making it appear that God follows a set formula when dealing with each person. And Christians make the exact same limiting mistake when they assume that God works only through the traditional church. The apostle Paul coun-ters this human tendency when he breaks into the doxology: "O the depth of the riches and wisdom and knowledge of God! How unsearchable are his judgments and how inscrutable his ways!" (Romans 11:33).

The ancient Israelites had a God who was too small. They wanted a national God who would help them when times got bad and help their country to prosper. But God has never limited his aims to one nation. The story of Jonah and his missionary trip to the foreign city of Ninevah paints in clear colors the great concern of Israel's God: the salvation of all people. Through the prophet Isaiah, God tells Israel of his plan for them: "I will give you as a light to the nations, that my salvation may reach to the end of the earth" (Isaiah 49:6). This was not an easy message to hear. The Israelites' pride was in the fact that they were God's chosen people, the treasured possession (Deuteronomy 7:6). To follow God's greater vision, they had to go through a paradigm shift: "Enlarge the site of your tent, and let the curtains of your habitations be stretched out; do not hold back; lengthen your cords and strengthen your stakes" (Isaiah 54:2).

Using this metaphor of a tent, God taught the people of Israel that their conception of God's work was too small. The nation of Israel was not geographically defined, and not a private club with an exclusive member-ship, but a nation that was to expand and include every foreign nation—a holy kingdom of God. The small tent had to be enlarged; the people's conception of God's kingdom had to be broadened.

An analogy can be made between the paradigm shift Israel had to go through and the position of the Christian church at the beginning of the twenty-first century. The Catholic Church has long had a broad accep-tance of various orders and societies that also pursued ministry. But after the Reformation, the Protestants frowned on such orders "outside" the church, and the traditional church became the prime vehicle for all ministry. Throughout this time, there were still individuals and organizations that pursued ministry beyond the sacred walls of the traditional church, and many of them were cautiously accepted by Christians, but there has always been an unvoiced guilt as well. Individuals who chose to work beyond the church have had to be defensive and to explain why they chose to minister independently of the traditional church.

There is a message for us in the well-documented trend of parachurch growth, and it is similar to the message Isaiah brought to his fellow Israelites: the tent must be enlarged. Christians in North America and all over the world have drawn the boundaries for God's work woefully short. We have set up our own tent and defined how and where God may work. The stunning success of the parachurch forces us to pull up those hammered stakes and enlarge the human boundaries that limit God's work. This book is a continuation of the long process of adjusting human understanding to the true extent of God's kingdom.

2

DEFINING THE PARACHURCH BOUNDARIES

AS WE HAVE SEEN, the parachurch is significantly influencing individuals throughout this country and the world. Robert Bork, in his book *Slouching Towards Gomorrah* (1996), credited the parachurch organization Promise Keepers with doing more to restore the moral tone of society in a few years than traditional churches have achieved after decades of effort. Yet, even after all this success, the word *parachurch* remains poorly understood. Although the names of specific parachurch organizations are recognizable to almost every Christian, even people who are connected to church life will respond to the word with a quizzical expression. Chapter One provided glimpses of how the parachurch has prospered, and now Chapter Two turns to explaining the concept, to drawing boundary lines, or parameters, for the parachurch, so that it can be more readily understood.

The word itself is easy to define. The prefix *para* comes from the Greek and means "beside" or "beyond." In its most general sense, then, the parachurch is made up of organizations that are not part of the traditional, organized church, yet that are engaged in churchlike activities. The parachurch is the *beside-church*, trying to do God's work alongside the traditional church.

Theological tomes through the centuries have discussed and analyzed the church, but only recent books will mention the word *parachurch*. The word was not coined until the late 1960s, when it was first applied to small gatherings of Christians that took place outside institutional churches. We can learn something more about the parachurch from two similar words that entered our vocabulary at roughly the same time, *paramedic* and *paralegal*. The paramedic is the person who arrives with the ambulance and is trained to give emergency care but whose primary job is to get the patient to a doctor. This paramedic supplements and extends the work of trained doctors. The paralegal provides a similar service for the legal profession. Both of these services take on a naturally subordinate position to the professions they assist.

What makes the parachurch such a lightning rod of controversy is that its subordinate role is often questionable. It is as if the paramedics who arrive in response to an emergency were to become so proficient at their jobs that a trip to the hospital would be often unnecessary. In that scenario a rivalry would quickly develop between the "real" doctors at the traditional hospital and the paramedics with their mobile hospital (offering in-house service and cheaper rates!). The parachurch faces a similar controversy. Groups like the Promise Keepers grab headlines with stadiums full of spiritually hungry men and have budgets in the millions of dollars after a few short years, but meanwhile there are local churches, both small and large, that are struggling to survive and that feel their resources being drained off by these parachurch organizations. These groups that by definition are beside the church have taken on a life of their own.

By 1981, the word *parachurch* was familiar enough to be on the cover of *Christianity Today* ("Parachurch Proliferation"), and it has now become widely used. Of course not everyone has taken to it. When Robert Wuthnow discussed groups like Campus Crusade and World Vision in his book *The Restructuring of American Religion,* he opted to call them *special purpose groups* (1988, pp. 181–182). And church historians often call these groups *voluntary societies.* But it appears now that after almost two thousand years of church life, many people are adopting the new word because it provides a succinct way to refer to a recognizable type of organization that has become increasingly visible in religious life.

There are basic areas of agreement as to what constitutes a parachurch organization. *The Dictionary of Christianity in America* gives a definition that covers the main points: "Voluntary, not-for-profit associations of Christians working outside denominational control to achieve some specific ministry or social service" (Reid, 1990, p. 863). J. Alan Youngren, defining the term in an article for *Christianity Today,* touched on the same points: "not-for-profit, organized Christian ministry to spiritual, mental, and physical needs, working outside denominational control" (1981, p. 39).

Since these definitions were written, parachurch organizations have multiplied and taken on a life of their own so that refinements are needed.

Here are four litmus tests that an organization must pass to qualify as a parachurch organization:

○ Test 1: Is the group organized as a nonprofit?

○ Test 2: Does the group have a Christian mission statement?

○ Test 3: Is the group independent of traditional church structures?

○ Test 4: Does the group work at one or more specific ministries or services?

These four tests, taken together and with reasonable allowance for exceptions, provide a good means of determining what constitutes a parachurch organization. And within each test, there is a broad spectrum of acceptability. The first two tests separate parachurch and church organizations from the broad array of secular nonprofit organizations. The final two tests separate the parachurch from denominational enterprises.

Most religious organizations that are not churches are parachurch organizations; they fall clearly and obviously into the parameters represented by these tests. Mission Aviation Fellowship (MAF) is a textbook example. Its specific ministry is to "multiply the effectiveness of the church by using aviation and other strategic technologies to reach the world for Christ" (Christian Management Association, 1997, pp. 5–6). Missionaries need not be part of any particular denomination in order to be assisted in their work by MAF. Because its technicians and pilots raise their own support, MAF is not under the authority of any larger group, and it is organized as a nonprofit.

Other groups do not fit so neatly into the definition. Consider a number of women who work at the same crowded downtown office and discover that they share a common Christian faith. They may decide that during their lunch hour they will have a short prayer meeting or Bible study. When they gather in a group, they meet many of the criteria for being a parachurch: their mission, though maybe not written down, is Christian; they are outside denominational control; and their specific purpose is spiritual encouragement. The test this group of women does not pass, however, is the nonprofit organization test. The women are not quite organized enough to be classified as a parachurch group.

Even though most religious organizations that are not churches are, like MAF, easily recognizable as parachurch organizations, many more do not fall so neatly into the category, and this makes it helpful to consider the four tests more closely. Perhaps the story of Stan will make the parameters clearer. Stan is fictitious, but his story is typical.

Stan the Carpenter

Stan is a carpenter—has been since he was nineteen. He lives in a city nestled quietly someplace in America. Since he was a kid, Stan has attended the small local church in his neighborhood, but once he gets into the work world his attention is concentrated on his job and making money for his family. For years he has given little thought to his church. Then, as happens with many people, there comes a time when he is not satisfied. He looks around at all the wonderful things he has acquired and at the family he loves, but something is missing from his life. For Stan this happens when he is in his late thirties. He is financially secure and now owns his own construction business, but spiritually he feels empty. One Sunday the pastor of the small church seems to be talking directly to him. The text for the pastor's sermon comes from the Sermon on the Mount. Jesus urges his disciples not to store up treasures on the earth but to strive to lay up treasures in heaven. Stan has heard those words many times before, but this time they are different. It dawns on him that he has worked hard to surround himself with treasures on earth, not in heaven. The pastor ends the sermon with a challenge to his small congregation, sitting in their slightly uncomfortable seats. He challenges them to look at their lives, and find ways to store up eternal treasure, working for what will truly last, not what will fade away.

That week Stan talks with his pastor about how to use his time and money to help the church. Stan's ideas are far-fetched at first: Should he sell his business and devote all his time to serving God? But his pastor has a different idea. He points out to Stan that God has given him certain skills and resources. Their small church is in poor repair. It needs fixing here and there, and there are always the expansion plans the church has dreamed about. Stan has noticed the problems many times, but never considered what he could do. Of course Stan cannot do everything or provide all the materials, but the pastor challenges Stan to find ways to use his talent for God—and that talent is his expertise as a carpenter and handyman.

Stan volunteers one day each week to work on the church, carrying out the church's dream of refurbishing the sanctuary. Stan's newfound energy is contagious, and a number of other men and women from the church show up to help him in this project. Stan feels that finally he is working for more than just his own selfish goals. As Stan matures in his Christian commitment, he meets men and women from other churches and finds that he has much in common with their spiritual commitment. When, after several months, his work on his own church is done, he wonders if perhaps he can extend his new ministry to other local churches, whose buildings are also in need of repair. He begins to offer his services to these churches and finds that many of them are eager for his help. Several men from various churches volunteer their services one day a week as well. Now Stan has a small group formed, which is able to provide services for the local churches. However, it is still just a group of volunteers, with no formal structure.

Yet this nucleus of men and women meets with unanticipated demand. Stan sees that churches all over his portion of the county need minor repairs and help on expansion projects. Stan sets his sights high and envisions a large network of people who volunteer their time and work to repair old church buildings. To reach his new goal, he must raise support from people who appreciate his ministry, and he must make churches and potential volunteers aware of his work. To accomplish these latter goals, Stan decides to start a formal organization. The most natural structure for it is that of a nonprofit organization, which will allow him to receive tax-deductible donations and let him promote an official group: the Christian Carpenter Squad.

At the level of parachurch, there is plenty of room to grow. Stan is limited only by his own vision, by the demand for his services, and by donor support. If the physical decay of church buildings were a national crisis, the Christian Carpenter Squad could find itself with a million-dollar budget in a few short years. More likely the group will have moderate success on a local scale. Stan will probably never make the cover of *Christianity Today*, but a parachurch organization has been born!

Test 1: Is the Group Nonprofit?

Test 1 in particular can be visualized through Stan's story. At the beginning Stan simply started doing individual volunteer work. By taking this step, he joined the millions of men and women who do volunteer work for a group or cause they believe in. Thousands of church treasurers, Sunday school teachers, pianists, and choir directors will recognize the impulse of faith that drove Stan to volunteer his time working for his church.

A further step was taken when a number of other men and women in the church regularly volunteered their time to help with the work. As soon as a number of people volunteer their time, some kind of informal structure is added. By the nearest estimates, some four out of ten Americans are involved in small-group gatherings, whether they be for Bible study, book discussion, or support groups (Wuthnow, 1994b, p. 369). The women mentioned earlier who meet for a prayer meeting during their lunch hour fall under this category of small groups. These unstructured groups do not meet the first parachurch litmus test of being organized nonprofits. Such volunteering is certainly important in U.S. church life, but parachurch organizations have a higher level of structure than these loosely formed groups.

At the point a formal nonprofit group is established, it has met one criterion for moving into the realm of the parachurch—the center portion of Figure 2.1. Certainly Stan's work before he formed a nonprofit organization accomplished the same things it did afterwards. But incorporation as a nonprofit nevertheless makes a needed distinction between the thousands of groups that do regular volunteer work and those that are part of the phenomenon of the parachurch.

Some organized groups do avoid becoming nonprofit organizations—perhaps they want to avoid paperwork or the time demanded by incorporation. For this reason there is no absolute wall at the left end of the parachurch portion of Figure 2.1 signifying which groups are in or out; the oval representing the parachurch should be thought of more as a semipermeable membrane. Yet most groups find the advantages of nonprofit status to be desirable. The handbook *How to Form a Nonprofit Corporation* (Mancuso, 1996, p. 12) gives a few of them. Incorporating as a nonprofit

- Is required to get grant funds
- Provides tax exemption to donors
- Makes low-cost mailing permits available
- Affords protection from individual legal responsibility
- Establishes organizational structure

Any group that involves a large number of people or that has a need to raise money will find it helpful to incorporate. As Stan raised his sights to helping a large number of churches, for example, the step of incorporation became necessary.

Figure 2.1. Test 1: Is the Group Organized as a Nonprofit?

Independent/ Unorganized	Nonprofit Parachurch		For Profit
Individual/Group Volunteering	Loosely Organized	Highly Organized	

Within the parachurch, there are of course different degrees of structure. At one extreme, for example, there are small Christian camps with budgets that barely meet the expenses. At the other extreme are those parachurch organizations that resemble multinational corporations, complete with CEO and board and huge budgets. Yet all these groups, from the smallest to the largest, are included in the spectrum of parachurch organizations. They are united in being structured organizations that work at a Christian ministry or service independent of for-profit companies or the traditional church. The first test for defining the sprawling parachurch, with its vast array of services and differences in size, is to recognize the importance of nonprofit status. This is the test that separates loose volunteerism from the phenomenon of the parachurch.

Test 2: Does the Group Have a Christian Mission Statement?

Traditionally we have thought of the United States as split into two major sectors: public and private (Drucker, 1995). The public sector is represented by the government, and the private is made up of businesses. Politicians and writers of editorials haggle over how much power should be left in the hands of the government and which social problems may be best combated by the private sector, but in recent years the growing third sector has become a major force. This third sector of our society is made up of voluntary organizations; it is the *nonprofit sector*. Peter F. Drucker, in his book *Managing in a Time of Great Change,* states that there are now about one million organizations registered as nonprofit in the United States (1995, p. 255). Of these, roughly 70 percent have formed in the last thirty years. The parachurch is a slice of this nonprofit sector, and the growth of the parachurch is connected to the growth in importance of this large sector of our national life.

What distinguishes a parachurch organization from the crowd of other nonprofits is the *church* part of the word. This identifies the organization as having a special purpose and a specifically religious—and Christian—orientation. Thus, part of the job of defining the parachurch is to define what it means to be a "Christian" organization, and the harder one looks, the harder it is to define a Christian organization. This would seem to be an easy task: broadly speaking we can say that a Christian organization in some way draws its purpose and goals from the New Testament message of salvation through Christ. So groups interested in evangelism and conversions are obviously Christian. But many are not so obvious. An organization may have the word *Christian* in its title simply by the accident of historical origin, and when asked about religious matters, its leadership may deny any particular religious stance. Other organizations, such as some hospitals, may have a driving Christian vision behind them, but it can be difficult to pinpoint in what way they are Christian when they perform the same service as many secular hospitals and when so many of the people who are employed are doctors or nurses with no specific religious convictions. Once again there is a continuum: on the one side are groups that are unquestionably Christian, and on the other side are groups that are secular, with perhaps a tenuous faith connection. Between these two extremes fall many organizations, scattered all over the spectrum.

Thomas Jeavons has analyzed how a religious organization may be identified (1992, pp. 10–28) and has proposed several questions to determine the degree of religious commitment.

○ Do most of the participants in the organization share a common faith?

○ Does the support for the organization come from religious donors?

○ Is the end product connected to religious values?

Along with these questions, Jeavons formulated some charts that hone the definition of a religious organization. The questions can be answered by conducting interviews with everyone involved, and that may be the most accurate way to identify a religious organization, but it is also time consuming. A look at the organization's mission statement is the quickest way to determine whether it has a religious orientation (see Figure 2.2).

A mission statement is a legal necessity for a nonprofit organization. In this mission statement, the nonprofit puts forward its intended purposes and goals. In the case of a parachurch organization the mission statement will reflect Christian values and goals. All the activities of the organization

Figure 2.2. Test 2: Does the Group Have a Christian Mission Statement?

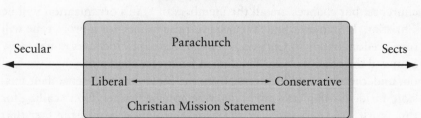

should flow from this short statement, and the primary purpose of the organization's board is to make certain that everything the organization does is true to this statement. Because the mission statement is so crucial to the functioning of a nonprofit organization, its content can test whether the organization can be called Christian and therefore defined as a parachurch organization and distinct from the larger category of nonprofit organization. (The reason this cannot be the only test is that the degree to which an organization is faithful to its Christian mission statement can vary greatly.)

The importance of the mission statement in identifying a parachurch organization may be illustrated with the example of the Union Rescue Mission located in Los Angeles, California. Its mission statement sets forth these goals and objectives: "The purpose of the Union Rescue Mission is to disseminate the Gospel of Jesus Christ. It is a community designed Mission to communicate principles of Christian living and relieve suffering in a wide variety of ways including the provision of food, lodging, hygiene facilities, clothing and medical care . . ." (Evangelical Council for Financial Accountability, 1996, p. 371). Although the rescue mission's actual tasks may differ little from those of many other secular organizations that are working to relieve suffering, its mission statement gives clear evidence that this work is done with another goal in mind: service to the Gospel of Jesus Christ. Such a goal allows us to define this nonprofit organization as a parachurch organization.

If we could examine the mission statement for our imaginary Christian Carpenter Squad, we would certainly find Stan's religious convictions present. Most likely he would begin by setting forth his faith and desire to work out his Christian faith into life, and then he would state the specific ministry that he would pursue—repairing and upgrading the churches where Christians worship. Such a mission statement will leave no doubt that the Christian Carpenter Squad is a parachurch organization.

If we apply Thomas Jeavons's questions to the Christian Carpenter Squad, then once again we will be confirmed in our decision. Most of the people who volunteer to work on churches will be Christians themselves. It is conceivable that a nonbeliever might find it delightful to work on churches, but chances are all the members of Stan's organization will be Christian. If Stan ever finds the need to raise money for a project, he will turn predominately to Christians. His fundraising brochures might show Stan and the other workers standing in front of a church they had worked on, underneath would be a verse from the Bible that represents their mission. Inside the flap Stan might describe how he first felt God's calling for this work. All these parts of the brochure would betray the fact that mainly Christians are supporting his ministry, and thus the second question proposed by Jeavons could be answered in the affirmative. As to the final question, we can see that the product aimed at by the Christian Carpenter Squad is strongly related to its members' Christian faith. On the spectrum that ranges from overtly Christian to completely secular, we can place Stan and his group squarely on the Christian side.

There are many Christians who serve God in secular organizations, many who find a ministry in their work, but for the purpose of defining the parachurch, we must recognize a rigorous definition of Christian organization. It is something more than a nonprofit group that was founded by a Christian, or a philanthropic group with which a Christian may wholly sympathize, or the organization of a Christian businessperson who works "for the glory of God." Instead, it is a group that is largely made up of Christians, whose financial support comes largely from Christians, and whose end product or service is related to its members' Christian faith. Such a group is usually best recognized by a look at its mission statement and the values and objectives set forth there.

A word must also be said about the Christian diversity within the parachurch. Although a large percentage of parachurch organizations have arisen from the Evangelical world, there are many groups that would not label themselves as conservative. Robert Wuthnow, for example, describes the two clusters of organizations shown in the following list (1988, pp. 181–182).

CONSERVATIVE	LIBERAL
Healing ministries	Protest activity groups
Prison ministries	Antinuclear coalitions
Hunger relief groups	Holistic health groups
Bible study groups	Therapy groups
Charismatic groups	

There is some overlap between these clusters, but they usually remain quite distinct. And neither can claim the parachurch as its own. Wherever there is conviction as to the truth of the Christian message, there will be parachurch organizations.

Test 3: Is the Group Independent of Traditional Church Structures?

The word *parachurch* itself reminds us that we are dealing with something different from the traditional church. An essential part of understanding the beside-church, or parachurch, then, is knowing what the church is.

We can imagine a few knee-jerk definitions. What Protestants generally mean by the *church* is the invisible body of believers scattered around the world. In other words, every Christian by virtue of his or her faith is a constituent of this invisible body. Most Roman Catholic believers will no doubt differ, and claim instead that the church properly extends only to the borders of the Roman Catholic Church. There is one church, and it is headquartered at the Vatican.

Both of these are definitions of church with a capital C. The church in parachurch has a small *c*. This lowercase church invites no high-sailing definitions or theological controversy. This church is simply the institutional church that is a reality in this pluralistic world. Parachurch organizations put aside any question as to which denomination or definition is the true church. Each and all are surrounded by local churches that give structure to American religious life. These are the buildings located on Main Street or built out on the wheat fields, the places where Christians come to fellowship with their friends, sing the newest praise choruses, repeat the creed, get healed, celebrate the Eucharist, or kneel on prayer benches. Most of these churches fall into larger organizations called denominations, which string together the smaller churches into national or regional organizations. With the lack of any official state church, the religious life of the United States is made up of these competing denominations, or sects. This is the reality of the church in America, and it is with this meaning in mind that this book uses a word like *parachurch*. The word does not imply that there are Christian organizations that work outside of the universal Church. Instead it simply describes an alternative institutional form in God's kingdom.

Not only do parachurch groups usually shy away from competition with the local church but most of them depend upon churches for their support. A group that runs a Christian camp in the local mountains may not receive any money directly from a church, but it may count on being able to put out fliers in the foyer on Sunday morning or perhaps even get a live pitch from the church youth pastor. The same is true for a rescue mission in the heart of some great city. It depends on churchgoers to be sympathetic to its efforts and to give money. The moment it becomes a competitor with donors' churches, its support will dry up. Even a large group such as the Prison Fellowship would lose support quickly if its leaders began to promote their own competing church actively.

The *Mission Handbook* identifies a number of areas where friction is possible between the church and parachurch. These range from conflicts of authority to suspicions about finances. "When two groups (one church, one parachurch) want the same programs, the same dollars and the same authority, a clash is inevitable and both ministries suffer" (Roberts and Siewert, 1990, p. 29). The church is hurt because its resources are drained, and the parachurch is hurt because it loses its base of support. In nearly every case, the parachurch is well served by drawing firm lines between its work and the work of the institutional church.

It is true that there are groups that have made the jump from parachurch to church. The Christian Missionary Alliance is now a denomination, but at its beginning it was a missionary sending agency, only gradually did it evolve into an actual denomination. It is easy to imagine a tight-knit campus Bible study becoming something of a substitute for a church, and in the first chapter we saw how Chris Grace, when he was a student, found his primary source of spiritual life in such a setting. But these instances are not the norm. For example, InterVarsity Christian Fellowship states in one of its tracts: "InterVarsity is not a church. Inter-Varsity's job is to enhance the work of the local church. We desire and earnestly seek a spirit of cooperation. Staff members are vigorously encouraged to get involved in the activity of a local church in the area where they serve. They, in turn, encourage students they work with to take an active role in a local church. The majority of the students in our chapters are active in a church" [InterVarsity, n.d., n.p.].

Such a clear statement seems almost geared to set the local pastor at ease. It is a clear statement that InterVarsity is not out to supplant the church, but to strengthen it through its ministry with students (see Figure 2.3).

An essential part of the definition of the parachurch is that it is separate from the traditional church. Yet perhaps these organizations that are beyond or beside the institutional church have something to teach us about God's Church, with a capital C. Traditionally we have identified God's institutions with the buildings with steeples and filled parking lots

Figure 2.3. Test 3: Is the Group Independent of Traditional Church Structures?

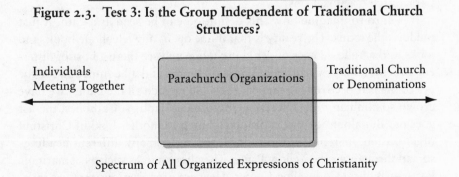

Individuals Meeting Together — Parachurch Organizations — Traditional Church or Denominations

Spectrum of All Organized Expressions of Christianity

on Sunday morning. We assume that God is working and accomplishing his plans through these staples of religious life. Yet there is no doubt that God is working through parachurch organizations in addition to the traditional churches, and this enlarges our conception of what God's Church is—God is not limited to any one institutional pattern.

However, a definition of the parachurch that differs considerably from the one presented here has grown out of this enlarged vision of the Church. It has been best expressed in Howard Snyder's book *The Problem of Wine Skins* (1975, pp. 151–168). From the outset Snyder rules out the possibility of there being a biblically sanctioned institutional face for the Church. He proposes that what we find in the New Testament is the Church presented as a "Charismatic organism, not an institutional organization" (p. 157). In other words, the Church is the supernatural core, the community of those with faith. Only this core is valid throughout every culture and time. Any institutional structure is therefore a culturally relative venture. Snyder defines any institutional face for this core, whether it be a Presbyterian church or Campus Crusade Bible study, as a *para-church*. (These ideas were also presented to the 1974 International Congress of World Evangelism, held in Lausanne, Switzerland, and included in the official publication of the conference, *Let the Earth Hear His Voice* [Douglas, 1974].)

Jerry White, in his book *The Church and the Parachurch: An Uneasy Marriage,* writes that "we must recognize every ministry structure other than a local congregation as a para-local church structure" (1983, p. 64). This is the same basic idea as first put forward by Snyder: every kind of institutional structure is a part of the parachurch—or as White calls it, the para-local church. According to this definition, every Christian organization falls under the category of parachurch: denominations, missions, seminaries, Sunday schools, and so on. Suddenly the Southern Baptist denomination and InterVarsity Christian Fellowship are both defined as parachurch organizations.

It is hard to imagine how this definition can be seen as a gain. It just muddies the terms. The reality is that if one opens any telephone book, and looks in the Yellow Pages under church, one will see there a host of different churches, all from different denominations, and all competing for the eye of the prospective churchgoer. They will include all the names we have grown so familiar with: Lutherans, Reformed, Baptists, Catholics, the list goes on. But alongside the traditional church is another kind of Christian organization. Its representatives are listed under many different headings spread throughout the Yellow Pages. They have names such as Samaritans Purse or Biblical Counseling Center. They are organizations that are independent of the traditional church and begun by the individual initiative of their founders. They are a different kind of organization than those found under the heading churches. The word *parachurch* has come into existence and has caught on so well precisely because it is a useful word to describe these Christian organizations that work beyond the church yet often work for the same goal—the advancement of the Gospel. To follow the solution proposed by Snyder is to lose a useful word and end up with a gray and amorphous word that tries to cover every Christian institution.

Although the definition of a parachurch organization that Snyder proposes does not adequately draw distinctions between the institutional faces of Christian work, still it captures a larger point. God's work is not bound up with any one kind of organization. The traditional church on the corner is important, but God is working through the parachurch as well. Its upstart organizations are part of God's Church, with a capital C.

Test 4: Does the Group Work at One or More Specific Ministries or Services?

Test 4 is the final litmus test in the four-part definition of a parachurch organization. The traditional church by its nature must be a generalist, whereas the parachurch organization is a specialist.

The specific ministries of parachurch organizations vary considerably. It seems that as society becomes more complex, there arise new niches and new specialties for parachurch groups to grasp. The Evangelical Council for Financial Accountability releases a directory with a short profile for each of its 750 members (all Evangelical organizations), each of which has agreed to financial accountability. The members are only a small slice of all parachurch groups, yet one can see the immense diversity in ministries as one flips through this thick directory. The final group in the directory, for example, is the Zwemer Institute for Muslim Studies. Its stated ministry is "serving the Church by bringing the worldwide needs and opportunities for ministries to Muslims into focus" (Evangelical Council for Financial Accountability, 1996, p. 407). A glance through the directory brings to light many other groups that have focused their resources on a single need. The American Scientific Affiliation seeks to integrate the discoveries of science with the knowledge given through scripture. The Alternatives of Kalamazoo Crisis Pregnancy Center aims to provide alternatives to abortion, offering free care and practical help to women in need. The Long Beach Rescue Mission provides shelter and counseling to the homeless. Each of these groups meets the definition of a parachurch organization, and each focuses on a single ministry.

Lesslie Newbigen (1980, p. 41) has described three roles for the church: community (*koinonia*), servant (*diakonia*), and messenger (*kerygma*). Each function of the church may be classified under one of these headings. Community has to do with the fellowship, discipleship, and teaching that goes on between believers. As a servant the church reaches out its hands to help those in need, the poor and hungry inside and outside the church. As a messenger the church shares with nonbelievers the message of salvation. The healthy local church engages with all three of these roles. If it is missing one, then something has gone wrong. It is in this way that the church is a generalist; it must take up each of these roles.

The parachurch, in contrast, is most effective when it latches onto a single ministry and carries that ministry to perfection (see Figure 2.4). The various ministries of the parachurch take on one or another of the three main roles of the church. A group like Ligonier Ministries takes up the community role. Through its tapes and broadcasts, it promotes its own vision of Christian truth. It is a ministry of discipleship and teaching for those who seek after a deeper understanding of the Bible. The many rescue missions spread over the country testify to the servant role of the church. They witness to the Gospel through caring for the homeless and the poor. Likewise the prison ministries and mission agencies take up the messenger role, taking the Gospel to those who have not heard. By choosing a single role, the parachurch organizations show themselves as particularists. When all works well, the particular focus of the parachurch meshes well with the steady rhythm of the local church. When the parachurch takes on a broader ministry and threatens the church, or when the church wants to monopolize Christian service, then problems arise.

The complementary nature of the church and parachurch was drawn on by missions scholar Ralph Winter (1970, pp. 52–56) for his definition of the parachurch. He looked back through the history of the church and

Figure 2.4. Test 4: Does the Group Work at One or More Specific Ministries or Services?

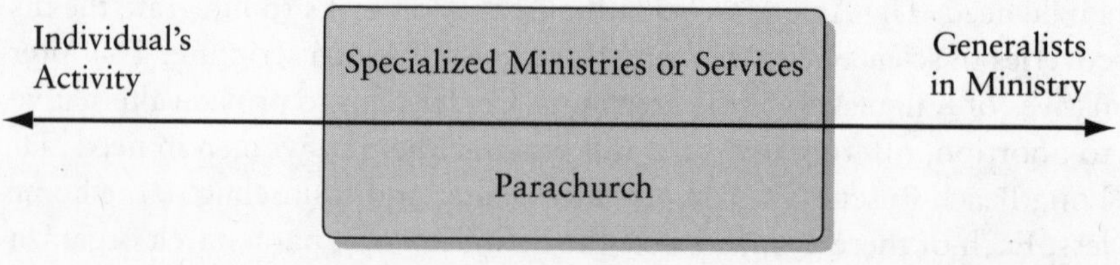

noticed that there has always been an interplay between two principles in Christian life. He called these two principles *modality* and *sodality*. Modality refers to the general structure of the church. The church harbors great diversity in its membership and tends toward bureaucratization as the forms harden into a tradition. The second principle is sodality, referring to voluntary groups focusing on a more narrow objective. The strength of sodality is that it has greater mobility and efficiency. One historical model that Winter uses is the Roman Catholic Church and the various religious orders such as the Jesuits that functioned alongside it. The church was the modality, and the religious orders were the sodality. Winter would have us see this same dualism at work today in the interplay between institutional church and parachurch.

Although it is possible to find some good insights with this pattern, it neglects history for the allure of an easy picture. The fact is there was no Focus on the Medieval Family to minister exclusively to the needs of families centuries ago, no Fellowship of Christian Knights to provide spiritual nourishment to the brave jousters. Nor are modern parachurch groups the equivalent of Christian orders. They make no claims to offer a spiritual life that is deeper than the spiritual life of a Christian who attends church faithfully. These groups simply offer avenues of service. The current explosion of the parachurch is not the rebirth of historical structures but the advent of a new structure that allows Christians to organize as a nonprofit, to raise funds, and to tackle a highly specific problem or need in fulfillment of a Christian mission.

Although we may not accept the large picture that Winter draws, we can appreciate the basic truth that lies at the base of his explanation. The institutional church and the parachurch are not meant to be enemies but, ideally, to occupy complementary places beside each other. One focuses on the general needs of the people of God, whereas the other finds a specific goal and trains all its energy on accomplishing it. Recognizing this difference between the church and the parachurch goes a long way toward answering the question of how they can work together.

Community, servant, and messenger are the broad categories into which the various ministries of the parachurch may be classed. Yet the huge network of groups may be broken down in other ways also. To introduce the reader to the many different kinds of ministries found in the parachurch, a taxonomy is provided in the Resource. To browse through it is to see that every need of life is covered by some parachurch group. From the performing arts to health care to church growth consulting, the parachurch is involved and carrying forward its specific part of the work of the universal Church.

Back to Stan

The definitions proposed by Howard Snyder and Ralph Winter foundered because they failed to appreciate the relative newness of parachurch organizations. Just as the professions of paramedic and paralegal arose only recently because of the changing needs of our complicated society, so the parachurch too is a recent arrival. The explosion of specialized ministries that work outside the institutional church is fueled by modern realities.

Perhaps both of the definitions were correct in this: they looked for a universal principle with which to understand the parachurch. But perhaps the principle is much more basic than they realized. To find this principle we must see Stan sitting in church, listening to his pastor. His intense gaze betrays that now, for the first time, he is hearing the message. He knows now that he has been storing up for himself treasures on earth, where moth, rust, or some modern disaster may rush in and destroy the hoarded goods. He knows now that his true work is to store up treasures in heaven. By faith Stan changed his life. By faith he began to give, and not simply take and enjoy. This is the impulse of faith. Christian workers down through the centuries know this impulse well. From Paul to the early and anonymous missionaries, to the dedicated Catholic bishops, to those in the monastic orders, to the reformers, to those in faith missions—all these Christians know the feeling that Stan had on that Sunday morning. The impulse stays the same, but the way that impulse is embodied in an institutional structure varies over time. In this day, because of great personal freedom, easy travel, and helpful tax codes, the form this impulse takes is very often the parachurch.

In the next chapter the historical roots of the parachurch will be examined. Yet it is important to always remember the thoughtful gaze of Stan as he sits in the wooden pew of his small church, listening to his pastor speak. The individual is touched by God, and out of this comes the energy out of which all organizations are formed. This impulse of faith is not limited to Baptists or Presbyterians or Catholics, or to Evangelicals or mainline believers. The energy of conviction is spread throughout the church spectrum, and there are parachurch groups that reflect every shade of Christian belief. Every parachurch organization begins with the conviction of Stan.

3

THE ROOTS OF THE PARACHURCH BOOM

FAITH HAS MANY different looks. In one place it is rigid lines of author-ity; in another it is a ricocheting ball with little apparent direction. In one place it is a crowd of thousands hearing an evangelist; in another it is a small group quietly discussing private issues or praying. Attempts to round up and classify different expressions of faith prove impossible.

Jesus once had to answer the questions of those who thought they knew how faith ought to look. Some people asked Jesus, "Why do we and the Pharisees fast often, but your disciples do not fast?" (Matthew 9:14). Jesus had two responses. First, he pointed to the unique situation of the disci-ples: just as the wedding guests would not think of fasting on a day that should be spent celebrating with the bridegroom, so the disciples do not fast on the few days when their Lord is with them. The second response seems to embody a much wider principle: "No one sews a piece of unshrunk cloth on an old cloak, for the patch pulls away from the cloak, and a worse tear is made. Neither is new wine put into old wineskins; oth-erwise, the skins burst, and the wine is spilled, and the skins are destroyed; but new wine is put into fresh wineskins, and so both are preserved" (Matthew 9:16–17).

The wine is spiritual life—all the energy that accompanies the Kingdom of God. The wineskins are the human containers for that spiritual life. Those people who wanted the disciples of Jesus to fast and to do other expected actions wanted to put the unique present life into the old con-tainers. How many times since have new Pharisees tried to put the new wine of their time into the old containers of the past?

Americans are awash in new wine. It is generally agreed that the vital-ity of spiritual life in the United States is astounding. New containers are not lacking either. One of the containers that has proved most efficient at

channeling the spiritual life of the United States is the parachurch organization. It is prospering; it overflows with people and energy and money.
To understand the present reality of the parachurch, we must look to the
past to see the reasons that the parachurch has grown so strong.

At the outset here, God's sovereignty over the affairs of humanity and
especially over the church must be recognized. But in searching for human
explanations, we look back on American church history and can identify
six main roots in U.S. church history that explain the proliferation of the
parachurch:

- ○ Root 1: the serious search to know God
- ○ Root 2: the ability to move beyond traditional lines
- ○ Root 3: passionate founders and leaders
- ○ Root 4: the freedoms found in America
- ○ Root 5: strong convictions of faith
- ○ Root 6: the challenge of secularization

Each of these historical roots has strong implications for the management of the parachurch today. Perhaps it is a good time for this new wine-
skin to take stock of the wines and wineskins that came before it.

Root 1: The Serious Search to Know God

When John Wesley was a missionary in Georgia, a Moravian asked him
a troubling question: "Do you know Christ?" Wesley had no positive answer for the question and felt instead that "vain words" defined his dry
faith (Stoeffler, 1976, pp. 190–191). That simple question led him to a
time of searching for an experiential knowledge of God. His search ended
in 1738, after he had returned to England. He found the inner certainty
of forgiveness through faith in Christ, and finally he could answer that
Moravian question: "Yes, I know Christ." This direct knowledge of God
marked the preaching of John Wesley and marked the denomination that
came about through his labors. And when the Methodist denomination
spread throughout the United States, having two hundred thousand members by 1816 (Noll, 1992, p. 173), it was this message that came with it.

This was not a new message. Wesley found himself in a long line of believers who knew that Christianity was not about belonging to a certain
church or about reciting a certain creed; instead it was about heart knowledge of God through Jesus Christ. The Moravians and other Continental
Christians who influenced Wesley were part of a movement known as

Pietism, and Pietism itself was simply a reawakening of the personal zeal that had characterized the earlier Reformation. And the stream goes back even further—to medieval mysticism and the devout monastics. Church historian Ernest Stoeffler clarifies the situation when he refers to an *experiential tradition* in which faith is not a creed but a heartfelt belief (1965, pp. 6–7). It is too easy to confine church history to the external structures of the major organizational branches—Catholic, Lutheran, Orthodox, Reformed. The experiential tradition runs within each of the major branches of Christendom and their many offshoots. Speaking of this tradition, Stoeffler writes: "Whether it occurs in England, in Scotland, in Wales, in the Netherlands, in Germany, in Switzerland, in Denmark, Norway, Sweden, Russia, or North America, whether it is linked with Calvinistic, Lutheran, or Arminian theology its main features are always the same. Whether we look at it from the point of view of its major emphases or from the point of view of the sense of world-wide fellowship which has always characterized its adherents it is one historic reality" (1965, p. 7).

Running alongside all the major Christian traditions are movements of renewal, sparked by those who thirst for more than "vain words." This search to know God is the source for the new wine, the new spiritual life of every century.

This spiritual vitality led the Continental Pietists in the seventeenth century to create *conventicles*—small groups that met in homes to discuss scripture and spiritual topics. These conventicles are examples of the new containers that fresh faith instinctively finds. As people's needs were not being fully met in the established church, people formed independent groups in which to nurture their faith. Despite this growing independence, Pietists made it clear that they operated within the framework of the established church. Leaders like Philipp Jakob Spener wrote against separation from the established church, even if it had become corrupt (Brown, 1978, p. 62).

The experiential tradition found many bridges across the Atlantic to North America. The writings of John Wesley drew heavily from Pietists, and through these writings the members of the burgeoning Methodist denomination were introduced to the heart knowledge of God. George Whitefield was another bridge for the experiential tradition. Despite the often discussed differences in theology between him and Wesley, the two agreed on the importance of the *new birth*. Immigrants from Germany, the Netherlands, and Sweden brought with them their devotional literature, hymns, and most important, their living faith. All these Pietist influences mingled with the strong Puritan presence in America, which already shared many Pietist beliefs.

American evangelicalism is simply a continuing manifestation of this search to know God. It shares at least two major characteristics with the Pietists. First, both emphasize a "personally meaningful relationship of the individual to God" (Stoeffler, 1976, pp. 13–14). It was belief in this relationship that enabled Wesley to finally answer the Moravian question, "Do you know Christ?" This is the same question that evangelists have long asked their overflowing crowds. From George Whitefield's ministry in the 1740s to Billy Graham's more recent ministry (and, through television, much more widely spread), this call for a personal relationship with Christ has been a dominant theme in American evangelicalism. A second shared characteristic is a religious idealism that sets itself up against what it sees as a cold, self-assured orthodoxy. The Pietists combated this orthodoxy with their conventicles and devotional books, but they also kept within the bounds set by the state churches of their countries. On American soil the authority of these "true" churches would fade, and few doctrinal or social barriers would keep a conventicle from splitting from its parent and forming its own separate church.

This Pietist energy would lead to the flourishing of the parachurch. Americans who had discovered for themselves the experiential knowledge of God would look around for ways to work that faith into life. Instead of forming conventicles, as the Pietists had done, they would form voluntary societies aimed at a specific Christian service. Still later, these voluntary societies would evolve into the parachurch organizations that we recognize today. When the old containers of faith harden into shells, then a new life emerges. This is the new wine of the parable, and it has an unerring ability to find new containers to hold it. At one time the new container was the monastery; once it was the Pietist conventicle; today it is the parachurch. As the parachurch looks to the future it must recognize where its strength comes from, and strive not to become like the inflexible institutions that have historically opposed new spiritual life. Instead the parachurch must continue to be a vehicle for the search for God—the source from which the new wine springs.

Root 2: The Ability to Move Beyond Traditional Lines

Martin Marty has called the U.S. religious map a "crazy-quilt" (Carroll, Johnson, and Marty, 1979, p. 89), and after one sees such a map with its colored zones illustrating denominational strength in each region, this seems an apt comparison. Although European nations have their own complexities, their religious patterns seem simple compared to that in the United States. In those countries, a state church dominated for many years, and when dissenting groups were finally allowed, they were still secondary to the monolith of the official church. The United States inherited numerous congregations from these state churches (Reformed, Presbyterian, Anglican, and also Lutheran from Sweden, Norway, and Germany), each of which now had to coexist and even compete with the others for members. Add to these Reformation-descended churches a new breed of dissenters led by Baptists and Quakers, and we may begin to see the religious complexity that was present at our nation's inception. Since then splits and resplits, along with new movements such as Pentecostalism or Adventism, have only further complicated the religious map.

Within the framework of a fragmented religious map, individuals have been able to speak for large numbers of Christians more effectively than any single organization tied to a party line. To be broadly effective any coalition of Christians or national religious movement must get beyond denominational differences and speak for the plurality of Christians spread throughout all that map's fragments. The most visible leaders in U.S. church life have been the great revivalists. Names such as Charles Finney, Dwight L. Moody, Aimee Semple McPherson, and Billy Graham are easily recognizable to those who take an interest in church history, and countless other men and women could be included in this list. Each of these major revivalists downplayed denominational divisions, working instead to focus on the essentials that united the fragments of the religious map. How many people know what church Billy Graham attends on Sunday? Who besides a scholar would know in what denomination Dwight L. Moody began his ministry? Moody himself exclaimed: "I hope to see the day when all bickering, division, and party feeling will cease, and Roman Catholics will see eye to eye with Protestants in this work. Let us advance in a solid column—Roman Catholics, Protestants, Episcopalians, Presbyterians, Methodists—against the ranks of Satan's emissaries" (Findlay, 1969, p. 248). The major focus for these revivalists was the individual's personal faith in Christ. The factions that grew out of denominational rivalries were a hindrance to the main pursuit of the revivalists, and so each found a way to transcend these barriers between Christians.

Parachurch organizations are effective for the same reason. By refusing to limit themselves to a narrow band of Christians, they speak for believers in all denominations. The complexity of the U.S. religious map makes the parachurch a necessity. When an individual catches a vision for a certain ministry, that person has two choices. Either work with a traditional church, in which case the ministry is often limited to a single portion of the religious map, or organize a parachurch organization. For many people with a vision, the choice is easy. Although it may be harder to begin with no institutional backing, they see broader horizons from within a parachurch organization than from within a traditional denomination.

Root 3: Passionate Founders and Leaders

It is no accident that many of the largest parachurch organizations formed around the vision and passion of a single individual. Before there are budgets in the millions of dollars, before there are hundreds of employees, there is usually just a single person with a dream, a single person who desires to work out his or her faith into this world. The Billy Graham Evangelistic Association is an obvious example of a parachurch organization that has formed around a dynamic Christian leader. Other well-known groups, such as Campus Crusade, Navigators, Focus on the Family, and Wycliffe Bible Translators, also sprang from the vision of a single person or small group of people. The beginning strength of the parachurch is not found in marketing strategies or slick tracts; instead it is found in passionate leaders who are willing to follow God's call.

The prototype for the strong leaders in American church history was George Whitefield, and through his life and ministry, we can see the kind of leadership that has made the parachurch so dynamic (Stout, 1991). By the time of his death in 1770, he had become what no one previous had managed—he was a religious superstar. All over the Western world he could draw thousands of people to listen to his drama-tinged sermons on the new birth. At the age of twenty-three, he could pack the largest churches in London, and on his sweeps through the thirteen American Colonies he preached to the same overflowing audiences. Benjamin Franklin amicably described one of Whitefield's revival gatherings:

> The multitudes of all sects and denominations that attended his sermons were enormous, and it was matter of speculation to me, who was one of the number, to observe the extraordinary influence of his oratory on his hearers, and how much they admir'd and respected him, notwithstanding his common abuse of them, by assuring them they were naturally *half beasts and half devils.* It was wonderful to see the change soon made in the manners of our inhabitants . . . it seem'd as if all the world were growing religious, so that one could not walk thro' the town in an evening without hearing psalms sung in different families of every street [(1868) 1996, p. 82].

Unknowingly, Whitefield had stepped into a religious landscape with entirely new possibilities. Just one hundred years earlier such a ministry would have been unthinkable. He would have faced a more closed-up religious world, and although he might have shone locally, he could not have contemplated an international career. Now, new social realities had formed a world that had the leisure, money, and freedom to support this itinerant preacher. Religion had an untapped market value, and people were eager to hear him speak. If they could not hear him in person, they could read about his triumphs in his *Journals*. He had a natural gift for advertising, promoting, and publicizing his revivals, long before the importance of such marketing activities was realized. In short, Whitefield was a religious entrepreneur. Yet this is not to imply that he was insincere or manipulative. Over the course of his thirty-three-year career, he preached some fifteen thousand times (Noll, 1992, p. 93), and the motive for this draining work was a clear passion to tell others about the new birth through Christ. Whitefield is an example of the Christian leader who works out a personal vision into the reality of the culture. He found himself in a world with new possibilities, and he was able to take his message to larger crowds and larger numbers of people than the preachers who preceded him, precisely because he could promote and advertise his meetings so well.

Whitefield was simply the first in an illustrious line of American revivalists and religious leaders. Billy Graham has many of the same strengths as Whitefield, and Nathan Hatch and Michael Hamilton have written that "it would be difficult to overestimate Billy Graham's importance over the last 50 years of Evangelicalism" (Hatch and Hamilton, 1992, p. 23). Just as Whitefield helped to unite the fragmented colonies, so Graham has helped to unite a large constituency of people of different backgrounds into a semicoherent evangelicalism. To do this he has toned down the vitriol of fundamentalist rhetoric, easing the fears of moderates; he welcomed into fellowship groups such as the Pentecostals, who had traditionally been on the fringes of U.S. church life; and he made efforts to include Roman Catholics in his crusades. He also paved the way for Evangelicals to regain a public voice through his espousal of several progressive causes and his friendly relations with many elected leaders. Just like Whitefield, he has been able to rise above denominational infighting and find a position that transcends the fractured U.S. religious map. The parachurch has proliferated because God has raised up leaders such as Graham, and it will continue to proliferate as a new generation of leaders catches a vision for ministry and finds new ways to communicate that message.

Root 4: The Freedoms Found in America

As Alexis de Tocqueville toured the United States in 1831, he was impressed with the vitality of American life. "No sooner do you set foot upon American ground than you are stunned by a kind of tumult; a confused clamor is heard on every side, and a thousand simultaneous voices demand the satisfaction of their social wants" (Tocqueville, [1835] 1956, p. 249). De Tocqueville saw that democracy, with its loosening of authority, brought about a groundswell of popular associations. Within this clamorous environment, religious associations arose for every belief and cause.

It is easy to forget that the freedoms of associations and speech have not always been the norm. In modern America it is possible to take them for granted, but for much of the world's history, people were not allowed to meet freely or form organizations. In the seventeenth century, for example, John Bunyan, the author of *Pilgrim's Progress,* wrote of being imprisoned for the audacity of holding independent religious meetings: "After I was indicted for an upholder and maintainer of unlawful assemblies and conventicles, and for not conforming to the national worship of the Church of England, and after some conference there with the justices, they . . . did sentence me to perpetual banishment, because I refused to conform. So being again delivered up to the gaoler's hands, I was had home to prison and there have lain now complete twelve years" (Bunyan, [1666] 1948, p. 109). Where there is a despotic government or a repressive and jealous state church, people's natural impulse to work out faith into life is quickly checked. John Bunyan felt the same call as many modern religious leaders, yet because of the time in which he lived, he spent many of his days behind bars.

The parachurch owes its life to the freedoms found in U.S. society. This new container for the wine of faith could not have materialized without the First Amendment, which bars Congress from making laws "respecting the establishment of religion, or prohibiting the free exercise thereof." Another freedom that has been crucial to the parachurch is the freedom to raise money from donors. By allowing such gifts to be tax deductible, the U.S. government has even encouraged people to give money to religious organizations. From the beginning, U.S. religious leaders were aware of the new possibilities that lay before them. The missionary Rufus Anderson wrote in 1837: "The Protestant form of association—free, open, responsible, embracing all classes, both sexes, all ages, the masses of the people— is peculiar to modern times, and almost to our age. . . . Never, till now, did the social condition of mankind render it possible to organize the armies requisite for the world's spiritual conquest" (Walls, 1990, pp. 3–4).

Voluntary societies were the first new containers to arise from U.S. freedoms. Because they were independent of the traditional church and addressed a specific ministry, we can see them as protoparachurch organizations. The structure these voluntary societies adopted was much like that of the secular joint stock companies so common at the time, illustrating the timeless pattern in which religious impulses adopt the organizational structures of the times. The parachurch organization, with its CEOs and boards and presidents, borrows a distinctly modern method of organizing.

Some of the voluntary societies that arose in the first half of the nineteenth century are the American Bible Society (1816), American Tract Society (1825), Young Men's Christian Association (1844), numerous mission societies, and groups associated with causes such as abolition and temperance. All of these grew from the fecund soil of American democratic culture. Sunday School had its beginning in England, yet its story illustrates the crucial connection between freedom and the parachurch.

Sunday School has become such a ubiquitous fact of U.S. church experience that it is hard to imagine church life without it. Yet Sunday School had a beginning, and its founder was a man named Robert Raikes (Rice, 1927). Like so many later parachurch organizations, Sunday School began with the vision of an individual. Raikes was disturbed at the condition of children in late eighteenth-century England. In those days before public schooling or child labor laws, many children were illiterate and their habits coarse. Raikes envisioned Sunday School as a way to change that. In 1780, he held his first Sunday School in a kitchen rented expressly for the purpose. He taught the children to read the Bible and instilled them with a sense of right and wrong. By 1783, he had given tours of his work to John Wesley and other English leaders and had published an article on his work in a journal. The idea of educating the poor children turned out to be popular, and soon Raikes was explaining his idea to the Queen herself.

Although the idea of educating poor children seems simple and obviously beneficial, there is a reason such a movement did not come about until 1780. Up until the passage of the Enabling Act in 1779, English laws prevented anyone who did not conform to the Church of England from keeping a public or private school or even acting as a tutor. Given the Church of England's opposition at the time to the education of these children, it is unlikely that anything like the Sunday school could have arisen without the legal sanction of the Enabling Act. Once again we see the clear connection between a free society and the growth of independent religious organizations. Prior to 1779, the philanthropy of Robert Raikes (or anyone else) would have been stifled by the laws of the country and the prejudice of those in ecclesiastical power.

The Sunday School movement reminds us of the energy that can be harnessed by a group that captures the popular imagination in a free society. The freedom that allowed Robert Raikes to begin his first Sunday School in a rented kitchen is still with us in the 1990s. This freedom is the necessary environment for the parachurch. As other nations in the world come to have the same religious freedoms, the parachurch is finding a home within those nations also. Wherever faith is a powerful force in people's lives, and wherever they have freedom to join and begin new organizations, the parachurch prospers.

Root 5: Strong Convictions of Faith

What will lead a person to spend his or her life in a foreign country, to leave behind home and beloved relatives, to leave behind comforts and status? Many throughout history have abandoned their homes because they have been forced to do so by circumstance or have been drawn away by the promise of money and a better life. There are, however, a small percentage of people who have traveled to the uttermost parts of the earth from no outer necessity and for no benefit to themselves—missionaries. These voluntary sojourners have been energized by the knowledge that there are needy people in the world—needy both spiritually and physically. In response to this need and the call of the Great Commission, "Go therefore and make disciples of all nations" (Matthew 28:19), these men and women leave behind a comfortable life to serve God in a foreign country.

Missionaries have spread Christianity to every corner of the globe. Missionary work has thrived as individuals have had a sense of calling and strong personal conviction. Often the missionary vision of these individuals could not be expressed through denominational outlets, and they turned instead to parachurch organizations to fulfill their calling. Through the stories of such missionaries and the mission agencies they founded, we can see the importance of convictions of faith in the prospering of the parachurch.

William Carey is known as the father of modern missions. Certainly there were many missionaries before him, but his arrival in India in 1793 marks the beginning of large-scale missionary work from the English-speaking world. What sent this onetime cobbler to India was his belief that it is the duty of all people to accept the salvation offered in the Gospel and that the church must be diligent to proclaim the Gospel message to all people. Such convictions went directly against the prevailing ideas in Carey's Baptist denomination, which saw little need to tell the world about Christ. The year before he left for India he set down two principles of action: "Attempt great things for God; expect great things from God" (Neill, 1964, pp. 261–262). These beliefs led to the forming of the Baptist Missionary Society, and with the support of these like-minded Baptist believers, William Carey went to India to spread the Gospel.

Mission societies such as the Baptist Missionary Society were part of the general proliferation of voluntary societies in the early nineteenth century. This method of financing missions proved effective, and before long many more mission societies were formed. As with the case with the society that supported William Carey, many of these societies were independent of any denomination, yet it did not take long for the denominations to recognize a good thing. By the time of the American Civil War most of the denominations had either formed a mission society or adopted an independent society as their own (Walls, 1990), and the once independent movement became tied to the institutional church. Soon a new style of mission organization regained independence from denominations—the faith mission.

James Hudson Taylor began his missionary work in China with one of the many mission societies. Yet Taylor had his own unique vision for carrying out missions. After seven years he left the mission society, eventually forming the China Inland Mission. Taylor chose to rely on God for all his needs, thus shunning the security of a mission society and its moneyed subscribers. He also introduced his own principles of missionary work, the best known of which was to self-identify with the Chinese people through adoption of their dress and manners (Neill, 1964). Before long this upstart organization would be the largest mission agency in the world, having 641 missionaries only thirty years after its modest beginnings. Other faith missions sprang up quickly, including the African Inland Mission, Sudan Interior Mission, and the Gospel Missionary Union.

One of the most important reasons for the success of the faith missions was their openness to those without formal education. As the older mission societies were taken over by denominations, the missionary opportunities for laypeople became fewer. Only those with professional training were able to follow their convictions through these societies. Women also benefited from the new faith missions. No matter what her educational background, many denominations would not let a woman serve as a single missionary. Many faith missions would take whomever had a clear conviction and desire to serve God—and that included many women. Once again the old pattern is repeated: when new wine is dammed up within rigid institutions, new containers must be formed to hold the new energies.

There were also many new ideas in the air during the late nineteenth century. At times it has been easy, even fashionable, to ignore the driving force of new ideas and to concentrate solely on the external realities of history. Yet the great institutional changes in missions came about because of the convictions of the leaders. Carey believed that everyone needed to hear the Christian message, and Taylor knew that all people could be used by God on the mission field. Those convictions and these men's sense of calling came out of the way they understood their world and God.

Missionaries, along with those in other ministries, not only have been concerned with the eternal welfare of people but also have had compassion for their physical well-being. Marvin Olasky, in his book *The Tragedy of American Compassion,* points out how compassion was once a strong motivator for action. In early America, "the need to offer personal help and hospitality became a frequent subject of sermons" (1992, p. 7). Along with convictions of faith, compassion was a strong motivator for the formation of faith missions.

Many of the early faith missions, precursors of parachurch organizations, are now structured like any other parachurch organization, complete with boards and mission statements. And all parachurch organizations can learn a lesson from such early faith missions as the China Inland Mission—the lesson of conviction. No one turns away from his or her ambitions and livelihood for fun. No one works to help the poor because it is an entertaining way to spend the weekend. These are sacrifices, and they come from strong convictions that a certain action is true or right. There is power in an organization only as long as its ideals and its vision can inspire people to work and to give. For the parachurch to prosper, it must keep its convictions of faith firm and clear.

Root 6: The Challenge of Secularization

For a moment let us imagine a culture in which there is broad agreement over Christian ideals and values. In such a culture, citizens would go about business the same as in any other place. Ordinary people who want to make a living would run or work for companies that produce services and products, including books and movies. They would run the schools and other public endeavors. Given the broad Christian consensus in this make-believe society, the movies and books that draw the crowds would naturally be Christian. There would be no need to open specifically Christian schools because the public schools would be taught from the Christian worldview that underlies society.

Whether such a society is possible or good is not the focus here. The point is that in such a world, the parachurch would have almost no place. Having specialized Christian radio stations, Christian schools, and Christian publishers is important now only because the culture has become so secularized. When the general values of the country come to contradict the values of millions of religious believers, then the need for a separate network of alternative organizations is compelling. The parachurch has responded to the challenge of secularism.

Perhaps there has never been a truly Christian society. Always there have been religious attitudes and beliefs that to a later generation of Christians seem time-bound, wrongheaded, and even sinful. U.S. Protestants are prone to look back wistfully on a nineteenth-century culture that was largely Christian; yet on closer examination, there were many people for whom this Christian culture was oppressive. Despite this fault, Christian values were embedded in nineteenth-century America to a much greater extent than they are in the late twentieth century. But that earlier era was short-lived, and by the dawning of the twentieth century, cracks were beginning to appear in the Protestant dominance. A new social reality was being created by the rapid immigration of non-Protestants, and pressures from within denominations were also beginning to fracture the previous unity of thought.

The Fundamentalist-Modernist clashes represent for many the bitter transition from a culture dominated by Christian values to a more secular culture. John Scopes's trial, the so-called monkey trial, is the best known of these clashes (Marsden, 1994). The agnostic Clarence Darrow defended the right of Scopes to teach Darwinism in the public schools. Opposed to him stood William Jennings Bryan, a crusader against Darwinism and a leader among the conservatives. Scopes was found guilty, but serious damage had been done to the conservatives, who now bore the label, derisively applied, of Fundamentalists. They were portrayed as standing against progress and against science. When the smoke of battle cleared, those who considered themselves conservative heirs of American Protantism found that they were now outsiders to the secular world. The popular view was that these Fundamentalists were an outgrowth of small town rural America, who would fade away as enlightened ideas slowly penetrated. Instead of fading away, however, the Fundamentalists turned their energies to grassroots organizations, working through local churches, independent mission agencies, and Bible schools and developing new ways of communicating their message. After being disengaged from the "official" institutions of mainstream culture, the Fundamentalists developed a network of parachurch organizations.

Bible colleges offer a picture of how the parachurch has risen to the challenge of a society whose values are becoming secularized. These conservative schools began as a way for laypeople to get involved in Christian work without all the professional training demanded by the established seminaries. After the Fundamentalist-Modernist split, these small colleges found themselves at the center of the rising parachurch network. Many of the faith missions and independent churches came to rely heavily for workers on schools such as the Moody Bible Institute in Chicago or the Bible Institute of Los Angeles (Biola) (Carpenter, 1990). Unlike the established seminaries, these Bible colleges often had no official denominational support. They were parachurch organizations that had found a new niche—the training of religious conservatives who were locked out of the mainline denominations that had traditionally harbored them. The demand for this education was so great that in the 1930s, in the midst of the Depression, twenty-six new Bible schools were founded, along with such other conservative bastions as Bob Jones University and Dallas Theological Seminary.

Christian radio ministries offer another example of how parachurch organizations were a way to rise to the challenge of a secular society. Fundamentalists were among the first to realize radio's potential to reach huge audiences, but even on the radio network airwaves they were outsiders. Early in the days of radio, by the arrangement of the Federal Council of Churches, NBC excluded Fundamentalist broadcasters (Martin, 1988). As with the Bible colleges, being excluded only drove the Fundamentalists to develop organizations of their own, and in 1922, Paul Rader set up his own radio station, WJBT (Where Jesus Blesses Thousands). His lead was followed by many others, and names such as Aimee Semple McPherson and Charles Fuller became nationally known through radio programs.

From the example of Bible colleges and Christian radio we can learn a major reason for the growth of the parachurch. If there had never been a Fundamentalist-Modernist split, and if U.S. culture had gone on united under Christian values, then the parachurch would likely never have developed to its present strength. Although many independent organizations such as the American Sunday School Union and the China Inland Mission had existed in the nineteenth century, the traditional churches and denominations had remained strong. The denominational schools and societies were unavoidable for most Christians. The Fundamentalist-Modernist split meant that a large number of U.S. Christians had to survive without much denominational support, relying instead on the loose network of independent Christian organizations. Soon independent Bible colleges were attracting students away from denominational colleges, independent publishers were selling Fundamentalist books, and independent radio stations were broadcasting the Gospel. This change to independent parachurch organizations could take place so rapidly because it built on many trends already running throughout U.S. church history. From the time of Whitefield, there had existed a strong impulse for independent organizations, but after the split between the liberals and conservatives, the parachurch became a powerful way for Christians to work out their faith into life. The increasing secularization of society did not put an end to Christian faith, it simply forced that faith into new channels.

After World War II in particular, a roller coaster of changes came to the United States. The only Christian organizations that could fully keep pace with these changes were in the parachurch. The collision between culture and the demands of faith led to the maze of parachurch organizations that we know today. The next chapter examines more closely the way the parachurch has interacted with, and often countered, modern culture.

4

KEYS TO ENDURING
EFFECTIVENESS

IF SOMEHOW AN American could travel back to the year 1948, he or she would find a different country. Fast-food chains, buy-everything supermarkets, and malls were still nonexistent. Items that many people in 1998 could not imagine life without—household air-conditioning, freezers, dishwashers, and ballpoint pens—were unknown. But not only the gadgets were different; it was a completely different way of life. Only about one-third of the population lived in cities with more than fifty thousand residents. Historian James T. Patterson writes that "culturally as well as demographically the United States remained in many ways a world of farms, small towns, and modest-sized cities—places where neighbors knew each other and in which people took local pride" (1996, p. 11). A time-traveling American would be bewildered at the changes that separate 1948 from 1998, at the quick urban lifestyle of the 1990s and its accompanying fax machines, personal computers, and sleek cars.

The religious climate in the United States has changed dramatically as well. Following World War II, there was a steep upward climb in church membership, peaking at an astounding 69 percent of the adult population in 1959. Most of this growth took place within traditional denominations, which still held the loyalty of most American Christians (Patterson, 1996, p. 17). In the 1990s, the best words to describe the U.S. religious climate are *secular* and *fractured*. It is in these same years that have seen so much change that the parachurch has prospered tremendously.

Parachurch organizations that have endured have had the uncanny skill to be biblical and at the same time be relevant to this culture that is inexorably changing. The five keys that will be examined in this chapter are the common attributes that have been shared by parachurch organizations that endure through change.

Culture's Crucible

The word *culture* means many things to many people. For the purposes of this discussion we can think of culture as a pair of glasses. From childhood a person is taught a language, learns how to act around neighbors and friends, believes certain ideas about his or her world, lives by definite moral values—these elements form the glasses through which every person interprets the surrounding world. Each culture sees the world through different glasses, with its own worldview.

In the half century since the close of World War II, the worldview of most Americans has shifted dramatically. Not only the United States but the West as a whole has gone through a change. One way this shift became visible is described by Lesslie Newbigen, who left England in 1936 as a missionary to India: "Before we left India in 1974 we had become accustomed to the sight of young people from affluent homes in England, France, or Germany roaming the streets in tattered and unwashed Indian clothes, having turned their backs on Europe in the hope that—even as beggars—they might find in India something to make life worth living" (1983, p. 1). And Newbigen goes on to identify "the disappearance of hope" as the prime cause of this aimless searching. The shifting worldview has eroded the values and beliefs that gave hope and ideals to the youth of the past.

The cause of the emerging worldview is complex. Historians have sketched out the basic path: the old Enlightenment certainties that the human mind could know objective truth and that human culture could solve its own problems came crashing down. The twentieth century brought a number of developments that destroyed these assumptions. Freud's psychology, two great wars, and quantum physics are just three of the major events that over time shaped the new worldview (Van Gelder, 1996). Modernism is becoming postmodernism, and this is manifested by a cynicism as to whether a person may know or find objective truth and as a relativism that accepts any and every religious belief as valid (Leffel and McCallum, 1996). Yet the paradox is that in a cynical and doubting culture, there is still so much obvious longing for stable spiritual truth.

One of the major challenges now facing Christianity is how to minister effectively to a culture that is dominated by the postmodern worldview. The spiritual void must be filled with timeless and unchanging truth. Both parachurch and local church, in trying to meet this challenge, find themselves between two competing forces. On the one side is the timeless and universal Gospel that holds out Christ as the answer for every person. The other side is culture, with its local customs and time-bound ways of seeing the world. The local church and the parachurch, as the two dominant institutional expressions of Christianity, are faced with the task of translating the timeless message for contemporary culture. It is much the same job that faces any missionary, except it is not foreign words and syntax that must be translated but the foreign ideas and beliefs that make up the Christian worldview. In this crucible between two opposed forces, the demands of the Gospel and the needs of culture must both be met.

Many parachurch organizations are finding innovative ways to reach the doubting postmodern culture. The Crossroads Project, in Columbus, Ohio, is a parachurch organization that aims directly at finding ways to communicate the Gospel to those with a postmodern worldview. Part of its strategy is to host an event called Conversation and Cuisine (Leffel and McCallum, 1996). After dinner is eaten, a topic is discussed that involves moral judgment. The facilitator tries to bring out the differences in worldview that lie behind the answers of those attending. The goal is not to evangelize but to prepare those who are participating to hear the Gospel. Once people are made aware of the presuppositions in their own arguments and the logical conclusions to their ideas, they may be more open to hearing an opposing belief—and accepting it.

Even though the Crossroads Project is an organization focused narrowly on apologetics and evangelism, all parachurch organizations can learn from Crossroads the importance of paying close attention to differences in worldview. Any parachurch organization that hopes to endure into the next century must be willing to reinvent itself in order to answer the questions and needs of the surrounding culture. Through an examination of successful parachurch organizations it is possible to find five keys to enduring impact.

- Key 1: approach ministry as an entrepreneur
- Key 2: recognize the needs
- Key 3: provide an alternative solution
- Key 4: understand the possibilities
- Key 5: take advantage of emerging technology

Key 1: Approach Ministry as an Entrepreneur

One reason the parachurch has prospered over the past few decades is that confidence comes naturally to many individuals in North America. The culture applauds entrepreneurs in any field who can leap with vigor into a new situation. Competition and free enterprise are values that few people question, and culture as a whole has benefited from the energy and creativity parachurch organizations unleash.

J. Alan Youngren (1981) has pointed out the influence of the *frontier mind* on the parachurch. He draws upon the popular historical thesis of Frederick Jackson Turner that the American mind has been formed to a large degree by frontier values. These values include self-reliance, low respect for tradition, and infatuation with the new. Of course the results of these values have not always been positive, and Youngren points out the irrepressible, and often unneeded, multiplication of parachurch organizations as one negative result. Certainly parachurch organizations could often be more effective if their leaders learned to work together and to pay more attention to history, yet many healthy results have come out of these frontier values as well. Successful parachurch leaders have a readiness and confidence to try new ideas, to be different. The parachurch has prospered because, among other things, it has been a vehicle for entrepreneurial leaders who are finding fresh ways to meet the demands of the changing culture.

An example of this entrepreneurial spirit is Bill Bright, founder of Campus Crusade for Christ. He found the ministry at which he would work for the rest of his life when he was a senior at Fuller Theological Seminary in Pasadena, California and "discovered that we had to wait our turn to go to jail services and skid row missions because there were many other churches covering this area of service. One day it occurred to me that there were no waiting lines to reach college students or the top executives of the city. Here were the neglected leaders of our world, both today's and tomorrow's" (Bright, 1985, p. 5).

Just as we might imagine a businessperson or investor taking stock of market possibilities, so we find Bright at the outset of his ministry considering what his future ministry ought to be. And it should come as no surprise that Bright approached the question like a successful businessman. Even while a student in seminary, he maintained his position as president of the business he had previously founded, Bright's Fancy Foods.

It should be noted, though, that his ministry was not based solely on calculation. Bright writes about a specific night in which he felt a definite call from God toward this ministry. In the days and weeks that followed he sought confirmation of this call with spiritual leaders and peers. Once sure of the call, he left seminary, never to return, and sold off his business. The events of the days that followed were framed in prayer and meditation. "'Lord, where do you want us to launch this ministry?' was a prayer that [my wife] Vonette and I and our friends uttered frequently" (Bright, 1985, p. 8).

Shortly thereafter Bright and his wife established their ministry at the UCLA campus. As Bright tells the story of early Campus Crusade, although they had a budget of only $200 per month, God provided for them a house that was only one block from sorority row and that had a large living room in which they could hold Bible studies with students from the nearby campus. The next step was getting good personnel to help with this ministry. Bright again thought like an entrepreneur: "As in any expanding business, we needed new personnel. We needed dedicated, qualified staff" (1985, p. 12). Just as with the house, God provided a number of energetic and godly workers.

Today, more than forty-five years after this pioneering ministry got its start, most Christians in the United States know about the success of Campus Crusade for Christ. As of 1996, Campus Crusade was established on more than 752 university campuses in the United States and an additional 750 campuses abroad. The scope of this ministry, which began from such a small seed in 1951, is now much broader than college-age students. *Jesus,* a film produced by Campus Crusade, has now been seen by more than 766 million people, and in 365 languages (Bright, 1985, pp. xiv–xv). The organization's campaign Here's Life, America, attempted to saturate an entire city with the Gospel, using mass media and a trained corps of volunteers. The ministry of Bill and Vonette Bright has followed their early motto: "Win the campus to Christ today, win the world to Christ tomorrow."

The story of Bill Bright and Campus Crusade exemplifies a can-do approach to ministry. Any person who feels that God is calling him or her to a certain ministry should move toward this goal with energy. Of course such a calling needs to be confirmed with prayer and the advice of respected spiritual leaders, but once the calling is sure it ought to be followed. The person who is called must learn to think like a business entrepreneur. That means analyzing the situation and planning ways to make the goal a reality. As the story of Bill Bright shows, God will open doors and provide for needs, but energy and effort must be given by the person who is called.

This entrepreneurial spirit is important not just for the small parachurch organization that has recently begun its ministry. Even seasoned organizations and veteran leaders face new challenges and opportunities. Bill Bright kept himself open to new and larger ministry opportunities, and when the time came he took on projects that would reach millions of people all over the world. If an organization is to continue to grow and influence modern culture, it must have creative leaders that can look up to find the next challenge on the horizon. Leaders must never be content simply resting in the green valley of success. The energy to take on new challenges comes when leaders have confidence that God will use them to change lives.

Key 2: Recognize the Needs

Along with the shifts in worldview came changes in moral values. These changes blossomed in the late 1960s into what is now called the *sexual revolution*. Although many of the forces behind the changes had been simmering for decades, the outward changes came startlingly quickly. Books such as those by Alfred Kinsey claimed to reveal the sexual practices of Americans. In the mid-fifties, *Playboy* openly promoted hedonistic values, popularizing the twin ideals of complete freedom and happiness in material things. In books and movies as well, the walls that upheld traditional values were cracking. By the late 1960s, the cracks were gaping holes, and the moral changes were at flood tide (Patterson, 1996).

This was the world into which James Dobson stepped in 1970 with his first book, *Dare to Discipline*. "Many young people," Dobson said, "are now playing another dangerous game, packaged neatly under the title of sexual freedom. The rationale sounds very plausible: Why should you be restricted by the hang-ups of the past generation? Why shouldn't you enjoy this greatest of life's pleasures? Now that God is dead, who has the authority to deny you this fulfillment? . . . The 'Playboy Philosophy' has been accepted as the banner of the new generation" (1970, p. 17). This book sold over three million copies—and continues to sell in the 1990s. It struck a chord with the millions of Americans who did not agree with the flood of secular values. The success of Dobson and Focus on the Family, the parachurch organization that he leads, stems from his ability to recognize a need, an emptiness, in the culture around him, and build a ministry aimed at that need.

Dobson's ministry began with no special calling and no divine illuminations. In his first year at college he knew that he would be a psychologist, and through methodical work, he did just that. "His career," says Tim Stafford, "has been a straight line of rising success. . . . He always seemed to know exactly what he wanted to do with his life" (1988, p. 20). While pursuing his doctorate at the University of Southern California, Dobson was speaking to any audiences he could find, working constantly on his speaking abilities and on honing his message. It was during this time, in the late sixties, that he came upon the topic of discipline, which seemed to rouse strong interest among his audiences, and out of that interest came his first book.

Until 1976, Dobson was speaking at seminars on the weekends, but his full-time job was in pediatrics, at the Children's Hospital in Los Angeles. He took a yearlong leave of absence, and then he left the hospital for good in order to devote himself to his expanding ministry. In retrospect it seems like an obvious move, but it is not easy to give up a profession for the insecurity of weekend seminars. He turned his seminars into a series of films that could be watched by church congregations or small groups, multiplying the number of people he could reach. He also began to broadcast a weekly radio program that would one day reach millions. Twenty years later the ministry is thriving. Focus on the Family, based in Colorado Springs, has a budget of over $100 million (Evangelical Council for Financial Accountability, 1996). Through radio, books, magazines, and videos, the organization is fulfilling Dobson's vision of strengthening the family against the ravages of modern culture.

Each successful parachurch organization has zeroed in on a need in modern culture. No matter how strong the leadership or how professional the board, if the ministry is not addressing a real need, it will not prosper. Thus the first job of a parachurch leader is to identify the needs of the surrounding culture. Dobson did just this when he answered the need for a defense of traditional values.

A parachurch leader need never be discouraged by thinking that all the ministry niches have been filled. Dobson stepped in to fill a gaping hole, and new demands and niches are constantly being opened by an ever-changing culture. What are needed are people patient enough to find and study these needs and dedicated enough to be used by God to meet those needs.

Key 3: Provide an Alternative Solution

Culture is highly pragmatic. The parachurch must provide solutions that work, that change the culture for the better. Information about these organizations spreads quickly by word of mouth—"you can get a meal there," a homeless person might whisper to another, or, "*Moody Monthly* had a good article on this problem," a woman might tell her friend. To continue to endure, the parachurch must address the physical and intellectual needs of the culture.

Christian education has arisen as one of the primary needs of the present culture. Thousands of private elementary and secondary schools have as their goal the training of children in Christian values. Often these schools are closely affiliated with a church (Roman Catholic and Reformed churches are known for their school systems), but just as many schools are run independently of any denominational control. Even if these schools meet in a church facility, they retain the power to make their own decisions, and may thus be counted as parachurch organizations. Independent Christian education has also flourished in postsecondary schools. Numerous Christian universities, Bible colleges, and seminaries compete for the young people who want more from education than a truckload of facts and skills.

The reason for the growth of Christian education is not hard to find, and it becomes especially clear when we consider higher education. A secular worldview has spread like wildfire among academics, and the curriculum and ideas that are presented at many schools are often directly opposed to the worldview held by many Christians. This secular worldview has been clearly articulated by historian Carl Becker, professor at Cornell University from 1917 to 1941 and president of the American Historical Association: "It is still quite impossible for us to regard man as the child of God for whom the earth was created as a temporary habitation. Rather must we regard him as little more than a chance deposit on the surface of the world, carelessly thrown up between two ice ages by the same forces that rust iron and ripen corn. . . . What is man that the electron should be mindful of him!" (Marsden, 1994, pp. 371–372). When a large number of professors and administrators hold these bluntly secular views, then it is no wonder that many Christians began looking for a more friendly alternative in which to get the skills and knowledge they needed.

Biola University in Southern California is an example of the way parachurch organizations involved in education have prospered by providing clear alternatives. Biola (the Bible Institute of Los Angeles) was one of a number of Bible institutes that sprang up around the turn of the century. The original purpose of these schools was to provide basic Bible teaching and professional training to those for whom graduate-level seminaries were out of reach or unnecessary (Marsden, 1980). But as time went by and new needs in U.S. culture became evident, the nature of these schools changed also.

At its inception in 1908, the curriculum at Biola included "Books of the Bible, The Great Doctrines, Chapter Studies, Homiletics, Church History," and so on (Williams and Miller, 1983, p. 16). Gradually Biola began to broaden, from a school offering almost exclusively Bible courses to a liberal arts college that gave bachelor's degrees in subjects as diverse as English literature, art, and accounting. The change came as new needs became known. As many of the traditionally conservative Protestant seminaries began to turn their backs on the "fundamentals" of the Gospel, Biola began to consider the possibility of opening its own seminary, and in 1952, it added Talbot Seminary to its educational system. At about the same time, Samuel Sutherland, president of Biola, wrote: "Today's needs differ from those which existed in the early period of Institute life. . . . The curriculum of the Bible Institute twenty-five years ago never would suffice for the needs of the present time" (Williams and Miller, 1983, pp. 71–72). He went on to emphasize that Biola's purpose and goals had not changed at all, only the methods and structures had been changed to meet the changing demands. Today Biola University still has a number of required courses in Bible, but the prime reason for its success is its quality alternative to the secular education offered at other universities. Biola is only following a path that many other Christian institutions have followed, finding a need in modern culture and then offering a Christian alternative. Today Biola is the only national university whose faculty and students are Christian and that requires thirty units of Bible for all graduates.

The example of Biola teaches us that it is not enough to see a place where modern culture is failing and then raise a furor over that need with angry speeches and articles. To recognize a need is only half the job. Once the cultural need is understood, a tangible alternative must be found. For those who want their children to have a college education but who do not relish the thought of paying for them to learn a secular worldview, a Christian university has been a welcome alternative. Those who simply denounce the secular system are not the leaders who have an impact in the long run. A concrete alternative and answer to the problems must be established.

Key 4: Understand the Possibilities

One particular tangible and inescapable reason for the growth of the parachurch in the past few decades is the economic strength of the United States as a whole. In a poor country, where so much of the energy available for living is taken up by the business of survival, it is hard to imagine a prospering parachurch. Even if the people have great entrepreneurial spirit and their leaders are gifted at seeing the needs in their culture, if there is not a surplus of resources and personal energy, the parachurch will not have the same strength as it does in more prosperous countries.

The United States after World War II was anything but a poor country. In fact, the prosperity that came to the United States from 1945 until the mid-1970s is nearly unprecedented in world history. At the end of the 1940s, the United States had only 7 percent of the world's population, yet possessed an amazing 42 percent of the world's income and 50 percent of the world's manufacturing output (Patterson, 1996, p. 61). This boom continued through the 1960s, and with each passing year the Gross

National Product and the standard of living edged upwards. Business-people took advantage of this economic prosperity and offered an array of new products and gadgets to lure the consumer. The sales of household appliances, jewelry, clothing, and furniture jumped from three to five times their previous levels (Patterson, 1996, p. 70).

In these years the parachurch experienced the same type of exponential growth. It is estimated that more parachurch organizations have been founded in the last four decades than during the previous 150 years of our nation's history (Wuthnow, 1988, p. 112). Just as secular business-people were able to take advantage of the economic growth, so religious leaders in the United States were also able to expand and offer services that were unthinkable just a few years previously. That parachurch growth is connected to the growth of the nation's economy in no wise detracts from the parachurch accomplishment; it simply points out that wise leaders are able to harness modern possibilities and openings to further extend their ministries.

World Vision International is an example of a parachurch organization that has prospered because its leaders could see the possibilities that were opened up by the economic boom in the United States. The organization was founded by Bob Pierce in the 1950s to help children who were orphaned by the Korean War (World Vision International, 1997). Through a sponsorship, individuals or families from the more prosperous United States could support a child from South Korea, caring for that child's food, education, health care, and training. With the success of this program, World Vision expanded into a number of other ministries, including disaster assistance and more time-consuming projects geared toward bringing long-term hope and well-being to a community. Support for this humanitarian work often comes from individuals, but corporations often donate gifts-in-kind that go toward specific needs, and even the U.S. government gives support in the form of transportation and food grants.

All of this has been possible because individuals, corporations, and the U.S. government have had money and resources to give out of a surplus. If Bob Pierce had gotten his idea of supporting Korean orphans in the 1930s, in the midst of the Great Depression, it is doubtful whether a country hardly able to feed its own citizens would have been able to give substantially to help orphans overseas. He was able to implement his vision of giving aid to the needy all across the globe because of the economic resources available in the United States in later years.

Today the possibilities are different. The economic dominance of the United States is not so pronounced, and other countries rival it in standard of living. Individuals, corporations, and government are not able to give as freely. If World Vision International had continued to rely solely on the United States for support, the ministry would likely have felt the need to cut back on its ambitious programs or grow more focused on a certain need. But once again the key for an enduring parachurch organization is to see new possibilities in the present world. The United States alone cannot support the world's poor, but there is now a vast First World of prospering countries, each of which can support the poor within its own borders and in neighboring countries.

Recently, president and chief executive officer of World Vision International Dean Hirsch (1996) has pointed to a new direction for that organization, stating that the traditional distinctions between the rich nations that give and the poor nations that receive aid are being obliterated. The trend now is for World Vision regional offices to be self-sufficient, relying less and less on the support of the head offices in the United States, and Hirsch points to the offices in Taiwan and South Korea, which have gone from relying on outside funds to financing local and international programs. To Hirsch, these two offices are examples of the new philosophy of *partnership* that must be adopted by all the offices: "There would be no more dichotomy between 'support office' and 'field office.' No longer would one office understand that it carries out certain parts of the mission statement while other offices do other parts. Every office is a resource office. Every office is a ministry office. Every entity is pursuing the whole mission of World Vision" (Hirsch, 1996, p. 5).

In fact, this change, manifested in words like *partnership,* is a reflection of the world's changing realities. Today South Korea is no longer a war-ravaged country without the economic wherewithal to support its orphans; it is an economic power. World Vision International is able to keep growing because its leaders have not bound it to old ways of seeing the world. The diminishing ability of the United States to meet all the demands of the world is not being met with disappointment or denial; instead World Vision International sees new possibilities for funding its ministries.

We learn from World Vision that dreams must be wedded to reality. A dream that can be put into action in an affluent neighborhood may find little monetary support in places where the ministry is most needed. The parachurch leader must take the time to think through the possibilities in the culture. Perhaps the old ways of carrying out a ministry and the old ways of raising funds are no longer effective. Direct-mail appeals and door-to-door solicitation may have worked in the past, and may work today for certain types of ministry, but these methods will be unsuccessful if the goal is to reach a younger generation. The parachurch leader must fit dreams to modern possibilities. This is a project for which there are no ten-step guides—each situation is different. The leader needs wisdom and insight from God to see the new possibilities and new methods that are always at hand.

Key 5: Take Advantage of Emerging Technology

Most parachurch leaders are just the same as millions of other Americans: they are bewildered at the quick pace of technological change in this country. Every two years the speed of computers doubles, and the old computers and programs suddenly seem antiquated. Many smaller parachurch organizations have been slow to establish a website on the Internet. Almost all of the larger parachurch organizations have already taken this step, but for others the need for a website is less than obvious. It is imperative for a leader to have a wise outlook on technology, both a respect for its benefits and a skepticism for its wilder promises. Once again, by looking to a recent example we can find a proper attitude toward technology.

Wycliffe Bible Translators exhibits many of the same features as the other organizations mentioned in this chapter. It was founded by a strong and energetic leader, William Cameron Townsend, who at the age of twenty-one arrived in Guatemala as a Bible salesman for the Bible House of Los Angeles (Hefley and Hefley, 1974). While selling Bibles among the Cakchiquel Indians, Townsend saw many needs. What had begun as a short trip to Central America turned into a lifetime of work. In 1919, he put his convictions into practice by opening a school for the Cakchiquel Indians where they would be taught in their native language, not Spanish. He also became convinced that these people needed the Bible in their native language. This was an unheard of idea (previously it had been expected that the Indians would need to learn Spanish to have access to the Bible). It was also an idea that did not win the support of the missionaries in Guatemala. The Presbyterians and the independent Central American Mission (CAM) were working in Guatemala, and neither would support Townsend in his vision to translate the Bible into the Cakchiquel language.

Ten years after he began his work with the Cakchiquel Indians, the translation was completed. Townsend then lifted his vision to the many hundreds—and as would later be clear, thousands—of languages that still had no readable scripture. To meet this need Townsend began to recruit more workers, and this group became Wycliffe Bible Translators. The Summer Institute of Linguistics was founded in order to train this new breed of missionary in linguistic principles. By early in the 1970s, graduates from this linguistic school would translate the Bible into five hundred languages, spoken across South America, Indonesia, Asia, and Africa.

Townsend's vision would become a reality, but many seemingly insurmountable walls stood in the way at first. A primary reason that many languages were unrecorded was the inaccessibility of the people who used them. It would be technology put into service of ministry that would enable Townsend and the Wycliffe missionaries to overcome the walls. In 1926, Charles Lindbergh had not yet made his flight across the Atlantic Ocean. The airplane had been around for a number of years, but people were just beginning to see the possibilities it offered. As early as 1926, Townsend realized the immense help an airplane would be for missionaries. Without air transportation, places like the Amazon Basin were missionary graveyards. Disease and hostile Indians were constantly a threat, and supplies were many days away. With an airplane the dense jungle could be bypassed entirely. A trip that would otherwise take weeks could be made in a matter of minutes. Although Townsend saw the possibilities early on, it would not be until after 1949 that the Jungle Aviation and Radio Service was to meet these needs and provide access for many missionaries to the jungles of South America and Indonesia. The incredible growth of Wycliffe Bible Translators in the years following is due in part to Townsend's vision of putting to use the new technology of the airplane. For Townsend new technology was not something to be shunned but an opportunity to extend the ministry.

After Townsend's resignation as general director of Wycliffe Bible Translators, the organization continued his open approach to new ideas and technology. Perhaps its current use of computer aids to translation best illustrates this attitude. Necessary reference works for the translator have now been put onto a CD-ROM, the *Translator's Workplace*. This disk includes the major English translations of the Bible, along with French, Spanish, and Portuguese versions. Included also are the Greek and Hebrew scriptures with lexicons, exegetical summaries, and translators' notes. Even maps and illustrations come with the CD-ROM. Wycliffe has also developed CARLA (Computer-Aided Related Language Adaptation), a program that can help directly in translating the Bible into another language (Fultz, 1995). Each technological advance makes translating the Bible an easier and faster task, and this in turn enables more peoples to read the scripture in their own languages.

Many other parachurch organizations have put technology to good use as well, but Wycliffe points the way to the proper view of technology. Technology should be approached as a friend and with some caution. A couple of caveats must be given here. First, it is important to remember that a ministry is to people. A computer or some other machine can increase efficiency, but if this comes at the cost of human connectedness then the parachurch ministry is not served well. The ability to communicate quickly with many people is a gift of modern technology, but when only impersonal form letters are sent, then that ability may be a setback rather than a help. Technology must always be subservient to the biblical value of love—person-to-person contact.

The second caveat to remember is that technology should never be used just for the sake of technology. Cameron Townsend did not insist on the fanciest and most expensive airplanes. He used the airplanes that were available and that met the organization's particular needs. All technology must be evaluated through a biblical grid for its appropriateness to advance the organization. Technology, especially in the fundraising arena that manipulates supporters or that tricks them (such as computer-altered photos, presidential signatures generated by a machine, and so forth), deserves careful scrutiny by leaders.

For all the outward change, the inner needs of people are still the same as always. The parachurch endures and prospers because it continues to meet people's deep spiritual needs and communicates its message in a contemporary and accessible format.

PART TWO

WHO MAKES UP THE PARACHURCH?

THIS SECTION DESCRIBES the people who make up the parachurch, and especially those who are most responsible for keeping the parachurch prospering. It answers the following questions:

- ○ Who are the people who make up the parachurch?
- ○ What are the responsibilities of an effective parachurch board?
- ○ What are the qualities of a parachurch leader?
- ○ Who are the people who support the parachurch?

5

APPRECIATING THE STAKEHOLDERS AND THEIR DIVERSE NEEDS

IN MANY BIBLES there is a map on the final pages that traces the missionary journeys of Paul. The red lines mark his path through Asia Minor and from Jerusalem to Rome. The chapters in the book of Acts that sketch his heroic travels are some of the most exciting in the Bible. Paul can easily be seen as something of a cowboy missionary, traveling of his own volition from city to city to spread the Gospel. In reality there was an important supporting cast. At the end of many of his epistles, Paul gives brief instructions or encouragement to those who have helped him. In Romans 15:24, Paul writes of his hoped-for trip to Spain: "For I do hope to see you on my journey and to be sent on by you, once I have enjoyed your company for a little while." Reading between the lines, scholars guess that Paul was hoping for monetary support from the Romans to help him on his trip. In chapter 16 of Romans we find a whole list of various people who have supported Paul: Andronicus and Junia are greeted as fellow apostles (16:7); the members of the church that meets in the house of Prisca and Aquilla are greeted (16:3); many more people who are otherwise unfamiliar are listed and thanked for some work they have done. The unavoidable conclusion from this and similar chapters is that Paul was no lone cowboy but a person surrounded by a team of helpers.

It would be anachronistic to call Paul's mission work a parachurch organization, but some comparisons are valid. Many parachurch organizations seem to be headed by a single person—the voice coming over the radio, for example, is imagined as the sole force behind the parachurch organization. But just as in Paul's ministry, for every visible leader there is a cadre of *stakeholders* who often go unnoticed. If Paul's supporters were taken away, his early ministry would not have succeeded. In the same way, if the stakeholders of any parachurch organization are removed, the organization will collapse.

A stakeholder may be defined as "any person, group or organization that can place a claim on an organization's attention, resources or output or is affected by that output" (Bryson, 1988, p. 27). Another definition provides a different angle: "Stakeholders are individuals who perceive themselves to have an interest in the actions of an organization" (Boskin, Aronoff, and Lattimore, 1997, p. 160).

An effective organization is a balanced constellation of stakeholder groups. At the center of this constellation is a sun, around which all the stakeholders revolve. In a parachurch organization this center should not be a gifted individual but a mission statement and core values. These are the forces that keep the stakeholder groups within an organization moving in a common orbit. This principle is reflected clearly by Paul in 1 Corinthians 1:12–13: "Each of you says, 'I belong to Paul,' or 'I belong to Apollos,' or 'I belong to Cephas' . . . has Christ been divided?" Paul's goal was not to center the church around the person of Paul but around a life-changing message. Similarly, a central message ought to be the center of every parachurch organization. A primary challenge for parachurch leadership is to keep the different stakeholder groups orbiting smoothly around the Christ-centered values and mission of the particular organization. Supporters and volunteers, for example, are the stakeholders who keep a parachurch organization running through their prayers and monetary support. The challenge for the parachurch leader is to communicate with this fluid, often somewhat invisible body of stakeholders in order to keep its members committed to the vision that drives the organization. It is not a common community that keeps these individuals in the orbit of the parachurch but a shared sense of mission.

Identify the Stakeholders

There are a number of stakeholder groups that nearly every parachurch organization has in common. Figure 5.1 represents these different groups, ranged around the rim of a wheel, with their different demands shown inside the spokes.

Board of Directors

A board of directors (usually from five to twenty-five people) is key to the success of any parachurch organization. Group members are united by a strong interest in the core values and mission statement of the organiza-

Figure 5.1. Parachurch Stakeholders and Their Agendas.

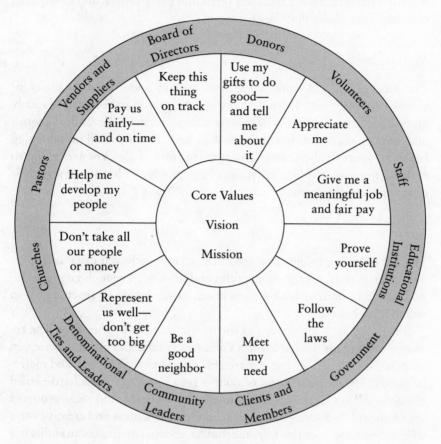

tion. Their primary purpose is to see that the parachurch organization is true to its mission statement and that it remains financially solvent. (Chapter Six expands on the responsibilities of the board.)

Staff

In regard to staff, at the low end of the spectrum are parachurch organizations that are simply coalitions of volunteers and in which nobody gets paid for the ministry or service. At the high end are organizations that employ trained professionals and use few volunteers. Organizations that rely on professionals (for example, those who use media such as radio or television) must pay increasingly high salaries to acquire the full-time services of trained workers. Although salaries are usually higher in the secular world, staff of a parachurch organization often find extra satisfaction in working toward a core vision that they believe in.

Volunteers

Common values and vision are the best way to understand the phenomenon of volunteering. The main reason for a person to volunteer a steady amount of time to an organization is that he or she believes in the work and want to make a difference with their lives. In this world of tightening budgets, successful parachurch organizations of all sizes are trying to make better use of volunteers from all age groups who want to give their time for a worthy cause.

Donors

The act of giving money and resources to a parachurch organization is also clearly based on common values and mission. Through giving, a donor is able to partner with a parachurch organization to reach a goal in which both believe.

It is possible to see donors as the mirror image of volunteers. The resource most easily available for a volunteer is time and effort. Donors, in contrast, are limited in time but are able to give of their money and material goods. The major demand of donors is to know that their hard-earned resources are not being wasted but used cost effectively. And because donors are often widely dispersed, the parachurch leaders must find creative ways to communicate with this key stakeholder group. (Again, because this is a key group to understand, a separate chapter looks at its needs.)

Vendors and Suppliers

Vendors and suppliers make up a broad stakeholder group that will vary according to a parachurch organization's needs. This group is not as interested in values and mission. Its members deliver services or products that are essential, but because they are for-profit organizations, their primary concern is prompt payment of bills. A large segment of the consultants offer marketing, management, and fundraising services. These support industries are frequently run by Christians who aid the parachurch organization by brokering radio time, producing direct mailings, or assisting the strategic planning process. The expertise of these service providers is essential to the success of parachurch organizations.

Clients and Members

Within a for-profit setting clients and members would be thought of as *customers*. Within the parachurch, there are two types of clients. On the one hand are those who receive a charitable ministry. They include, for example, the homeless people who come to a rescue mission for a warm meal. These clients do not support the organization with resources, yet the success of the organization still hinges on their acceptance. On the other hand are those receiving a spiritual ministry. People in radio land, for example, tune in to a specific program. They listen on a purely voluntary basis, and if they enjoy the program enough they may feel led to support it with a monetary gift. Both these types of parachurch client have some need that makes them responsive to a parachurch organization. Perhaps they are without a home or food, and thus they come to a local rescue mission. Perhaps they are hungry for good Bible teaching, in which case they may listen often to a certain television preacher. Whatever the exact nature of a ministry, the bottom line is that its clients and members are the people to whom the ministry is directed, and the benefit these people experience is the justification for the existence of that parachurch organization.

Community Leaders

Depending on the exact type of ministry, friendly relations with these leaders are increasingly important for an organization. Negative media exposure can mean fewer enthusiastic volunteers and fewer generous donors. Simply being open and communicating an organization's goals can often stave off negative criticism in the media. The relationship can even be turned positive by purposefully building friendships with key opinion makers. Community leaders can also be great allies if they lend public support to the work of the parachurch organization. This support will come as the local leaders see the beneficial work done by the organization for the community.

Churches and Pastors

As Chapter Fourteen will explore, churches and pastors often form the stakeholder group with which the parachurch organization encounters the most friction. The reason for this is easy enough to see: the visions of the parachurch and local church are apt to overlap, and questions of spiritual territory arise. But with a little effort and good communication, local churches can be the best allies of the parachurch. Through the local church the parachurch may be able to make connections with potential volunteers or donors. When understood correctly, the parachurch–local church relationship can be a win-win situation. The local church gets leaders, and the parachurch gets spiritual and theological accountability for its leaders.

Government and Educational Institutions

The two most common outside organizations for parachurch organizations are government agencies and institutions of higher education. Some parachurch organizations may be eligible for government funding, and this means that attention must be paid to the concerns and interests of various government agencies. Others may nurture a close relationship with a Bible college or seminary from which they often recruit staff and volunteers. Each parachurch organization must examine itself to identify the outside organizations that ought to be included in any list of its stakeholders.

Meet the Challenge of Balance

With a dozen or more stakeholder groups, the parachurch organization is inevitably faced with juggling their various needs and agendas. And like a good juggler who scans the field where the balls are going up and down, the parachurch leader must keep the large picture in mind, not letting any one group dominate the organization's actions. The needs and agenda of each of these groups are usually legitimate, and each of these competing groups contributes something very important to the overall health of the organization. What makes the task of leading a parachurch organization so alternately invigorating and bone-crushing is that each of these positive agendas pull at finite resources. Leaders have a finite amount of time in their day, organizations have a finite amount of money and space, and volunteers are finite in number and have finite time to give.

This problem of competing agendas and needs is common to almost every kind of organization, but parachurch organizations are unique because they are held together by core values that are set upon a Christian understanding of the world and by a mission that grows out of those values. In the business world the stakeholders are kept in a common orbit by the understanding that some monetary gain will accrue to them. In the world of the parachurch, monetary gain is only rarely the center that holds together the various stakeholder groups, the real energizing force is the power of a shared mission.

This can be visualized as the wheel in Figure 5.1. At the center of the wheel is the hub of core values and mission. Arranged around the circumference of the wheel are the various stakeholder groups. Each of these groups functions like a spoke for the wheel. According to this model the wheel will work fine as long as two things remain constant. First, the values and mission must remain the hub for each of the groups making up the rim. The moment that the vision begins to lose its hold on the imaginations of the various individuals, then the wheel begins to collapse. Clarifying this vision of the organization is done through strategic planning. Second, each individual spoke must support its area of the wheel. If one or two stakeholder groups let up on their efforts, then the wheel begins to wobble and will eventually collapse. Leading a parachurch means that careful attention must be paid to all the various stakeholders and their needs. With this done the organization is able to prosper and roll forward.

There are many reasons for a stakeholder group to lose sight of its vision or to flag from its work. An organization that tries to minister to people with drug or alcohol problems may have a poor success rate, or at least not enough success stories, and when this information gets back to the donors, they find another organization to support. The donors are a major stakeholder group for the parachurch, and their demand is that the resources they provide be used to accomplish definite goals. In contrast, the people who work directly with the alcoholics or drug addicts may demand time and freedom to use the methods that produce the best results over the long term. In the estimation of the workers, perhaps stories of quick success are not signs of lasting success. This is a tug in a different direction than the desires of the donors.

For each of the other stakeholder groups around the wheel, similar problems could be described. The volunteers want to help the organization, but their limited available time might be difficult to coordinate with the preferred times of those being ministered to. Local churches may support the ministry verbally but shy away from letting the parachurch organization make a direct appeal for support from their congregations or use their facilities. The ministry may have many opportunities to grow, but the board must keep its eye on the organization's overall solvency. These are just a few of the many pressures that each ministry will feel at some point.

The balancing act faced by parachurch organizations will never go away. The future is certain to hold yet more stakeholder divisions to be added to the wheel. Many of these new divisions will cut across already existing stakeholder groups. Gender and ethnic issues may unite people from different stakeholder groups. Political and theological positions may further divide the members of an organization. Advancing technology and communication abilities may disperse and fragment stakeholders into yet more subcategories.

The effectiveness of a parachurch organization is determined to a large extent by how well the stakeholder groups are kept working together despite organizational distance and division. The organization must articulate a strong vision of the future that energizes the diverse stakeholders to keep focused on the organizational mission. The skill that is most needed to keep the stakeholders moving together is old-fashioned communication. In a world growing more complex every day, it is a necessity to develop an organizational culture that allows for honest and easy communication between members from each of the stakeholder groups. The only way to reconcile their competing agendas and needs is to strive for open communication between those involved and work for compromises that allow win-win solutions. Communication skills are also vital as members of stakeholder groups become more spread out over the geography of North America and it becomes more challenging to keep the dispersed contributors in contact with the organization.

Know Your Stakeholders

An organization is able to judge its balance only when it has done a good job of knowing stakeholders. This is an indispensable step for good communication between the leadership and various stakeholders. A stakeholder analysis is also important for the strategic planning process. Unfortunately this crucial step is one of the most neglected. In the study funded by the Lilly Endowment of the financing of selected American Protestant parachurch religious institutions, leaders were asked whether they had surveyed their constituencies within the last three years. Only one in ten organizations answered yes to the question, and the final report of the study was negative on this topic: "Most ministries spend little effort and research to learn who their constituencies are" (Willmer, 1996, p. 12). But if a leader is to successfully balance the competing needs and agendas of stakeholder groups, then that leader must know clearly what those needs are and how to best energize the various groups. In addition, beyond simply analyzing the needs of stakeholders, parachurch leadership demands working at a genuine relationship with stakeholders.

There are four steps to knowing the stakeholder. The first step is to identify an organization's stakeholder groups. Figure 5.1 illustrates the basic categories, but each parachurch organization will differ in its exact constituency. For example, a parachurch organization may have two separate staff stakeholder groups. One for those who work at a central office and another for those who are on the front line of the ministry, whether that front line is in Asia or downtown Seattle.

The leaders of the organization ought to spend some time brainstorming the identity of the basic groups that support the ministry. As precisely as possible each group should be identified and written down. In considering this question it is important to look beyond the internal groups and to recognize all the informal groups that "perceive themselves to have an interest in the actions of an organization."

A second useful step is to specify the criteria stakeholders use to assess their relationship to the organization. Often the leaders have a good idea what the demands of each group are and can make informed guesses about a group's criteria for judging the organization. But as good as intuition may be, nothing takes the place of actually asking the stakeholders themselves, through surveys, interviews, and group discussions. This kind of direct information gathering is absolutely essential as the organization works out its mission and approach to ministry. At these crossroad times it is foolhardy to rely on intuition to understand the demands of the stakeholders.

The third step is to make a judgment about how strong the organization-stakeholder relationship is according to stakeholders' criteria. For example, if the donors demand cost efficiency, is that being delivered to them, and do they know it? Simply knowing whether organizational performance is poor, mediocre, or very good compared to the criteria is enough to spark useful ideas and discussion. The places where the demands of the stakeholder group are not being met are where the leadership of a parachurch organization ought to focus its efforts. The stakeholders whose needs are not being met are in danger of letting their spoke of the wheel come loose. The leadership of the parachurch organization should spot this before it happens and communicate to the stakeholders how the organization is working to remedy the situation.

The fourth and final step in the stakeholder analysis is to ask this question: How should we serve our key stakeholders? Out of the analysis the organization gets an idea of which stakeholder needs are not being met and what can be done to fix the problems.

The parachurch organization ought to react differently to the needs of its key stakeholders than would a for-profit corporation. In the business world, the dictum "the customer is always right" rules. The bottom line for each corporate stakeholder is money—is there a profit? The values that hold together the parachurch organization are much different. As already noted, these values are founded on a Christian faith. A radio ministry that preaches the traditional Gospel might find that its listeners would prefer an easier message. Smart business would dictate changing the message to meet this demand. Faithful ministry dictates that if the ministry believes it is called to preach the Gospel, then it must persevere in that calling. The mission and underlying values of an organization must set the pattern for the way it responds to the demands of its stakeholder groups.

There is a give-and-take between two realities. The nucleus of values and mission must do all it can to meet the legitimate demands of the surrounding stakeholder groups, but at the same time, these demands cannot be allowed to take over the organization. The exterior is fluid; the interior remains always constant.

Supply Intangible Resources

Each of the stakeholder groups that makes up an organization needs resources if it is to function effectively, and the resources demanded are not solely the tangible ones of money and time, although these are certainly important. Each stakeholder group also needs intangible resources.

The first intangible resource that each stakeholder group needs is strong leadership. Leadership style and content may change, but each group requires senior leadership to set direction for its participation and contributions. Instead of leadership, management is all that too many organizations know about. Management's focus is on the day-to-day workings of an organization—its scheduling and daily work. Leadership is a resource that organizations need every bit as much as money and time. When there is vision-setting leadership, all the members of an organization are galvanized behind a single focus. The vision-setting leader uses communication skills to transfer that vision to other members of the organization. The leader of the parachurch organization also needs a spiritual dimension. The leader needs to have the moral qualities that many churches look for in elders or deacons. If these qualities are absent, he or she will find it hard to be the leader that spiritually motivated people need.

The second intangible resource that a parachurch organization provides is recognition. Although the individuals who belong to a parachurch organization make countless sacrifices, and ask little in return, they still need to be publicly acknowledged for the time and energy that they give. Each stakeholder group contributes something unique to the overall work of the organization. An organization must find creative ways to pat individuals on the back for their hard work. For example, this recognition might come in the form of a newsletter article that explains a volunteer's recent work, or it might be a small Christmas gift given to a friendly delivery person.

It will often be the case that some group has gone virtually unnoticed in its day-by-day work, and this sacrificial work ought to be applauded. A characteristic of a Christian organization is its ability to instill within people the knowledge that what they do is important. One remembers Paul at the conclusion of the book of Romans, and his recognition of the many people who had helped him and his ministry. We can imagine how those people felt on hearing their names and efforts mentioned by Paul. The modern parachurch leader must strive to give this same feeling to his or her organization's stakeholders.

The third intangible resource that is owed to stakeholders is a meaningful role. Increasingly, individual stakeholders desire work or tasks that they know are counting in the overall mission of the parachurch organization. Parachurch organizations can be careless about how they place people, rather than placing them according to their gifts, expertise, or passion. Misplaced individuals often languish in an unrewarding position and slowly slide out of the organization. This bloom-where-you're-planted mentality is a relic of past leadership styles and does not fit the context of twenty-first century ministry. Individuals know what their strengths and enjoyments are, and the parachurch must strive to let them work in positions that take advantage of their gifts.

One final note: parachurch organizations have historically operated on little or no margin. Their visions are big and their resources few. The budget is filled out to the last dollar, and the work week is scheduled to the last minute. One of the challenges for parachurch leaders moving into the twenty-first century is to build system margins that allow breathing room in time and money. If stakeholder groups are to continue doing effective work, they must have a secure envelope of time and money in which to work. This means that the parachurch leader must structure budgets and schedules that are realistically attainable. "Just getting by" may be appropriate for a start-up organization but should not be the hallmark of a mature organization. A mature parachurch organization owes its stakeholders sufficient margin to take risks, experiment, and work normal hours.

People who are attracted to the parachurch are not looking to own the biggest house or nicest car but are looking instead for a meaningful role working to accomplish a mission they believe in. Intangible resources are the strength of the parachurch, and instead of trying to look more like a for-profit corporation, the effective parachurch organization must sharpen its use of native strengths. Every stakeholder of a parachurch organization should experience quality spiritual leadership, serve in a meaningful role within the organization, and receive public recognition for work done. It is the leadership of the parachurch organization that must set the tone of the environment in which these resources can be distributed to the stakeholders. And it is this and other crucial roles of the parachurch leader to which we turn in the next chapter.

6

BUILDING AN EFFECTIVE CHRISTIAN BOARD

FROM THE ONE-PERSON ministry to the complex, multifaceted organization, one of the groups most important to the overall functioning of the parachurch organization is its board of directors. As Edward L. Hayes has written, "The survival and vitality of a Christian organization depends in large measure upon how effectively board responsibilities are carried out" (1987, p. 37).

There are plenty of books, pamphlets, articles, and seminars available on how to be a board member of a nonprofit organization, but little has been written for board members of parachurch organizations. This chapter focuses on eleven responsibilities common to every parachurch board. But first it is important to understand what is distinct about the board of a parachurch organization as opposed to its secular counterpart.

The Distinctiveness of Parachurch Boards

At a casual glance, there may seem to be no difference between a parachurch board and the board of a secular nonprofit: both meet at scheduled times, have similar responsibilities, and attempt to run the organization efficiently. What is unique about the boards of Paxton Ministries, Mission Aviation Fellowship, World Vision, Promise Keepers, Prison Fellowship, and Campus Crusade for Christ or any of the thousands of other parachurch boards, big or small? How is their work different from the work of any other governance board with a nonprofit organization?

The attempt to integrate Christianity into the work of the organization is a large part of what makes the parachurch board unique. There are four facets to this uniqueness: a common Christian faith, the Christian worldview, doctrinal distinctives, and accountability to God.

Distinctive One: Common Christian Faith

As outlined in Chapter Two, one of the defining marks of a parachurch organization is a Christian mission statement. Consistent with this mission statement, and frequently at the top of the characteristics sought in members of a parachurch board, is a strong Christian faith and spiritual commitment. When presidents from the Coalition of Christian Colleges and Universities were asked to evaluate a list of characteristics for recruiting new board members, spiritual commitment ranked number one—above leadership, financial support, or professional experience (Andringa, 1996, p. 151). A survey of Christian Management Association members reflected a similar practice: almost half of the parachurch organizations responded that they required board members to have a personal Christian faith, and asked them to sign a written statement of faith (Christian Management Association, 1986, p. 6).

This is not a negative requirement. The Christian mission statement of the organization motivates parachurch board members to serve. C. William Pollard, chairman of ServiceMaster Company (listed in the Fortune 500 as the number one service company), serves on the board of directors for the Billy Graham Evangelistic Association and is chair of the Wheaton College board. He has many opportunities to serve on boards and says, "My motivation is the underlying Christian mission of the organization. That is what captivates me and is my incentive to serve. I ask, what eternal difference does the ministry make in the lives of people?" (1997, p. 4). This spiritual motivation is common to all kinds of volunteerism. A *U.S. News and World Report* survey on volunteerism found that 56 percent of the people who volunteer said it is important that their services have a spiritual basis (Gerson, 1997, p. 34).

Distinctive Two: Christian Worldview

As a result of the board members' common Christian faith, an entire set of values comes into play that dictates the way each board member views the world. This worldview also dictates the way the parachurch board formulates policy and devises strategy.

The Christian worldview is distinct from that held by society as a whole. Christians acknowledge God as Creator and Sustainer of life and the purpose for living. They also believe there is eternal life after death. The evil in this world is the result of sin, which separates humans from God. The solution for this separation is Jesus Christ, who gives a personal relationship with God and eternal life in heaven. All people have been created in the image of God and therefore have value as individuals. With this understanding of life, the parachurch board member takes on a role that requires him or her to be a good steward of the time, talents, and resources that God has provided and to labor faithfully at God's eternal work here on earth.

When Home Free Ministries in Placentia, California, works with former gang members, recovering drug addicts, street people, and others who need help, it starts with the belief that the basic problem is spiritual. At the root of these people's struggle is a spiritual issue. Upon acceptance of Christ as Lord and Savior in their lives, they come to realize there is an eternal purpose to life and that they can overcome life's problems (Hodgins, 1997). Similarly, the Los Angeles Union Rescue Mission has a goal to meet the spiritual needs of the urban poor and at the same time to meet their physical needs. As parachurch board members oversee programs and policies that reflect this Christian worldview, they operate on a level distinct from that of board members of secular nonprofit organizations.

Marvin Olasky (1992) points out that in recent years the emphasis in our culture on spiritual improvement has shifted to an emphasis on the material. This supports the concept that individuals can live any way they choose, without thought of consequences. The common practice used to be for recipients of charity to attend church or perform chores in return for assistance they received. This is far from the current situation, where they are often told that they are victims of circumstances beyond their control. This shift results from cultural change. Our culture is no longer dominated by biblically driven Christian values but is now dominated by self-serving values that leave God out of the equation. Parachurch board members must work at seeing to it that the parachurch ministry is not run by the values of the broader culture but by the values of the Christian worldview.

Distinctive Three: Doctrinal and Behavioral Standards

Although a parachurch organization is not under the formal control of a church or denomination, many parachurch organizations require commitments from their board members that relate to doctrine, behavior, and denominational ties.

It is quite common for parachurch organizations to hold particular doctrinal distinctives rooted in theological convictions—Pentecostal, Wesleyan, Calvinistic, Dispensational, or Roman Catholic, to name a few. These distinctives make their way into the statement of faith that must be signed by each board member of an organization.

Another point that often makes a parachurch board unique is members' expected adherence to a set of behavioral standards besides the general commitment to be a professing Christian. These behavioral standards generally fall into three categories: to obey Jesus' commandment to his disciples to love one another, that is, to show respect for all people regardless of race, gender, or stage in life; to refrain from practices that are biblically condemned: drunkenness, profane language, harassment, dishonesty, occult activity, and sexual sins; and to abstain from alcoholic beverages, tobacco, substance abuse, gambling, and offensive behavior in personal relationships. All or a combination of these standards may be a prerequisite to board membership for a parachurch organization.

Another area of distinction is denominational representation. In certain cases, even though the parachurch board is independent, the bylaws stipulate that a percentage of board members must represent a particular church, denomination, or region. The board member selection process is then dictated by these expectations. For example, Seattle Pacific University has written into its bylaws that a certain percentage of its board members must be members of the Free Methodist Church (the founding denomination).

Distinctive Four: Accountability to God

Peter Bell's book *Fulfilling the Public Trust* makes a passionate plea for nonprofit boards to fulfill their role of public trust and accountability. He states that board members "are morally, if not legally, accountable to a broader public . . . [and are] only authorized by society in pursuit of some form of the social good" (1993, p. 2). Although parachurch boards would generally agree with these proclamations, their Christian worldview takes board accountability a step beyond a horizontal responsibility to society to a vertical responsibility and accountability to God. Out of a common faith and Christian worldview comes a belief that the board is ultimately accountable to God. Board members are serving as stewards, caretakers of God's creation; therefore their actions, plans, and policies are ultimately responsible for reflecting God's will for the organization. God is the owner; boards are stewards of the work, accountable to God (Jeavons, 1992).

Focus on the Family reflects this accountability in its literature: "This ministry belongs to God. . . . We will try to remember always that Jesus Christ is our possessor and our dispossessor. He ordained and blessed this ministry. It belongs entirely to Him" (Focus on the Family, 1997, p. 38). With this accountability comes the necessity to seek God's wisdom as revealed in the Bible, and in prayer to listen to God for direction. This accountability to God brings to the work of a parachurch board member an eternal perspective. The board member is not just accountable to constituents or to the culture at large but, most important, to God.

Eleven Responsibilities of a Parachurch Board

By law, the governance board of a parachurch organization is the legal owner and the final authority for the institution whose assets and operations it holds in trust. The parachurch board assumes ultimate legal, moral, and spiritual accountability for the work of the organization, and thus it must be satisfied that the organization is headed in the right direction (Ingram, 1996, p. 3). Aristotle wrote that our difficulties come from a failure to define terms. To operate effectively, it is imperative that a board have a well-defined set of responsibilities.

Responsibility One: Govern Through Policy

It may seem redundant to list the first responsibility of a parachurch governing board as governance. However, the literature and personal testimonies are filled with examples of boards that failed to understand their governance role. Out of this primary responsibility flow all the others. A governance board sustains the vision, articulates the mission, and makes the policy that conforms to the values of the organization.

Individual board members have power and authority only as they vote as members of the governance group. This means it is the wisdom and consensus of the total group that governs, not the whims of an individual. Meetings are run according to a set of bylaws that establish the procedures for doing business. Once out of a meeting, no trustees have authority to set policy for the organization or to speak in a manner that would hint they have special authority. Their responsibility is to communicate the actions of the board as a whole. When board members stay within these parameters, there is little room for confusion or other problems.

A significant part of this first responsibility is to govern by establishing policies that affirm where the organization has come and where it is going. *Policy* is a nasty word in today's world—it smacks of restriction and lack of freedom. But the point of policy is not to squelch individual thought and expression but to provide clear parameters within which the staff will work to achieve the mission of the organization. These policies should be open enough to allow freedom for the CEO and staff to move ahead aggressively. Boards formulate, determine, and monitor policy that the staff implement.

It is amazing how many boards rely on old minutes or the memory of senior board members to recall the policies they have passed and under which they are operating. Key to operating an effective parachurch board is a policy manual that records all policies. Policies help define the manner in which boards conduct their business. They set the parameters within which the president and staff are to accomplish organizational goals, and outline the board's own structure and process. The bylaws (which outline meeting frequency and timing, governance structure, term limits, board and staff roles, and the committee structure) should be included in the policy manual. Rarely will this manual be more than a dozen pages in length (Andringa and Engstrom, 1997).

As organizations move away from the pyramid structures of the past and into the team-building models of today, boards should be governing in a more fluid fashion. They should be concerning themselves predominantly with do or die issues, those central to the organization's success. Decisions should be driven by results that are linked to timetables, that have clearly defined measures of success, and that involve the organization's internal and external constituents (Taylor, Chait, and Holland, 1996).

John Carver, in *Boards That Make a Difference,* reduces the governance process to four steps: (1) project a vision, (2) infuse mission, (3) allow the staff to be all they can be, and (4) have the board grow in the governance process. Most often the board handles governance through policy clarification, which then becomes the central feature of board leadership. The policies established by the board reflect the core values of the parachurch organization and provide the foundation on which the more mechanical and visible aspects of the organization operate. Attention to policy allows a board to gain control over what matters in the organization and to be at less risk of getting lost in the details. The goal of an effective parachurch board is to make the board's policymaking process focus on ends to be achieved, the means to the ends, the relationship between board and staff, and the governance process (Carver, 1990).

Implementation of policy set by the board is usually the responsibility of a president and staff. Except in emergencies, boards get themselves into trouble when they get involved in implementation and execution. Only occasionally will the full governance board need to approve a committee or an individual board member to implement a policy on its behalf.

Some bylaws authorize an executive committee to act for the full board between meetings on most policy concerns. This implementer function is meant for specific projects that need to be accomplished before the next meeting. A board member is assigned because of some specific expertise brought to the task. An example is the sale of a capital asset, such as property. Board policy might state that the full board must approve all property purchases. However, if a transaction needs to take place before the next board meeting, the board can vote to authorize an individual board member or committee with relevant experience to implement the policy between meetings.

Responsibility Two: Select Quality Board Members

Most parachurch boards are self-perpetuating; the board nominates and votes on its own membership. (One exception is associations where the general membership approve board members.) Because of this responsibility, boards have in their control the quality and appropriateness of board members. As John Knudsen writes, "The most important job of the board is not the hiring and firing of the president, but selecting trustees" (Nason, 1989, p. 60).

Because the parachurch board members understand their accountability to God, they look to the Bible for direction in the selection process. Frequently they adopt the typical qualifications for church deacons or elders. Like church leaders, parachurch organization board members are expected to set a good example to others and to be worthy of respect. As Michael J. Anthony outlines in *The Effective Church Board,* the clearest teaching on these qualifications comes from Acts 6:1–7 and 1 Timothy 3:8–13. Qualifications include the personal characteristics of being dignified, having a respectful attitude and behavior, and being consistent in communication (not double-tongued). Board members should show temperate behavior (not be addicted to wine) and not be fond of sordid gain (for example, they cannot be improperly influenced, say, by bribery). They will provide good leadership for the family and, if married, will have a pure marriage relationship. Likewise, they will have good reputations by both Christian and non-Christian standards, exhibit sound decision making (as seen in James 4:14–17), and be trustworthy. They will also demonstrate spiritual maturity: being full of the Holy Spirit, not being recent converts, holding consistently to the faith, and involving themselves actively in a local church (Anthony, 1994, p. 46).

The goal in building a parachurch board is a professional team with varied talents and experiences. A good starting approach is to develop a profile of skills, experiences, and characteristics that complement each other and are desirable in board members. The categories might be law, finance, public relations, business, construction, fundraising, and education. Being a CEO of a similar organization is also a useful category. Board recruitment should also take place with an eye to diversified gifts and personalities and overall board chemistry.

In the study on the financing of American Protestant parachurch organizations (Willmer, 1996), the median size of the respondents' boards was eleven members: nine men and two women. The boards ranged in overall size from seven to fifteen. In an earlier study of the Christian Management Association membership, it was found that board sizes ranged similarly, from three to twenty-five (Christian Management Association, 1986, p. 6).

At the heart of a good board is a quality chairperson, or leader. Finding the right person takes discernment, an intentional selection process, and the foresight to groom successors for the job. The chair is often the conduit through which the CEO works (especially in larger organizations) and is an essential component of an effective board. A strong chair has the potential to let a board languish or help it be productive, therefore the working relationship between the chair and the organizational leader or CEO must be healthy, open, and have integrity. This relationship is a linchpin that must be strong. More than one parachurch organization leader has failed to take the time to build a solid relationship with the board chair, and then wondered why the board was uninformed or not enthusiastic about a vision or plan. A commitment to open, healthy communication will help ensure a strong relationship.

Parachurch boards can encourage quality membership by having each trustee sign an affirmation statement before being elected and annually thereafter. This statement is a commitment to the time required for the position and to the mission and vision of the organization. It may also include a statement of faith, expectations of giving, and anything else the board holds important. Without this affirmation, it is easy for board members to lose their focus.

Responsibility Three: Ensure Vision and Clarity of Mission

Carver suggests that "boards need to spend their time exploring, debating and refining their dreams . . . with impassioned discussion about the changes to be produced in their world" (1990, p. 25). Because the organization's vision focuses on the world external to the organization and gives a broad perspective on the organization's momentum, it is a critical board responsibility. Boards need to ask questions like, How is the culture changing? Is our organization competing with others unnecessarily? And each board member needs to ask, What can I bring to this parachurch organization that will help it be even more effective? The vision is the preferred future—the board's dream. This vision is embodied in the mission statement.

Because the parachurch board members are the moral and spiritual keepers of the organization's mission, they need to ensure mission clarity and focus. Drifting off course is not the exception—it is the rule in most organizations. Good ideas that are just a little off center can still be very enticing. Somewhere in the organization some set of people must exercise objectivity to check ideas against the plumb line of the mission. That is the role of the board.

As Edward Hayes stated when he was serving as executive director of Mount Herman camps, "The clarification of spiritual purposes and the careful preservation of charter statements of mission are essential duties of trustees" (1987, p. 37).

Responsibility Four: Provide Spiritual Leadership and Prayer Support

By definition, a parachurch organization has a Christian mission state-ment, and as explained at the outset of this chapter, this presupposes a common faith and worldview that puts a predominant value on spiritual leadership and prayer. If prayer is important, then board members should be encouraged to be faithful prayer partners.

Fulfillment of this responsibility requires the board member to spend personal time in reading, thought, contemplation, and prayer on behalf of the parachurch organization. A board member who is just attending formal meetings and events of the governance board and is not giving personal mental, spiritual, and emotional time to the ministry is not fully committed to board membership. A board member is an extension of the ministry and should always be considering how to improve the orga-nization. Liaison with God, through prayer, is an important part of this function. The move in recent years toward viewing the board as a con-stellation, rather than a collection, of stars places greater emphasis upon the personal values that a member brings to the meetings (Taylor, Chait, and Holland, 1996). These values, by and large, are shaped outside the boardroom as a result of quality personal time given to prayer, the read-ing of God's word, and contemplation about the vision and direction the organization is taking.

To facilitate faithful and consistent prayer, a number of mechanisms can be used. Biola University president Clyde Cook distributes to board members a quarterly prayer letter, which outlines specific prayer requests on a day-by-day basis. Other organizations periodically publish and distribute concerns that encourage consistent prayer. The Internet or e-mail makes a convenient method for facilitating prayer. When urgent or sudden concerns arise, it is not uncommon in many organizations for personal letters to go out to the board, explaining requests for prayer.

At some parachurch board meetings, members set aside time at the beginning of the meeting to pray. Others divide up into small groups or have a designated board member provide a devotional lesson from scripture. Whatever methods are used, spiritual leadership and prayer are the signs of a truly engaged parachurch board member.

Responsibility Five: Organize the Board for Effectiveness

No board member wants to waste time in scheduled meetings and work that add no real value to the organization. CEOs and board chairs share a joint responsibility to keep board contributors effective. Defining clear roles is the first step to an effective board. Confusion in the board's work is often the result of differing assumptions about who does what. Written job descriptions, reviewed and updated frequently, are essential.

The second step is sending the right communications. On the one hand most board members complain that they receive too little of the right information and too much of the wrong information. On the other hand CEOs complain that board members do not read what is sent to them. No question is more important to an effective board than this one from a CEO: What information will help you be a great board member, and how often do you want it? Armed with the answer to this question, CEOs can prepare and send the right information—information that adds value to the contribution of a board member.

A third step is holding productive meetings. Research on board function suggests that four elements are necessary to have meaningful meetings: a concise agenda; an effective chair; simple, clear committee reports; and good personal relationships among board members (Biehl and Engstrom, 1988, p. 171). With time and energy at a premium, most board members (especially baby boomers and busters) want just enough community to be effective and shorter, highly focused meetings.

A fourth step is seeing that those serving on a particular board get an orientation on the history, organization, and peculiarities of the parachurch organization. Parachurch organizations will often assume that a new board member automatically understands the organization's position, but this is seldom the case. The orientation process has two phases: preselection activities, before the person is asked and says yes, and activities that take place after the person is officially a member. Some common orientation activities include meeting officers; being interviewed; reading the organization's history and bylaws; and reviewing the strategic plan, the board reference book (discussed later), and board policy manual. Another important activity is a review of the process of work, the procedures for meetings, the time required, and so on. In addition to the initial orientation, an ongoing training system should be in place to keep board members informed on current issues within and outside the organization. Many boards make an annual retreat so board members can focus on training, orientation, and relationship building.

A fifth step is setting up meaningful committees. The purpose of a committee is to help the full board make policy. The committee speaks *to* the full board, not *for* the full board—it does not make policies independently of the board. Most committees will have a staff liaison assigned to help gather data, analyze options, and staff the committee work. However, the committee's purpose is not to do staff work or to direct staff in any official way. Preferably, committees meet before the full board so that they have time to prepare reports and so that the board can discuss their actions. Committees function best when they have job descriptions approved by the board.

There is no set number of committees or subdivisions needed to accomplish the work, and many boards use a variety of committees. A nominating or trustees affairs committee that is responsible for empowering officers and replenishing the board is common. A finance committee reviews and makes recommendations to the board regarding financial concerns (including the audit). A development or advancement committee oversees the public relations and fundraising concerns. Frequently an executive committee, composed of the officers, is empowered to act for the full board. Some groups have program committees that handle the particular program concerns of the organization. Increasingly boards are appointing a board development committee, which has the task of providing professional development for board members and of organizing the board's work. A good way to avoid committee problems is to keep in mind the specific role for which each committee was begun, and not let its work slip over those parameters.

One of the best ways for the board to fulfill the responsibility of organizing itself is to put all the information a board member needs into a board reference book (usually a three-ring binder) that is kept current by staff. Components include the board policy manual, organization mission, vision, bylaws, orientation check list, list of board members, forms the board uses, job descriptions, organization chart, minutes, history of the organization, and the like. The book becomes the "bible" of an effective board member.

Responsibility Six: Appoint, Empower, Support, and Evaluate the CEO

The most important decision a parachurch board makes (other than board selection) is the appointment of a CEO or president who will implement the vision, mission, and policies the board has established. Defining the CEO's responsibilities is critical, and after the board decides on a job description, the expectations ought to be written down as well. In the selection process, each of the constituents of the organization ought to be involved, and frequently an executive search firm is employed as well.

There are two unique dynamics in selecting parachurch CEOs that distinguish the process from the normal process of other nonprofit organizations. The first dynamic is that the Christian board member finds in scripture (1 Corinthians 12:7 and 1 Peter 4:10) that God gives spiritual gifts to all believers so that they can build up and equip the members of the body of Christ. Because God provides different people with different gifts, it is the job of the board to discern these gifts and to select a CEO accordingly. "The New Testament teaches that those with a specific gift ... must be placed in positions where they can exercise their gifts" (Anthony, 1994, p. 46). The second dynamic for the parachurch board is the members' common belief that people are called by God to serve, that God raises up people and provides gifts and leadership. Thus the spiritual maturity and qualifications of a CEO candidate have high importance in the selection process.

Once appointed, the CEO should be able to view the board as part of the leadership team, working together with the CEO and other leaders to accomplish the organization's vision. The CEO position is a lonely one and needs the ongoing encouragement and empowerment of the board. An important part of this process is a periodic evaluation by the board that holds the CEO accountable and provides suggestions of how to do a better job. In summary, the board appoints, empowers, encourages, and evaluates the CEO so that he or she can carry out the leadership and management directed by board policy.

Responsibility Seven: Facilitate a Strategic Plan

Another responsibility of the board is to assure that the CEO drafts and presents to the board a strategic plan that implements the vision and mission of the organization and provides a framework to assess current and future programs. Thinking strategically is of core importance to the board's role. As the article, "The New Work of the Nonprofit Board," suggests, "A board's contribution is meant to be strategic, the joint product of talented people brought together to apply their knowledge and experience to the major challenges facing the institution" (Taylor, Chait, and Holland, 1996, p. 42). The strategic plan translates the mission and vision into objectives and goals that can be measured and accomplished. This plan, once approved by the board, becomes the road map for the direction of the organization. The plan should be assessed annually and updated to stay as relevant as possible to the changing culture. (A more detailed description of how to develop a strategic plan is provided in Chapter Nine.)

Responsibility Eight: Oversee Financial Resources and Their Management

As the owners of the parachurch organization, the board members have an important responsibility to oversee the acquisition of financial resources and to manage those resources with integrity. The first part of this responsibility is a board task with which many parachurch leaders are particularly dissatisfied.

In the parachurch financing survey (Willmer, 1996), the presidents and CEOs of parachurch organizations expressed a good deal of dissatisfaction with their boards, particularly when it came to fundraising functions. More than half of the presidents were either very dissatisfied or somewhat dissatisfied with the board or had mixed feelings about it. When it came to deciding fundraising policy, making financial contributions, referring donor prospects, and soliciting donors, as many as 60 percent were not satisfied with the board performance (Andringa, 1996, p. 151). To fulfill this responsibility, a board member should give generously and encourage others to give generously.

The second area of financial responsibility requires oversight of the organization's budget, financial plans, investment strategies, and verification of internal financial controls. Approval of the budget signifies that the board agrees the budget represents an effective and efficient use of resources to advance the organization's mission. It is also essential to require a certified audit statement. Many parachurch organizations have joined the Evangelical Council for Financial Accountability as a way to stay accountable to others. The good management of financial resources is significant to fulfilling the public's trust and ensuring that resources are being used wisely to further the ministry's mission.

Responsibility Nine: Serve as Final Arbitrator

This responsibility is seldom called into action because usually the CEO handles these potential staff disputes. However, the parachurch governing board, as the highest court in a parachurch organization, serves in this role when the CEO cannot manage the problem or when it is necessary to prevent lawsuits, and should have an established policy to deal with disputes should they arise.

Responsibility Ten: Evaluate the Board and the Organization

Having the final say for all the operations of the organization, the board should see that evaluation of all aspects of the ministry is taking place on an ongoing basis. The board should require periodic external audits (program, legal, financial, structural, and so on) to ensure that the parachurch organization is functioning at a maximum level of efficiency and accountability. Internal evaluation should also be ongoing, including assessment of the board and the president. One way for an organization to evaluate itself internally and periodically is to have a person from outside the organization review its operations through site visits. That person can also observe board meetings and assess the board's effectiveness and progress.

Responsibility Eleven: Represent the Organization to the Public

Board members have a responsibility to represent the parachurch organization to its various publics. For example, board members might serve on a golf tournament committee, sponsor a table at a donor outreach banquet, meet with major donor prospects, meet with colleagues to interest them in supporting the organization, make a report at church about the activities of the parachurch organization, staff food lines, or coordinate a regional event.

As representatives, board members become important links among the organization's stakeholders. They must listen to the stakeholders' views, report the accomplishments of the organization, and help identify new individuals who can get behind the parachurch organization. These are the types of activities that are essential to being an enthusiastic and effective board member. But board members must remember that they do not speak for the organization or have its authority; each board member is a simply volunteer representative.

Plain and simple, it takes time to be a good board member. Many parachurch organizations are filled with board members who are too busy and overextended to be effective. Cleaning house is always in order—parachurch board members need to have the integrity to step down when they can no longer make a meaningful contribution.

Good parachurch boards are the result of many things; however, great boards work when organizations take time to make sure they function effectively. The parachurch board is effective when it understands its distinctives and responsibilities and acts upon them.

7

LEADING WITH
INTENTIONALITY

WHAT WAS IT that made the apostle Paul a strong leader? The Corinthians seem to have thought him unimpressive as a person: "His bodily presence is weak, and his speech contemptible" (2 Corinthians 10:10). He does not seem to have been a particularly attractive man, so why did such an extensive group of supporters form around him? The answer is that these people believed with all their hearts in the Gospel that Paul preached. The early church was not held together by personal charisma but by a powerful message. The growth of the church over the past two thousand years demonstrates that the message is larger and more enduring than the personalities who proclaim it.

The characteristics of a great Christian leader—and therefore a great parachurch leader—are not what would commonly be expected. Parachurch leaders are not a mirror image of smooth corporate leaders but more often a bit eccentric, a bit rough around the edges. They have not ascended to leadership because the stockholders felt they could be entrusted with the investors' millions but because they have proven themselves to be visionary and dynamic. Paul was no model of Roman leadership; rather he was a man driven by a mission and willing to press beyond his personal limitations to bring the Gospel to the world.

Billy Graham is perhaps the best known parachurch leader in the world. Without the backing of a denomination, he has stood up and preached from the Bible to millions of people. And just like Paul, the young Billy Graham had nothing that marked him out as a great leader. He was born with no special privileges and no marks of genius or prodigy. Graham writes in his recent autobiography that when he gets to heaven he has a question to ask of God: "Why me, Lord? Why did You choose a farmboy from North Carolina to preach to so many people, to have such a wonderful team of associates, and to have a part in what you were doing in the latter half of the twentieth century" (1997, p. 723). What marked him out was a heart for God's ministry and a vision of how people could be reached with the Gospel.

An event in 1994—nearly fifty years after the start of his ministry—illustrates why Graham has been such a powerful leader. 1994 was the year that Graham and his team came to a difficult realization: the traditional youth night of Graham's crusades was floundering. This standard feature of his weeklong crusades was not having the spiritual impact they desired—it was not connecting anymore with the youth. The question that faced them was how to present the biblically sound message in a way that was culturally relevant yet still palatable to ministry supporters. The solution was risky and required a large measure of faith and courage.

In his Cleveland crusade that year, Graham warned the adults throughout the week that the youth night would be different. Sure enough, when Saturday night came around, it was not the usual fare for a crusade. On the stage were rap group DC Talk, pop vocalist Michael W. Smith, and NBA star Mark Price as speaker. Wearing casual clothes rather than his customary suit, Graham preached to the 65,000 young people who filled the stadium. Fifty years into his ministry, Graham was still able to change and try something new if it meant furthering the message of faith.

What he exemplified was intentional leadership. The easy thing for Graham would have been to continue doing things the way he had always done them. It was not as though the old youth night was *un*successful—crowds were still coming forward at the end. However, leadership does not mean taking the easy road but rather heading toward resistance, intentionally. It means giving definite direction and purpose to an organization, even if that means departing from the way the ministry has always been done.

Defining the Parachurch Leader

Interest in the topic of leadership has surged over the past decade. Bookstores have an ever-growing section devoted to new books on leadership and management. Pick up most any book on leadership, and you will find the same qualities as are needed by a parachurch leader. Whether a person is in the military, business, law, or medicine, certain fundamentals of leadership can be applied across the board. In many ways the parachurch leader resembles every other effective leader, but there are core traits that make a parachurch leader unique compared to his or her secular counterparts. We now examine four areas that should define the uniqueness of parachurch leaders (although these beliefs and behaviors are not always practiced).

Christ is their ultimate authority. The secular leader is bounded by human authority. The leader of a large corporation must always consider the reactions of stockholders and the board of directors. The parachurch leader recognizes human authority as necessary and good, but ultimately his or her responsibility is to God. It was this that drove Paul to his fervent activity: "I press on toward the goal for the prize of the heavenly call of God in Christ Jesus" (Philippians 3:14). He recognized the need for human authority, but in the final measure his work was for the sake of Christ and the divine calling he felt in his life.

The Bible is their source of guidance. Where secular leaders turn to business publications like the *Wall Street Journal* or *Harvard Business Review,* the parachurch leader turns to the Bible. The overwhelming majority of parachurch leaders have a Bible on or near their desks, and are likely to turn to it in times of need. Many parachurch leaders do not need any lessons in the importance of seeking answers in scripture. If anything, their horizons need to be broadened to embrace that which is relevant from writers and thinkers who do not share their Christian convictions.

They understand their work as an extension of God's Church. That work is done "to the glory of God" is a deeply held value for most parachurch organizations. Ask about the motivation for their ministry, and most parachurch leaders will answer with a phrase along this line. Before Jesus was taken back to heaven, he gave to his disciples the Great Commission: "Go therefore and make disciples of all nations . . . " (Matthew 28:19). This is a call not only to evangelism in foreign countries but to taking up the cause of Christ and his Church wherever there is a need. Parachurch leaders connect their work with this ancient commission.

They live according to Christian principles. Here again we find a dramatic difference between a parachurch leader and a leader in the secular world. Few, if any, Fortune 500 companies care whether their senior leaders have a deep faith in Jesus Christ or even whether they adhere to any religion at all. Few corporations care whether their leaders actively pray for God's guidance or continued blessing on an organization. Few inquire whether a leader regularly attends church or has a healthy devotional life.

What secular leaders do with their private lives is nobody else's business; for the parachurch leader, a God-honoring private life is a requirement. A parachurch organization will not knowingly hire a non-Christian or a person not living by biblical standards to lead an enterprise. The Salvation Army is an example of this approach. People of all faiths may volunteer to work for the Salvation Army, but the uniformed and paid officers are followers of Christ. The same holds true in thousands of smaller Christian organizations. Every staff member of a parachurch organization may not be Christian, but almost all parachurch boards are interested in hiring a leader who will lead the organization according to Christian beliefs and who will live according to Christian values.

Defining the Intentional Leader

The more things change, the more they stay the same. For generations, writers have said with gusto statements like, "The times in which we live require a different kind of leadership," or, "Where are the leaders for times like these?" It seems that every generation feels the pinch of too few qualified leaders. Here at the dawn of the twenty-first century the situation is no different. We scan the parachurch landscape and look at the baby boomers now moving into leadership. We then turn our gaze to the generation Xers and the millennialists and gasp, "Where are the qualified leaders? Who has what it takes to lead the parachurch enterprise into the next century?"

If there is one quality that is needed for the parachurch leader now and in the future, it is *leading with intentionality,* that is, with purpose, confidence, and anticipation. Without intentionality, the parachurch organization is simply drifting lazily down the river of culture. The world today changes too quickly to be forgiving of this floating mentality. The traditional safety nets of organizational loyalty, unquestioning staff, and supportive boards are no longer in place.

Here are a number of characteristics that are seen in intentional leaders:

The intentional leader is authentic. In the well-known book *The Leadership Challenge,* authors James Kouzes and Barry Posner state that credibility is one of the foundations of effective leadership (1995, pp. 210–211). Credibility is sometimes expressed by phrases like "he practices what he preaches" or "she puts her money where her mouth is." Conversely, leaders whose words and values do not match their actions lack credibility in the eyes of those who are led, and this cuts into the effectiveness of the organization. The intentional parachurch leader spends significant time developing authenticity in relationships with others in the organization. Hiding and covering up are not descriptive of this leader. This authenticity is manifest not only in clear and honest relationships with fellow workers but also in an evident relationship with God. When authenticity is present, the work of ministry flows not from necessity but from an inner being that is deeply committed to modeling the values of the ministry. This modeling gives credibility to the leader and energizes others to follow his or her example.

The intentional leader pursues results over status quo. The intentional parachurch leader does not get caught tending a garden plot that produces no fruit. Often this leader must exist in an environment where funds are tight, workers are few, and time is stretched to the limit. Tremendous energy is exerted simply to keep the doors open. In such a hectic environment it is difficult to step back and ask the necessary questions: Do we know what results we are working for? And are we getting those results? In too many parachurch organizations, there is no agreement among the leadership, board, and staff members about the answers to these fundamental questions. The reporting that is done focuses on the amount of funds raised, but too often neglects finding out whether the main goals of the ministry are being met. The intentional parachurch leader is clear about the goals to be met by the organization, and works to find ways to measure the overall effectiveness of the ministry.

The intentional leader strives for vision. In larger and older parachurch organizations the temptation is to rest on the reputation of past ministry successes. This lack of vision is exacerbated by a strong corporate culture, complete with scores of functions and traditions that do not contribute to a healthy working community. The parachurch leader is often drawn into this culture, and the focus is then fixed on the inner machinations of the organization, not on the future. In contrast, the intentional leader works hard at developing a vision that rests on the far horizon of the future. With this vision, the leader sets about creating a working army committed to reach that preferred future.

The intentional leader focuses on the strategic. Urgency is a tyrant, never satisfied with what is given to feed it. One parachurch organization involved in Bible translation saw annual 5 to 7 percent increases from its supporters. But every year leaders would urge the board to "have faith in God's provision," and to approve budgets with a 15 to 25 percent increase over the previous year. As could be guessed, halfway through the fiscal year everything came to a screeching halt. Budgets were slashed and programs slimmed. Vendors were asked to wait 90 to 120 days to receive payment. The leaders of this organization were not intentional. In their desire to meet needs, they overreached what God had been shown to provide. They were unwilling to admit that God was entrusting them with more and more each year for ministry—they just did not like God's percentages.

The intentional leader preserves the core of the organization. Parachurch organizations have a strong propensity to go off course. They are prone to mission drift—losing focus on their main task. It takes intentional leadership to focus the organization on the major issues and challenges and away from the red herrings. To do this well, the parachurch leader must not just understand the core of the organization but be committed and passionate to preserve it. This core comprises the theological beliefs and moral values out of which the vision originated. It includes the organization's mission and vision. The forces at work eroding these core values are numerous. Both the external pull of postmodern values and internal lethargy conspire to pull the parachurch organization off course. The intentional leader does not sit back and passively watch this happen but gets in the middle of the fray and keeps reestablishing the core of the organization.

The intentional leader creates a productive work community. There are two key words in this leader characteristic: *productive* and *community*. On the one hand the parachurch leader must ensure that the ministry is effective and reaching its stated goals. But on the other hand the parachurch leader has the responsibility of creating a community in which people honor God and each other. In the ideal parachurch community, workers

- Are placed in positions that suit their temperaments and passions
- Receive affirmation for their contributions
- Have spiritual accountability to other members
- Have clear roles and expectations
- Are committed together to the organization's vision
- Have trust in their leaders
- Know that each person is respected, regardless of sex, race, and ethnic background
- Have personal growth opportunities
- Have a safe, enjoyable place to work

The intentional leader must manage to bridge the tension between productivity and community. It has to be recognized that the parachurch organization must reach goals if it is to justify its existence—it does not exist to provide group therapy to its workers. Yet because it is Christ's kingdom that is advanced, it is imperative that the organization exemplify Christian values of community and love. The intentional leader quickly finds that true leadership is servanthood. Intentional parachurch leaders instill in others the calling to ministry, and they learn to ask, How can I help you? instead of commanding selfishly.

The intentional leader thinks ahead. Just as a great chess player has in mind the next ten moves, so the effective parachurch leader must think one donor or ministry recipient ahead. This anticipation forces the leader's mind out of the present and into the future. The questions this leader asks are: Where will the next one thousand supporters come from? or, How are the needs of our ministry recipients changing? The moment parachurch leaders stop thinking ahead, the future is sure to catch them off-guard; just as chess players are caught off-guard by opponents if they cease to imagine the coming moves.

A second aspect of thinking ahead is the development of new leadership. John Maxwell writes that "excellent leaders add value to their people and help them become better than they would be if they worked alone. The first question a leader should ask is: 'How can I help make those around me more successful?' When that answer is found and implemented, everyone wins!" (1993, p. 130). The intentional leader works to share the spotlight with younger leaders, grooming them to one day take over the role of leadership. Parachurch leaders who neglect this grooming risk seeing the organization that they strove to build collapse as soon as they leave.

Understanding the Lack of Leadership

Some parachurch leaders who have been charged with the responsibility of providing solid direction to their organizations end up simply floating through their leadership tenure. These leaders may not perceive themselves as floating—they work hard, put in long hours, travel often, and speak often in public. They attend the National Prayer Breakfast each year; they prepare for board meetings well in advance; they are right on time with performance reviews; their files are in impeccable order and their time management admirable. But underneath the outer correctness is too often a leader in denial, a leader severely challenged and even frightened by the immensity of the leadership needs in a chaotic and complex world. If one were to examine the decisions made by these leaders, a passive and reactive pattern would be discovered—a pattern manifested by indecision and maintenance of the status quo.

However, there are also parachurch leaders who make choices different from those of their timid counterparts. Putting one foot in front of the other, day after day, these leaders make decisions with foresight. We could say that their intentional leadership is "on purpose," as opposed to the drifting leadership that is "by accident." On the surface these leaders behave like their passive counterparts—they work hard, travel often, speak frequently, use their time effectively. But underneath, the path chosen by these leaders is markedly different. Intentional leaders are choosing a definite direction and are being guided by a clear vision, and the ultimate success of their organizations will reflect this intentional style of leadership.

In today's parachurch world both kinds of leaders are present, which means there is not enough intentional leadership. There are several explanations for this leadership gap.

One major cause of the lack of sufficient intentional leadership in parachurch organizations is that the parachurch has no weeding-out system, and as a result an overall mediocrity has permeated its leadership until recent years. The for-profit world is terribly intolerant of floating leaders, and it has an extremely effective rule for weeding out nonperformers: generate profit—you're a keeper; lose money—you're gone. It is a very simple system. Even with all the gentler talk these days about corporate values, companies do not keep around visionaries who lose money or who cause shareholder losses. In the parachurch world the reality is different. These organizations find it notoriously difficult to fire people for lack of performance, and as a result, weak leaders move up the system. Increasingly, though, the trend of weak parachurch leadership seems to be reversing itself. There are more parachurch leaders who have come from the nation's top businesses, who have been well educated and groomed, or who are of the quality to occupy top positions in the business world.

A second cause for lack of intentional leadership is that there is often no entity that demands high standards of performance for a parachurch organization. Stockholders make this demand in the for-profit world and force leadership to focus on staying profitable. In theory, demanding high standards is the job of the parachurch board, but historically these boards have been lax in putting demands on senior leadership or even in holding them accountable. Ironically, over the past decade it has been the younger donors who have increasingly put pressure on parachurch leadership. They are asking to see how the organization uses its resources and just what its measurable results have been. But even though these donors have added an increased measure of accountability, there is still less demand in this area than is found in the for-profit world.

Another major cause of the lack of parachurch leadership is the manner in which leaders are found. Typically, parachurch leaders are drawn from within the organization. When the founder of an organization moves on, the board looks to its own ranks to fill the gap. Those who move up this ladder are individuals who have been successful in the ministry or mission for which the parachurch organization exists. So, for example, a missionary who is a successful church planter in the Philippines could one day lead a multimillion-dollar enterprise and yet know very little about how to do that. Or a person with a strong radio personality may one day be a station manager or owner. Because these people were effective in their work, they were rewarded with an opportunity to come back to the home office or with a step up the leadership ladder. However, these rewards based on performance in one area of the organization's ministry may have little to do with whether a person has the gifts to lead the enterprise.

Parachurch organizations also use other sources to find leaders. At times leaders will be hired from another parachurch organization or non-profit charity. In rare cases the path to parachurch leadership extends from the secular corporate world. A corporate leader will receive a calling to do something more with his or her life and will take a cut in pay to work for a parachurch organization. Another source for parachurch leaders is the local church. Daniel Watts was a children's pastor at Mariner's Church in Newport Beach, California, and on a short-term mission trip got a vision for a broader ministry. He saw the need for someone to equip Sunday school teachers for Evangelical churches in Poland. Because of this calling, he left his position as children's pastor and moved to Poland to start Every Generation Ministries.

A fourth reason for the shortage of quality parachurch leaders is that the on-ramps from colleges and seminaries are obscure, at best. Few schools offer coursework or career development paths for those aspiring to leadership in a parachurch organization. Although some parachurch organizations have established de facto relationships with independent Bible colleges or Christian universities from which they habitually recruit workers, very few official ties exist between institutions of higher education and the parachurch. This is quite in contrast to a traditional church, which often has several colleges and seminaries directly tied to it and offering coursework tailored to meet the educational needs of future church leaders. By comparison the parachurch often makes do with skills gained ad hoc rather than through formal training.

Lack of successful parachurch leadership is also caused by the lack of effective continuing education for leaders. Compared to the for-profit world, parachurch leaders have few affordable options available to them to sharpen their skills. Hiring an outside consultant is one of the primary means parachurch leaders have used to brush up their skills or to learn about new ideas and developments. Unfortunately, grabbing a workshop at the annual meeting of the Christian Management Association or the Christian Stewardship Association characterizes the education commitment of most parachurch organizations. What is needed is a renaissance in thinking, to see continual people development as an investment in the future—not as a luxury.

In recent years Peter Drucker and the Peter Drucker Foundation for Nonprofit Management have taken a noteworthy run at developing tools and training for the nonprofit leader. As a subset of the nonprofit world, parachurch organizations find value in much of this material; but many aspects of parachurch leadership are unique and cannot be fully addressed in material aimed at the larger nonprofit world. Much of the recent writing on leadership or management technique takes no account of the special Christian dynamic that is always present within the parachurch. This lack of quality materials is a contributing factor to weakness in parachurch leadership.

A sixth reason for the lack of leadership is that the parachurch has not done much better than any other part of society when it comes to making up for the values that moms and dads of the late fifties and sixties failed to give their children. At the very core of a great leader is sound character, but our culture has left behind many of the values that build character. Stephen Covey makes this point in his best-selling book *The Seven Habits of Highly Effective People*. After surveying the success literature published in the United States since 1776, he found a startling trend. For the first 150 years, these works were dominated by what he calls the *character ethic* (1989, p. 18). But in the last 50 years, success literature has been preoccupied with such issues as image, consciousness, and techniques. Covey's message is that the character ethic must be regained if effective leaders are to emerge. The dearth of parachurch leadership is in part a result of the common philosophies trumpeted by the current culture.

The parachurch leader must embody the character ethic, but leading the parachurch takes even more than. It also requires that a person be a close follower of Jesus Christ. Parachurch organizations often suffer because an anemic Christianity has been passed on to their members, particularly those of the baby boom generation. They received a Christianity that was centered on legalism or was not centered on a personal relationship with Christ, and this left many of them with a deficient faith. Without an energetic faith, potential leaders of the parachurch stall spiritually or drift out of the range of the parachurch.

The seventh and final reason for weak parachurch leadership is that the parachurch has often violated the central teaching that the Church of Jesus Christ is best understood as a living community or organism. In *A Theology of Church Leadership*, Larry Richards and Clyde Hoeldtke wrote: "Scripture teaches that in its essential nature, the church is a living organism. We are members of a body, not an institution. Any expression of the church must be an expression in harmony with its nature, not a stumbling copy of man's notions for organizing institutions" (1980, p. 37). In the Bible, it is Paul who develops the metaphor of the body: just as the body is composed of many different parts, each with its own role to play, so the church is put together of people who have many different gifts, each of which ought to be used (1 Corinthians 12:14–26).

Following this teaching from Paul, Christians believe that God has equipped each person with unique gifts. When people work in their areas of giftedness, they are more effective and successful. When they cannot use those special gifts, they are likely to be frustrated and less effective. One reason parachurch organizations have experienced weak leadership is that they have not always spent the time to determine the gifts of those within the organization.

This emphasis on giftedness is balanced by another factor that distinguishes the parachurch from the secular nonprofit and for-profit world. Many leaders have a powerful sense that God has *called* them to a certain position. Yet it often holds true that they are called to a position in which they may not be a perfect fit. Nevertheless the sense of calling will often supersede any other dynamic of leadership selection. In the for-profit world this sense of calling has no real parallels. Corporate boards select leaders from a candidate list. Rarely are leaders chosen based on their personal sense of God's hand on their lives and his direction. The parachurch board members must juggle this spiritual dynamic with more pragmatic concerns.

Identifying New Leaders

Just as pastors often look over their lay leadership and see aging faces, so the parachurch leaders look over their strongest supporters and see men and women who are in their twilight years. At the dawn of the twenty-first century we can see that there is a changing of the guard under way. The generation that saw the boom in parachurch organizations in the years after World War II and up until the 1970s has continued as the main pillar of support for parachurch organizations throughout the closing decade of the twentieth century. This older generation has had an unusual amount of influence, and the reason is obvious: they were friends, relatives, and supporters when the founders of parachurch organizations established their networks. Their support has worked well, but it means that many parachurch organizations now find much of their support comes from seniors. As baby boomers age, seniors will play an increasingly important role for the parachurch. But clearly, if parachurch organizations are to continue to prosper, they must find ways to make their message relevant to the next generation.

Many parachurch organizations have already begun to develop strategies to involve the current generation in their ministries. The young potential leaders they look for are those with excellent communication skills, those who are driven by Christian values rather than financial or personal gain, and those with technological savvy. It is imperative for every parachurch organization to work this fresh group of supporters into positions of leadership. If the vision of a parachurch organization is not able to inspire the upcoming generation, then it can expect its star to wane in the coming years.

The parachurch leader ought to be able to identify these four types of potential leaders:

○ Young people with influence over group opinion

○ Young people with a usable expertise or skill

○ Young people who are keenly energetic about the organization

○ Young people with a track record of providing resources for the organization

Identifying these young people, who are embedded within every organization, requires more than office interviews; it means relationship building on an individual level. Again, once these potential leaders are identified, every effort should be made to get them into places of leadership.

The apostle Paul did not neglect to develop new leaders. The churches he planted were not meant to be dependent on him but to be self-sustaining and independent. In his letters, Paul's frustration when they are unable to lead themselves becomes clear. In addition to encouraging independence, Paul also nurtured young people for leadership in the church. We get the clearest picture of Timothy, whom Paul addresses in a letter as "my beloved child" (2 Timothy 1:2). Paul intimates to Timothy that he expects to soon lose his life: "I am already being poured out as a libation, and the time of my departure has come" (4:6). But he does not spend time mourning his own fate. Instead, he devotes the time to encouraging Timothy: "For this reason I remind you to rekindle the gift of God that is within you through the laying on of my hands" (1:6). Most likely, Paul had laid his hands on Timothy as an ordination to ministry. At the end of his own ministry, he does all he can to strengthen the ministry of the next generation. And that is a lesson that can be taken to heart by all current parachurch leaders.

8

UNDERSTANDING
PARACHURCH DONORS

Figure 8.1. Profile of the Parachurch Organization Donor.

Wanted Dead or Alive

- Beware: This person is a part of the largest subculture in America and not afraid to call on allies for help.

- This person is an active Christian and can usually be found in an Evangelical church.

- This person is known to take the Bible seriously and feels responsibility toward the poor.

- An active giver to religious causes—this person provides two-thirds of all charitible giving.

- May often be found volunteering time for community work and is likely concerned about your spiritual condition (and not afraid to ask you about it).

- This person is an impressive giver by the standards of society, but rarely does that giving reach the biblical standard of 10 percent.

- This person is either in a high- or low-income bracket (not as often in the middle). If the income is under $20,000 the person gives a higher percentage of it than those who make over $100,000.

- Often spotted in the South and Midwest.

- Thirty-five to 44 years of age, or over 55.

- This person is probably a woman.

If found, please contact your nearest parachurch organization.

AS THE PARACHURCH has prospered, so has an entire posse of fundraising efforts aiming to catch the parachurch donor (profiled in the wanted poster in Figure 8.1). Millions of people are contacted through direct-mail appeals, telephone calls, radio and television programs, and personal visits. Outside of conducting a ministry, parachurch organizations do their most active work in the fundraising arena.

According to the Evangelical Council for Financial Accountability (ECFA), 51 percent of the income for parachurch organizations comes from cash donations (including foundations and government grants). Earned income accounts for an additional 37 percent; gifts-in-kind provide another 12 percent. Smaller organizations receive very little government support. Although some large organizations attract federal dollars (for example, World Vision), in general what nonprofits receive comes from cash donations, gifts-in-kind, or earned income.

Between 2 and 5 percent of the revenues for parachurch organizations come from foundations. There are about twenty widely known Evangelical foundations and scores of smaller foundations set up by Evangelicals. Some of the larger ones include Maclellan, Chatlos, Crowell, Fieldstead, DeMoss, Bakke, and Stewardship. These foundations give priority to missionary work, evangelistic activities, Evangelical education institutions (Bible colleges and seminaries), and general human welfare organizations. Although these foundations exert considerable influence in the parachurch world, they are a small group in light of the total number of charitable foundations. Significantly, the majority of the support for the parachurch does not come from foundations or corporations but from individuals. Individuals make up the financial backbone of nearly all parachurch enterprises. According to Paul Nelson, ECFA president, member organizations with budgets below $1 million derive 82 percent of their income from cash contributions and grants.

Who are these donors who keep the parachurch prospering? What factors will keep them giving? This chapter explores these questions by looking at

o Who gives to the parachurch?

o What do we know about their giving?

o Who gets their money?

o Who is the future parachurch donor?

Understanding the donor is crucial because, without these people and their support, the $100 billion global parachurch enterprise would be a bust.

Who Gives to the Parachurch?

Americans are generous. Robert Wuthnow's research has found that "total giving to charitable organizations of all kinds, both absolute figures and as a proportion of income, is higher in the United States than in virtually any other advanced industrial society" (1994a, p. 227). Robert Payton (1992) tracks this giving tradition to the Christian religious roots of the American colonists. They reacted against the European system of involuntary tithes by developing a religious system sustained by voluntary gifts. Out of all the money given by Americans, religion receives a larger percentage than any other category.

Although Americans are generous by the world's standards, they are not so according to biblical standards. The IRS reports that deductions for charitable contributions on tax returns represent only 1.6 to 2.16 percent of income. The American Association of Fund-Raising Counsel says that giving ranged from 1.7 percent to 1.95 percent of personal income over the last 20 years. Thirty-one percent of U.S. households say they give no money away at all. Many reports suggest that giving is up, but this is generally true only among those who were already giving. Overall, American giving seems to be holding steady at the level it has maintained over the past four decades.

One of the well-established facts about American giving and volunteering is that it is dominated by those most actively involved in organized religion (Yankelovich, Skelly, and White, Inc., 1986; Hodgkinson and Weitzman, 1994). Not only do these people support overtly religious causes, they also give to charities unconnected to religious aims. The study *From Belief to Commitment* (Hodgkinson, Weitzman, and Kirsch, 1988, p. 12) found that 73 percent of all contributions given to charities came from donors who support religion and claim religious affiliation.

But to understand parachurch giving we must take it a step further, there is a strong correlation between fervency of faith and levels of giving and volunteering. The most important indicator of who gives in the United States is a high frequency of church attendance, Bible study, and prayer (White, 1989, p. 8). Research also shows the converse: the absence of compelling Judeo-Christian religious convictions operates as a major factor to explain the lack of giving (Barna, 1994, p. 42). The statistic that 31 percent of households give to no charities correlates with the number of the unchurched in the United States.

Given this understanding, it is clear that Evangelical Christians are a major historical taproot for the strength of giving in the United States. The reality is that no group of U.S. citizens is giving more personal time and money to show compassion for the disadvantaged or to extend love to those needing love than those people who are strongly religiously motivated. This reality of American giving is largely ignored by sociologists and the media.

There are four reasons for the strength of Evangelical donors: they are the largest and most active component of religious life in the United States (almost one-third of the nation's population) (Green, 1992); a higher percentage of Evangelicals actively practice their faith than either of the two other major Christian groups—Catholics and mainline Protestants (Green, 1992); Evangelicals give as a percentage of their income about two times more than mainline Protestants (2.84 percent versus 4.79 percent) (Ronsvalle and Ronsvalle, 1992, p. 23), almost three times more than Roman Catholics (Hart, 1990, p. 8; Greeley and McManus, 1987, p. 17), and at least four times more than members of the general population; and 80 percent of all adults that give 10 percent or more of their income are born-again Christians (Barna, 1994, p. 56).

Moreover, Robert Wuthnow pinpoints this key factor in the making of a donor: "What makes a difference in giving is believing that the Bible should be taken literally" (1994a, p. 123). This belief is a major contention of Evangelicals. Similarly, Dean Hoge says that "those who say their primary duty is to help others to commit their lives to Jesus Christ gave more than any others" (Stafford, 1997, p. 22); again, this primary duty is a characteristic of Evangelicals.

All observers, Christian and secular, have debated how to define *Evangelical*. Today only 18 percent of the general population say they can define an Evangelical ("National and International Religion Report," 1994, p. 23). If the term *conservative Christian* or *conservative Protestant* is used, people conjure up a wide variety of images—some positive, some not so positive. Media polls, such as the *New York Times*/CBS News poll, often focus on Evangelicals because of their giving potential and clout.

In order to understand Evangelicals—the predominant group that gives to the parachurch—it is essential to know the theological foundations of their faith. In simplistic terms, the word comes from *evangelion* which means "gospel" or "good news." University of Virginia sociologist James Davison Hunter states that an Evangelical is a theologically conservative Protestant and can encompass a wide variety of religious and denominational traditions. Thus the term *Evangelical* is synonymous with Protestant orthodoxy and conservatism. Evangelicals are known for their tenacious insistence that the Bible is the inerrant word of God (Hunter, 1987).

The roots of the Evangelical faith go back to the Reformation principle of *sola Scriptura* (scripture alone). This Protestant belief permeated American life from the nation's founding. The Puritan reverence for the authority of the Bible endured through the nineteenth century, particularly at the level of common faith (Hunter, 1987). The Bible was factual, and it was assumed to be one's religious, moral, and social guide.

These assumptions began to erode when some Protestants started to pursue a social gospel or liberal Christianity that abandoned the cornerstone of scripture alone. Without an inerrant Bible as the final authority on spiritual, religious, and moral matters, there was no test by which to measure the ultimate truth or falsehood of any doctrine or spiritual innovation. In the past fifty years especially, an Evangelical has been defined as a Christian who holds to scripture as inspired, in contrast to the view of the liberal, or mainstream, side of Protestantism.

British historian David Bebbington has identified three other key ingredients of Evangelicalism: conversionism (an emphasis on the new birth of belief in Jesus Christ, the Son of God, as a life-changing religious experience—hence the *born again* label); activism (a concern to live life in a way that demonstrates and convinces others of this truth); and crucicentrism (a focus on Christ's redeeming work on the cross) (1989). These theological concerns are important because they give rise to the motives that cause Evangelicals to support the parachurch.

A 1988 Gallup survey suggests that Evangelicals have the following demographic characteristics: they are highly concentrated in the South (41 percent) and Midwest (29 percent), more likely to be over fifty years old (47 percent) than non-Evangelicals (35 percent), less likely to be under thirty (16 percent) than non-Evangelicals (24 percent), and more likely to be either married (68 percent) or widowed (12 percent) than non-Evangelicals (61 percent and 7 percent, respectively). More Evangelicals (56 percent) than non-Evangelicals (48 percent) were women, and more non-Evangelicals (52 percent) than Evangelicals (44 percent) were men. There was no statistically significant difference between the education of the two groups (Clydesdale, 1990, p. 199).

Perhaps the primary ingredient is the fervency with which Evangelicals ascribe to their faith. Billy Graham, sums up the fervor of Evangelicals with this statement: "My own purpose in life is to help people find a relationship with God, which I believe, comes through knowing Jesus Christ" (Billy Graham Evangelistic Association, 1994, p. 4). Their fervency is reflected in concrete ways: twice as many Evangelicals as others claim religion as "very important," and they are three times as likely to attend church (60 percent to 20 percent) (Clydesdale, 1990, p. 199). These are also characteristics of people who give generously.

What Do We Know About Their Giving?

Given the strong correlation between fervency of faith and generosity in giving, Evangelicals are clearly a strong giving culture. Approximately 36 percent of the born-again Christians give 10 percent of their income to churches and other charities.

Evangelical giving is generally characterized by giving to ministries that the individual donors can readily understand and put their faith in. They do not give much to causes of high culture, the arts, research, or endowed institutions (Hatch and Hamilton, 1992). They are often more concerned about an individual's accepting Christ than about changing large societal problems. An example of this is their heavy giving to foreign mission work; it dwarfs the money given by mainline denominations. Evangelicals sponsor over 90 percent of the foreign missionaries that go out from North America (Hatch and Hamilton, 1992, p. 23).

The explosive growth of parachurch organizations in the last fifty years has been funded largely by Evangelicals. Studies of selected Evangelical churches show that approximately 15 to 40 percent of their members' giving goes to parachurch ministries, and in a few congregations it reaches 50 percent or higher. The growth of the parachurch movement has paralleled the growth of the Evangelical movement over the last fifty years and reflects the causes that stir Evangelicals.

Who Gets Their Money?

More than 160 years ago, Alexis de Tocqueville ([1835] 1956) observed that Americans were noteworthy for their quickness to create voluntary associations to meet needs. The reason behind this energy, then and now, is compassion and a work ethic driven by spiritual values. It is commonly understood that the primary reasons people give are the values they hold, and for Christians these values are generally theologically defined. Parachurch organizations that have received sustained support from Evangelicals have the following concerns:

They support Christian values. With the secularization of the culture, Christians have moved aggressively to build parachurch organizations and institutions that uphold and support a Christian value structure. They are giving to causes that build institutions to support, sustain, and perpetuate faith commitments. These institutions include the burgeoning K–12 school movement; up to five thousand private (sometimes church-related) schools have been developed so that children can be educated with the values of the Christian worldview. Christian colleges, radio and television stations, publishing houses, social service agencies, camps, and rescue missions are also supported, as are other institutions that support and maintain Christian beliefs (see the taxonomy in the Resource for a comprehensive list of categories).

They help the needy. People who give to the parachurch have a genuine desire to help those who are in some state of need. Whether it is the local rescue mission raising money for the homeless, a relief and development organization, or a center for pregnant teenage mothers, Christians are willing to give when a compassionate plea is made for the needy. Giving increases when a sense of emergency exists—a fire destroys a crisis pregnancy center, world famine arises, a national disaster occurs. Those who give to the parachurch are quick to provide financial support to meet these needs. Once there is a sense of emergency, compassion is an impetus for generous giving.

They take the Gospel to the world. A significant segment of those who support the parachurch are motivated to give to reach those who have not heard the Gospel. At the heart of this Christian concern is a sense of a calling from God to share the good news. Recall once again that in the Great Commission Jesus said, "Go therefore and make disciples of all nations, baptizing them in the name of the Father and of the Son and of the Holy Spirit" (Matthew 28:19). According to Timothy Clydesdale, "Evangelicals want people to hear about Jesus and place a high priority on evangelism and missionary work. For them, the highest act of caring is the spiritual regeneration of a person" (1990, p. 208).

They work to preserve the nation. Most parachurch donors feel a strong sense of patriotism, and they have watched with fear as the moral values of the culture have been eroded. In the last two hundred–plus years, there has been a steady move away from the conservative Christian faith. As historian Mark Noll points out: "America was 'evangelical' not because every feature of life in every region in the United States was throughout dominated by evangelical Protestants but because so much of the visible public activity, so great a proportion of the learned culture, and so many dynamic organizations were products of evangelical conviction" (1992, p. 243). Noll also maintains that the largely Protestant culture–dominated society set cultural values, provided standards for private and public morality, assumed responsibility for education, and powerfully shaped the media. Today this influence is fragmented.

Parachurch donors feel a moral and spiritual responsibility to resist the cultural shift and to fight the cultural drift toward materialism and toward a person-centered rather than God-centered worldview. Many Christians would agree with William J. Bennett (the former secretary of education), who says our society is far more violent and vulgar than it used to be. This is evidenced by the enormous increases in violent crimes, out-of-wedlock births, abortions, divorces, suicides, child abuse, and welfare dependency. From his point of view the answer to much of what ails us is spiritual and moral regeneration (1993). This drive to see spiritual values rekindled and a more moral nation motivates giving.

They are known and trusted. Church donors make up a subculture that readily supports organizations the donors know and trust. These donors' giving is on both an organizational level and a personal level. Missionaries and others raise personal support by gaining the confidence and trust of their local church, friends, and other acquaintances. Organizations like Campus Crusade, Navigators, InterVarsity Christian Fellowship, and many missions organizations, rely upon the good character and trust their workers build up.

Donors also give to trusted figureheads of parachurch organizations. If Billy Graham asks for support, people will respond, almost irrespective of the project. The larger parachurch ministries (Focus on the Family, Prison Fellowship, and so forth) draw heavily on this good will because their leaders are trusted. Parachurch donors are less likely to give to a specific project than to give to an individual or name they trust. When Jim Bakker and Jimmy Swaggart betrayed the trust of their supporters in the late 1980s through moral failures, support that had taken years to build dried up in days.

They allow individuals to be a part of their efforts. An old adage says that involvement plus participation yields commitment. When individuals are actively involved as volunteers for an organization, they naturally are more willing to support the organization financially. Ninety percent of volunteers contribute to charity, and their households donate 2.6 percent of their income—almost double the national average. Fifty percent of Evangelicals versus 31 percent of non-Evangelicals feel that giving time through volunteer work to charitable religious organizations is absolutely or very important (Clydesdale, 1990, p. 200). Many parachurch organizations have giving clubs, auxiliaries, and other volunteer activities to build relationships with donors and prospects. For example, one woman is in a Bible study fellowship and is part of the women's auxiliary for the Colorado Springs, Colorado, Salvation Army. As a result, she and her husband have gotten to know and have confidence in the leadership and its programs—and now provide monetary support.

The donors who give to these types of organizations often share some common religious and pragmatic understandings. There are at least three of these understandings.

They respond to Bible truths. As already noted, a significant segment of parachurch donors view the Bible as the guide to all of life and take seriously its instruction about possessions. Martin Luther said there are three conversions for a Christian—head, heart, and pocketbook. Jesus evidently felt this too—seventeen of the thirty-eight parables focus on possessions. The importance of this topic is evident if one simply counts the number of times it appears in the Bible: 2,172 verses offer instruction about possessions and giving. In contrast, the important topic of prayer shows up 371 times, and loving, 714 times.

The primary reason for this concern with possessions is that God realizes, as stated in Matthew 6:21, "For where your treasure is, there your heart will be also," and that if God is not first with a person's money, God will not be first in matters of faith. There is a vital link between faith and finances, and it can become a major reason for giving. There is no single issue more important to Christians than how they deal with money. Parachurch donors would likely agree with the Hoge and Griffin research (1992) that indicates the three most important reasons for contributing were feeling gratitude to God, feeling that giving is a part of worship, and feeling it is a privilege to share.

They respond to biblical teaching about stewardship. An important theological underpinning of Christian giving is a keen sense of stewardship. This stewardship involves three beliefs: God has provided all resources, God has given the responsibility to manage these resources to each person as a steward (not as an owner), and God will ultimately hold believers accountable for how they use God's resources (Willmer, 1989). For parachurch supporters, stewardship is God's order for a person's relationship to God, not a relationship to an organization. Opportunities to give are evidence of God working in their lives to help them grow in their faith through the discipline of giving.

Dennis Bakke, cofounder and chief executive of AES Camp in Arlington, Virginia, is a Christian who has established the Mustard Seed, a foundation that gives predominantly to parachurch ministries. He has espoused this belief in *Forbes* magazine, saying, "Everything we have is not ours, it's the Lord's, we're just stewards of it" (Linden and Machan, 1997, p. 160).

These values and teachings are diminishing in our current culture. They are now found most often among older donors. The study *The Reluctant Steward* (Conway, 1992) has reached a similar conclusion. It seems that a seldom talked about but critical casualty of the current cultural shift, is Christian stewardship. This should be a significant concern for parachurch organizations.

They give for measurable results. By definition (see Chapter Three) a parachurch organization is a ministry focused on a specific need. George Barna's research shows that even though religiously motivated donors see value in the work being done by nonreligious organizations, they still choose to give the largest share of their money to religious organizations that are pursuing a specific ministry (1994, p. 43). All indications are that this concern for results compatible with a Christian worldview will increase in the future. In addition, donors want to know that their giving is going where they desire and that it is getting the results promised. Organizations that fudge in reporting back to donors what happened to their money can be assured of tepid commitment.

Who Is the Future Parachurch Donor?

All indications are that the typical parachurch donor of the future will be a very different person from that of the past. Along with the shifts in average age and in ethnicity, other demographic shifts, and value changes taking place in our culture, changes will also be reflected in giving patterns.

The vast majority of parachurch organizations was founded in the last fifty years, and as a direct result the core supporters are those fifty-five years of age and older (the *builders*). These people are loyal and faithful and give consistently. Many of them were *tithers*—systematic givers out of every paycheck to church and parachurch organizations. It was this kind of steady giving, brick by brick, that built up such a huge parachurch enterprise. This is the group that will likely transfer the largest estates in the history of the world (possibly $5 trillion). Indications at this time are that the generations that are following (boomers and generation Xers) do not place such a large value on loyalty and faithfulness, nor is there evidence that they will be able to accumulate comparable wealth.

The baby boomers and generation X groups are not rated high in institutional loyalty or faithfulness. They shift loyalties quickly. They are characterized as high-tech and high-touch generations that require regular servicing to keep them loyal. They give to specific projects, like to see results, expect to have a lot of say over how their money is used, and do not like to be taken for granted.

The parachurch donor of the future will be very different ethnically. In the Southwestern parts of the United States, by the year 2025, Hispanics will be the dominant ethnic group. The interests and concerns of such changing ethnic groups will effect giving to parachurch organizations. The parachurch fundraiser will need to find methods to keep up with the unique needs of the various groups.

The jury is still out on whether the parachurch donor of the future will have a steward's heart. It is possible that a spiritual renewal and revival of our culture will come as a reaction to secularization. Along with spiritual vitality generally comes increased giving. The attitude of the heart in the future—the vitality of faith—is probably the biggest unknown. Probably the one given about the parachurch donors of the future is that they will give to support organizations that respond to needs that are important for donors' lives and personal values.

PART THREE

HOW CAN THE PARACHURCH ENLARGE ITS IMPACT?

THE THIRD SECTION of this book turns a corner and explores ways to enlarge the scope of the parachurch's influence through strategic planning. Parachurch organizations can develop a strategic plan for the future by answering these four questions:

- What does the planning process look like?
- Where does the parachurch organization want to go?
- What is the current reality of the organization?
- How will the organization turn its vision into reality?

9

THINKING STRATEGICALLY
ABOUT GOD'S WORK

ENTERING PITTSBURGH, Pennsylvania, at night from the south is an unforgettable experience. After passing through quiet, unremarkable countryside, the driver approaches a large hill that is outlined in the darkness. Disappearing into that looming hill are the Fort Pitt tunnels. The dim tunnels envelope the driver for a mile; the only light is supplied by fluorescent bulbs. Suddenly the darkness of the tunnel is past, and the multicolored lights of a great city explode in front of you with all the vividness of fireworks on July 4. It is an invigorating experience: one minute a quiet countryside and a dark tunnel, and the next a vibrant city.

This experience captures the essence of the strategic planning process that faces every leader. The quiet countryside represents the place where the organization is right now. There may be good things happening here. The organization could be tempted to stay here but in doing so risks its future. The organization wants to reach the lights generated by greater activity and change. Those vivid lights and colors are the promises of the future—they represent an accomplished vision and mission. But getting to the lights means passing through that mountain blocking the path. The tunnels are the only way to reach the goal, and these tunnels are the plans and reality that must be passed through if the vision of the organization is ever to be fulfilled.

Effective strategic thinking can be reduced to three deceptively simple questions, each corresponding to the stages of the approach from countryside to city, from present to future. Despite the questions' simplicity, how they are answered will determine in large measure the effectiveness of the parachurch organization. The questions are

- Where do we want to go? (The destination.)
- Where are we now? (The current situation.)
- How will we get there? (Moving from the current situation to the destination.)

Each of the following three chapters will answer one of these questions. An organization's longevity and impact for Christ are directly influenced by how well it answers these questions. Although they are simple, it takes a concentrated effort to think strategically about their answers. But before we discuss these questions in detail, this chapter answers some questions about the strategic planning process for the parachurch organization. Can we do this and still get to heaven? How is the parachurch planning process unique? What are the benefits of strategic planning? And how do we get started on the process?

Can We Do This and Still Get to Heaven?

Some leaders secretly question if strategic planning is really a biblical approach to ministry. After all, isn't it God who provides the resources, blesses a ministry, and provides the vision? Who, then, are we to plan for his work? Many organizations move ahead in ministry with too little conscious planning or articulated vision—claiming to simply "lean on the Lord" for guidance.

The Bible certainly does not support a reliance on God without active use of planning and strategy. The book of Proverbs has a storehouse of verses that directly contradict this misguided fear. For example, it tells us, "Wise warriors are mightier than strong ones, and those who have knowledge than those who have strength; for by wise guidance you can wage your war, and in abundance of counselors there is victory" (Proverbs 24:5–6). This proverb addresses the needs of the Israelite king, but its advice is applicable to all who must carry out the work of the Lord. God and his word set the agenda and the values of an organization, but its leaders are expected and urged by scripture to use natural and spiritual gifts to further those goals. Thus thinking and planning strategically does not mean that a ministry will be manufactured solely by careful technique. Instead it means that the God-given ministry will be guided by thoughtful planning and foresight—always under the authority of Christ.

How Is the Parachurch Planning Process Unique?

Every kind of organization needs a plan. Whether it is the federal government or a family-owned business, it is important for the organization to formulate a plan to reach its preferred future. The parachurch tackles many of the same issues as any other organization, but there are at least four elements in successful parachurch strategic planning that distinguish it from the planning methods used by secular organizations.

First, there will be a passion to execute the plan whether it makes money or not. In the for-profit world the need for financial performance drives the majority of decisions. It is difficult to stir up any real passion for an activity that does not net a profit. In contrast, in a parachurch organization, financial performance usually is not the major criterion by which strategies are considered effective. Financial solvency is important, and a plan needs to be developed and executed with God-honoring stewardship in focus. But profitability is not the primary measurement of success. Organizations work hardest to execute a plan that aligns the organization with God's calling and leading. Sometimes leaders knowingly execute a plan that will be costly because it is the right thing to do to help achieve the mission.

A second unique element in successful parachurch planning is that the members of the organization see themselves as part of an extended family. The ministry of a parachurch organization is interrelated with the ministries of other parachurch organizations and local churches. Cooperative effort between parachurches should not be unusual. Whereas many for-profit firms move aggressively to increase their market share or to buy out a competitor, parachurch organizations need to seek ways to develop strategic alliances that will expand a ministry's impact.

This topic is developed further in Chapter Fourteen, but suffice it to say here that parachurch planning should work with local churches, not against them. Plans that build rapport and goodwill among Christian organizations and that are not redundant of the work of a similar organization are far more defensible than lone ranger plans.

A third unique element is that parachurch organizations have a commitment to integrate faith in God with their strategy. Parachurch leaders with a living and active faith have a constant awareness that they lack the wisdom and insight to guide an organization by their own light alone. They look to Jesus Christ—"in whom are hidden all the treasures of wisdom and knowledge" (Colossians 2:3)—to make sound strategic decisions. Parachurch leaders cultivate a posture of dependency on God for guidance and for resources. Ascertaining God's will is not optional but foundational for the parachurch leader.

This is not to say that the parachurch leader does not struggle with doubts or questions, but there is a prevailing sense in the parachurch world that determining the mind of God for future choices is the only sure path to peace of mind and direction. Because this is true, the parachurch leader develops strategy that is integrated with the Christian faith.

The fourth unique element in effective parachurch strategy is that the risks match the resources. In the for-profit world, high-risk actions are easily matched with a commensurate amount of capital. The parachurch cannot raise money from stock buyers hungry for a quick profit, nor can it easily find banks to back its Christian vision. Because of this, the parachurch must always be in the fundraising mode if it hopes to grow, and this in turn means that the pace of action at parachurch organizations is a step slower than at their for-profit counterparts. When formulating strategy, the reality of available resources must be taken into account.

What Are the Benefits of Strategic Planning?

Many leaders would agree that strategic planning is necessary for a parachurch organization, but the thought processes that ought to be second nature for parachurch leaders need to be further developed. There are four major benefits that come with effective and biblically led strategic planning.

The first benefit is that a leader becomes better at managing in turbulent times. Imagine a continuum with the word *chaos* on one end and on the other end the word *order*. Chaos represents the breakneck speed of change and the unpredictable nature of our world today. Order represents the desired peace and calm that most leaders seek for their organizations. In *The 500-Year Delta,* Jim Taylor and Watts Wacker point out the dominance of chaos in today's business world. They describe how each year about twenty-six million Americans change jobs, one in seven or eight Americans are divorced, and as many as forty-two million Americans change residences. They write, "In two generations we have shifted from a society that nearly sanctioned stability—in the workplace and at home—to one that can barely sit still for a half-hour sitcom, and then only with channel grazer in hand" (1997, p. 15).

With a proliferation of changes comes more chaos, and chaos brings challenges for management. In a world where employees and ideas seem to be new every day, it is hard for an organization to move along smoothly. The default position for most organizations is to practice crisis management—leaders respond to rapid change by moving from crisis to crisis, just staying above water. The leader who is constantly treading water may be exasperated by it, asking, "How am I supposed to think strategically when I can barely keep my head above this churning water?" But treading water is often exactly a result of *not* thinking ahead and *not* deciding upon a definite vision for the organization and a realistic plan to implement that vision.

But is a serene world of order any better than a world of chaos? No matter how alluring, a perfectly ordered world lacks vitality. It is often a sign in an organization of too much control and too little experimentation or risk taking. The ideal place for an organization to be on this continuum is right in the middle. This is the place where order and chaos converge—a point of complexity. Order is needed to lend stability, but the chaos of change keeps an organization from stagnating. Strategic planning is one tool that allows an organization to find its balance in the middle of two extremes.

The second benefit that comes from strategic planning is that good intentions get transformed into reality. Thus strategic thinking and planning become acts of stewardship. J. B. Crouse, the president of OMS International, an international missions organization, has said, "I spent my first three years as president fighting crisis fires. I knew we couldn't keep going this way. I felt the mission would go under within five years if we didn't start addressing the larger issues. But despite the fact that there was a new fire to fight every day, we launched a strategic planning process" (personal conversation, March 1996). This president leads an organization that has sent hundreds of missionaries to Asia over the past one hundred years. The organization exists to "share the gospel and plant churches." Its intentions were good, and it enjoyed a measure of success. But somehow it had lost sight of the future and had begun to focus its energy on just existing. A yearlong strategic planning process moved the organization out of the turmoil of crisis management and into a position to truly implement the purpose of the organization—thereby stewarding available resources.

A third benefit that comes with strategic planning is the renewed ability to say no. Peter Drucker reports that "about eight out of ten nonprofits in the country are small organizations whose leaders find it hard to say no when someone comes to them with a good cause. I advised some close friends of mine . . . that half the things they are doing they shouldn't be doing—not because they are unimportant but because they are not needed. I told them, 'other people can do those activities and do them well.' It is time for organized abandonment" (Peter F. Drucker Foundation for Nonprofit Management, 1993, p. 3). Parachurch organizations suffer from this trap every bit as much as secular nonprofits, and as a result their energies are siphoned off in directions that do not directly bear on organizational goals.

Parachurch organizations sometimes behave like a snowball rolling down the side of a hill. As it advances it picks up additional programs, policies, and services. Each of these may be laudable in itself, but together they distract from the overall goal of the organization. Strategic planning brings into focus the single objective and allows the organization to practice "organized abandonment" on the programs that do not move its guiding vision directly forward. For example, as a result of moving through a strategic thinking and planning process, the Salvation Army Eastern Territory leadership identified a series of policies and procedures that encumbered many people and their work. Abandoning them has freed people and ideas to move more freely.

The fourth benefit that comes from strategic planning is the new level of community that arises when all the stakeholder groups of an organization have input. It is common for the different constituencies of an organization to grow apart in their expectations and goals. Those on the front lines may desire the ministry to move in one direction, whereas the board and president may be pushing for other objectives. An organization may also lose touch with the donors that support it. But when an organization as a whole, with input from each group of stakeholders, begins to consider the vision and goals that it is working toward, then the organization begins to work as a team.

How Do We Get Started on the Process?

Just as organizational structures have evolved over time, so has the planning process. It used to be that the senior leaders of an organization would plan a major event. They would escape to some mountain top, literal or metaphorical, and spend a few days determining their organization's future goals and plans. Then, like Moses coming down Mount Sinai with the Ten Commandments, this handful of leaders would descend upon the organization bearing the new covenant. Parachurch organizations would do such a planning session annually, every few years, or perhaps just when a crisis arose. These planning events were stiff, rigid, and highly disciplined events.

Today the planning process looks much different. Two particular deficiencies of the old model have been corrected. First, the planning effort is no longer an occasional event, but a continuing process. The old model could be imagined like this:

WORK→WORK→WORK→PLANNING EVENT→WORK→WORK

The new model of planning looks quite different:

WORK→PLAN→WORK→PLAN→WORK→PLAN→WORK

Increasingly, planning and work are done continually.

The second difference between the current planning models and those of the past is that planning is no longer the domain of a few senior leaders. Effective planning includes all the different stakeholder groups. Only when all the different constituents of an organization and the entire range of goals, conservative to radical, have been voiced is it possible to set an organization's strategy. In light of this more effective model, the way most leaders envision the planning process must be changed.

Although planning is an ongoing process, there are times when an organization loses its way and desperately needs to determine a new vision or to decide on a new plan to implement its goals. When this is the case a special set of meetings and activities is necessary. This remainder of this chapter describes how this planning process looks and answers some basic questions about it.

A strategic planning consultant can be helpful to the organization during the process because the organization's leader may bias the planning sessions by his or her own set of preconceived ideas. The focus of every member of the senior leadership ought to be on contributing thoughts. Even the smallest parachurch organizations can find a quality facilitator whose job at the planning sessions is to focus people's dialogue in a neutral way.

Organizations often ask, How many meetings do we need? But there is no simple answer to that question. For organizations that simply need to refocus their plans, perhaps only one long morning session is needed. For organizations whose problems are systemic and profound, perhaps a year-long analysis is needed, with meetings spaced every month. The speed of strategic planning also depends upon the personalities of the leaders. Another determining factor is organizational size. The larger an organization is and the more stakeholder groups are involved, the longer the process becomes for even minor shifts in direction.

A second question often asked is, Who should be involved in the planning process? Once the need for a special process is realized, the next goal is to determine who will take part in the process. A *guiding coalition* is essential for a successful strategic planning session. A broad cross-section of the parachurch must be included in this guiding coalition. This does not happen automatically but depends upon the thoughtfulness of the leaders who put together the sessions. If this step is neglected, the effectiveness of the sessions can be nullified before they even begin. If it is successful, the sessions will have a broad range of voices that can give valuable insight into the direction of the organization. Each member will feel freedom to give input from the viewpoint of his or her stakeholder group but will also have an eye on the advantage of the entire organization. Meetings of this guiding coalition have generally replaced the older planning sessions that concentrated on a few senior leaders who escaped to a mountaintop to set the organization's vision and plans.

Members of the guiding coalition should also be chosen with an eye toward diversity in age, race, and gender. Large parachurch organizations must be especially careful to gather a diverse group. Oversights here, even when accidental, can cause bad feelings among those who feel that their input is not being heard. Also there must be diversity of mind-set. Some people must be present who are deeply committed to the current ideals of the organization, and others must think outside the common lines and want to push the organization in new directions. Often it is the tension between the conservative and radical factions in a planning session that brings about the best results. The one absolutely critical requirement for each person involved in the sessions is that he or she can think creatively and articulate clearly their thoughts.

"We don't want words but deeds" is a common sentiment, but in a strategic planning session it is important to get the words right. The answers to the questions being asked at the sessions need to be agreed on by all parts of the guiding coalition and then written down. Although getting the ideas right is supremely important, getting the words right does matter. For this reason it is helpful if a wordsmith can be identified among those present at the sessions. This person can craft the words so that they are easy to understand and can be agreed on by all who are involved. These answers must eventually be communicated to the rest of the members of the organization, and that is another reason it is imperative that they be written well.

Cycles of dialogue are crucial to developing a plan that can be agreed on by all parts of the guiding coalition. The planning team might draft a vision statement and then take that draft back to stakeholder groups to discuss and critique. At the next session the members of the planning team might explain the reactions to the draft statement and then incorporate that input into a further revision. The same circular process can then be repeated with the revised statement until a broad consensus appears. These cycles produce the broadest possible input and the most balanced final statement. This cyclic process will not happen over a weekend but over a period of a month or more. Meeting on Friday afternoons over a period of six weeks, for example, is one way to allow the time for this back-and-forth process to work.

A third frequently asked question is, How often should we have a planning session? This is another question that has no absolute answer, only some basic guidelines. As we have already seen, planning should not be limited to annual events. An organization must make micro-adjustments to its goals and strategies at each step of the way. If these incremental changes are made, then there will not be the pressing need for a major change each year in the course of the organization. However, these small steps need to be supplemented with a deeper process. Many organizations make a major review of their situation once every three years. This time period varies, of course. Some organizations feel the pull of change very strongly, and for them it may be good to reexamine the organization's strategic plan regularly until there is stabilization.

The end products of the strategic planning process are six:

- Mission statement (reason for existence)
- Vision statement (preferable future)
- Values statement (what is important to organization)
- SWOT analysis (internal and external assessment of strengths, weaknesses, opportunities, and threats)
- History and current position (life stage of organization)
- Specific strategies (goals, measurement systems, and actions)

The next three chapters discuss developing responses to those three questions that every parachurch leader ought to be able to answer. Where do we want to go? Where are we now? How will we get to our destination? In the course of these three chapters, the six products that result from the planning process will also be discussed further.

10

KNOWING WHERE
YOU WANT TO GO

IT SEEMS THAT it is always a small minority of people who are able to discern current challenges and future trends. In 1 Chronicles we read the story of a great army that came to Hebron to make David their king. Among the 340,000 fighting men of this army was a tiny group of men from Issachar, numbering 200 men plus their families. But there was something about these 200 men from Issachar that set them apart from the crowd. We find them described as "those who had understanding of the times, to know what Israel ought to do" (12:32).

The members of this small tribe had built a reputation for discernment. Somehow they were able to lift their eyes to the distant horizon and see further than those around them. They could read the signals of changing political climates, the movement of enemy armies, and the hand of God on their nation. Through effective analysis they were able to synthesize the facts and shape a strategic response for the army of Israel.

Every organization needs an Issachar factor—people who can look to the horizon and interpret the times, influences, forces, and trends facing their organization. Yet the Issachar factor is often missing from the work of parachurch organizations. Leadership in the parachurch tends to develop *managerial myopia*. In response to fast-paced change, leaders try to find stability by focusing solely on the present. What every parachurch organization needs is a set of headlights—a team of people looking out onto the horizon.

There are leaders who do not need any help looking to the future. This breed of leader seems to wake up in the morning thinking about trends and strategies. But these are a minority. Most leaders are not so visionary, and in the rush of day-to-day problems, they forget to ask key questions about their organization's future. The importance of the planning process is that it gets people thinking about the future, imagining what that future will look like.

Answering the question, Where do you want to go? is the first step to getting eyes for the future. There are three steps to answering this question:

o Clarifying the mission of the organization

o Developing a vision for the future of the organization

o Determining the core values of the organization

Taken together these three elements represent what we might call the *core essentials*. These are the ideas that really make up the cause. They capture the nonnegotiables, the compelling ideas that are magnetic. They are the expression of what leaders believe God is calling them to do.

We can think of each of these ideas as a horizontal thread in the organization. The vertical threads represent the personnel—the leaders, board members, donors, and other stakeholders. What binds these vertical entities together? What keeps them focused in times of change or discouragement or when a new leader takes over? Only the horizontal threads of mission, vision, and the core values will complete the weave—and then only if leaders have taken the time to articulate these core essentials that bind an organization together.

Clarifying the Mission

As we unpack the three subpoints of the core essentials, we begin with mission or purpose. Every organization must have an outer boundary, a fence if you will, that defines what is in bounds and what is out of bounds. Mission statements point to what is in bounds, why it exists.

At its simplest, a mission statement for any organization is much like a summary of the theme of a movie or the big idea of a sermon. It is a clear and concise statement that sets out the main purpose of the organization. If a parachurch leader were to be asked by an old friend, "Tell me again what this organization is about?" the response of the leader would closely resemble the mission statement. It would not be a full-dress litany of what the organization does but a broadly sketched statement that sets forth the nature of the organization's work and the purpose of its existence.

Most parachurch organizations have mission or purpose statements. They have to because the mission statement is a legally mandatory step in the creation of a parachurch organization. As mentioned earlier, among the requirements for gaining nonprofit status with the government is a mission statement that explains the kind of work in which the organization will be involved. This statement will usually be short—generally just a paragraph. And because parachurch organizations are generally classified as *religious* nonprofits, the mission statement must tie the organization's work to its religious convictions. To make this religious connection clear, the core values of the organization must be in complete harmony with the mission statement.

Mission statements should be the slowest of all directional statements to change. They need to be seen as nonnegotiable. Nevertheless, the single biggest need of most parachurch organizations is to refresh or clarify the words and ideas of an existing statement.

It is crucial to keep in mind that an organization should not be so confined by its mission statement that the mission restricts forward progress. Many organizations, both secular and religious, confuse what they are with what they do. This mistake was made earlier in the century by the companies that ran the railroads. They defined themselves as *railroad* companies, not as *transportation* companies that happened to be in the railroad business (Bryson, 1988). If they had not confused their method of transportation with their purpose, they could have adapted more easily to the new world of transportation that emerged with the trucking industry. However, these companies defined themselves as railroad companies, and therefore when the railroads declined, so did these companies.

Mission Aviation Fellowship (MAF) in Redlands, California, recently reassessed its mission statement and broadened it to include more than its traditional field of aviation and radio technology. President and CEO Maxwell Myers began this new look at the mission statement with the conviction that "if we are really the people of God, we need to ask ourselves, how have we changed in ways that are commensurate with how the world is changing today?" MAF's mission statement now reads, "multiplying the effectiveness of the church by using aviation and other strategic technologies to reach the world for Christ." Because of this rethinking, they developed an information technology division that handles millions of e-mail messages a month and allows prayer needs to be communicated instantly (Christian Management Association, 1997, pp. 5–6). All parachurch organizations, no matter how long they have been around, can take a cue here from MAF. The mission statement must be broad enough to allow for change in method and technique. If it is not, then when changes come over the next decades, the organization will find its efforts out of step with current realities.

An effective mission statement must be an idea large enough to meet the need. As we saw from the discussion of the parachurch's interaction with culture (Chapter Four), successful parachurch organizations have prospered because they have filled a need in culture. Recall how James

Dobson found himself surrounded by a culture that was rebelling from the traditional values of the past and countered that culture with an organization that "focused on the family" through books, radio, magazines, and seminars. The need was recognized, and the idea for the organization was large enough to meet that need.

It is at this point in writing or refining a mission statement that parachurch leaders must be very honest with themselves about their work. They must constantly ask themselves, What need are we seeking to meet? and then, Will our plans be large enough to meet that need? For example, perhaps an organization feels called to improve biblical literacy in this country. That is certainly an important goal, but what if the sole idea is to distribute Bibles. Even if it distributed Bibles to perfection, the organization would still not meet its stated goal, improvement of biblical literacy. The distribution of Bibles must be supplemented by some kind of educational work and values development. Only then will the idea truly match the need.

A third point that should be kept in mind when writing or refining the mission is that input should be gathered from as many sources as possible. For an organization that is just starting, that has only a president and a board, the mission statement will represent the hearts of these few people. But when an established organization is reworking its mission statement, it is a good idea to get reactions to refinements from each group of stakeholders within and outside the organization. But on this point we need to be clear: the act of writing and refining the mission statement should not and cannot be a group exercise. Missions and purposes need to flow out of the minds and hearts of a handful of people—those who have founded the organization or have a strong commitment to the founding purpose. These founders and other dedicated people may need to be challenged to contextualize the mission, but they know in their bones why the organization exists. Their long tenure brings stability to the enterprise, and their stabilizing role needs always to be in dynamic tension with the more innovative and risk-taking role.

When the mission statement is completed, the organization is one step closer to answering the question, Where do we want to go? With the mission statement the outline of the bright city of the future becomes visible. With the next step, not only the outline but the lights of the city become visible.

Developing a Vision: Imagining the Future

The story goes that when the Beatles were first getting off the ground as a band, John Lennon would turn to the other three mop-tops and ask, "Where we goin', boys?" And the other three would answer in humorous voices, "To the toppermost of the poppermost, Johnnie!" That quirky example of a vision statement helps to illustrate the way a vision to do something can empower a group of individuals. Certainly this vision empowered the four Beatles—it would be just a short time before their vision became reality.

It is difficult to overestimate the power of a well-conceived vision statement. Stephen Covey, in his book *First Things First*, has rhapsodized about the power of vision: "It taps into the deep core of who we are and what we are about. It's fueled by the realization of the unique contribution we have the capacity to make—the legacy we can leave. It clarifies purpose, gives direction, and empowers us to perform beyond our resources" (1994, p. 105).

Unlike the mission statement, the vision statement is not a legal necessity. Rather it is a chance for an organization to describe where it is headed, what its future will look like. It is dreaming on paper. Like Martin Luther King Jr.'s famous "I Have a Dream" speech, the vision statement says, "I have a dream for this organization, and it looks like this . . ." A well-written vision statement has several characteristics. It is

- Challenging: it moves people to consider work and ideas that are stretching.
- Visually stated: it paints a word picture for stakeholders.
- Stretching: it takes them beyond typical thinking patterns.
- Emotional: it generates enthusiasm and desire for change.
- Achievable: it can be imagined as possible.
- Clear: it can be understood—even by outsiders.
- Short: it can be a sentence, a paragraph, or a page.
- Future oriented: it is not a statement about the present.

A parachurch organization has to consider prayerfully what God would have the organization accomplish. The Beatles can aim at the "toppermost of the poppermost," but such a bluntly self-seeking vision is inappropriate for a parachurch organization. Just as the values and mission of the organization have come from the Bible and an understanding of God's will, so the vision statement must grow out of a deep desire to follow God's leading.

In his book *The Power of Vision*, George Barna makes clear this connection between an organization's vision and God's leading: "Vision for ministry is a clear mental image of a preferable future imparted by God to His chosen servants and is based on an accurate understanding of God, self and circumstances" (1992, p. 30). For a parachurch organization, operating from a Christian worldview, the question is not, How can we gain the most acclaim or influence? Instead the question is, How can we best impact the world for Christ? How do we augment the worldwide work of God? This question can only be answered as individuals seek knowledge of God's will and their own God-given abilities.

How an organization actually gets a vision is not nearly as critical as that it have one. When the territorial commander in the Eastern Territory of the Salvation Army developed a vision, he spent two years moving around the territory, gaining perceptions. Then he wrote a vision statement himself and presented it to the territory through a series of conferences. In the same organization on the West Coast, commissioner David Edwards chose to involve every Salvation Army corps in the Western Territory, for a vision development process that worked from the grass roots up.

Vision can come together in a variety of ways. Another method is for the parachurch organization's leaders to prepare a first rough draft and then involve other members of the organization in shaping the final version. What is common to most effective visions is that they are the product of a process that involves stakeholders. In today's cultural climate, stakeholders do not tolerate well leaders who develop a vision without input from stakeholder groups. Effective vision development results from two actions by leaders. They discern where God is saying to go and they hold enough conversations with stakeholders to ensure that there is a real buy-in from the necessary stakeholder representatives. Sometimes this can be achieved in a weekend retreat. More often it requires holding a series of meetings until a satisfactory vision has been hammered out.

Just like the mission statement, the vision statement, to be effective, must be thoroughly owned by the various stakeholders and leaders in the organization. More than being owned, it must be the driving force that inculcates every aspect of the organization—its strategic initiatives, goals, action plans, budgets, and even job descriptions. With an inspiring vision statement an organization is able to build a common sense of direction and hope for the future.

Conversely, the absence of a written vision statement is a clear signal of a mismanaged and underled parachurch organization. Instead of working toward a common goal, the workers and volunteers tend to drift aimlessly between discouragement and confusion. This can happen even when an organization does have a vision statement if there is no alignment between the different stakeholders as to the vision of the organization.

When the vision statement is completed, the parachurch organization should have a good idea of what the bright lights of their sought-for city will look like. All the stakeholders ought to be energized by that common goal and work for the day when the organization will drive out of the dark tunnel and be faced with the glittering city.

Determining the Core Values

In their book *Transforming the Organization,* Francis J. Gouillart and James N. Kelly write, "Values define the firm's non-negotiable behaviors as well as provide the guideposts for navigating through gray areas. They set forth the do's and don'ts, the always under any circumstances and the never under any circumstances" (1995, p. 193). Values keep a company together and give it resilience. Coming to understand these basic values and how they shape an organization's mission is vital, foundational work.

As discussed in previous chapters, what sets a parachurch organization apart from the thousands of secular nonprofit or for-profit organizations is its grounding upon a biblical worldview. The parachurch leader is not involved simply in doing a good deed or in making money, but in responding to the call of God upon his or her life. Here, at the core of an organization, should be values that are drawn from the Bible.

When identifying core values it is important not to confuse values with methods. James C. Collins and Jerry I. Porras write that they have "found that companies get into trouble by confusing core ideology with specific, non-core practices. . . . It is absolutely essential to not confuse core ideology with culture, strategy, tactics operations, policies, or other non-core practices. Over time, cultural mores must change; strategy must change; product lines must change; goals must change; competencies must change; administrative policies must change; organizational structure must change; reward systems must change. Ultimately the only thing a company should not change over time is its core ideology—that is if it wants to be a visionary company" (1994, pp. 81–82).

This concept can be visualized by imagining a sphere. The inner core of this sphere is stable and less prone to change than its rim. Within this inner core are the parachurch organization's guiding values—what is truly important. Hovering around this stable core is a fluid exterior—how this core is expressed. Strategy, goals, and structure are part of this exterior. These are parts of the ministry that change depending on cultural context and resources. Effective parachurch leaders will develop and protect the core ideology but establish flexibility in the noncore practices.

This differentiation between core values and noncore practices poses special challenges to the parachurch organization. A secular organization has to worry only about keeping up with the culture's prevailing values.

A parachurch organization does not simply listen to the culture but looks to the Bible for guidance with its values. The organization must also exercise much discernment to separate the essential from the time bound. When rock music came out in the 1950s and 1960s, many Christians called it the Devil's music. Forty years later it is clear to most Christians that rock music can be used for good—it is not essentially wrong, it is just often used to deliver wrong messages. Parachurch leaders such as Dawson McAllister are able to use rock music to reach out to today's culture. This is a positive example, yet there are many negative examples of instances when core values were betrayed by the adoption of modern practices. The parachurch leader must be ever on guard to see that core values are not violated by cultural adjustments.

The core values of an organization are useless unless articulated, made clear, and regularly practiced. A values statement is not a statement of faith or a list of doctrines that must be adhered to. It is also not a catalogue of all the values that the organization encourages. It is an aspirational statement. Values are concise statements of the qualities that govern the ministry of the parachurch. Smart leaders identify core values so that a plumb line exists to guide the way decisions are made, how money is spent, and how people are treated. So, for example, a rescue mission might state that "all people are created in the image of God and therefore deserve complete respect from workers." Such a values statement will help that rescue mission think twice about discriminating against any ethnic groups to which it ministers.

Typically a values statement will run anywhere from five to fifteen values, covering one to two pages. Figure 10.1 is an example of the values statement of the Salvation Army. Length is not important; what is important is that the foundational values of the organization are clearly communicated. The document should not require hours of study but should be immediately understandable. There is no correct form for or look to a values statement, and it is not a legal document. It can be included in the employee handbook given to all workers, or it can be posted on the wall, or it can be posted on the Internet.

Values have their greatest impact when leaders do three things:

- They mentor staff, instilling the values into staff via communication, messages, newsletters, summits, one-on-one meetings.
- They monitor the values. It *is* all right to treat people differently, according to how they adhere to core values. Compliance deserves rewards. Noncompliance deserves gracious but firm confrontation.
- They model the values. The old adage "pace of the leader, pace of the team" applies here. Both the walk and talk of leaders must line

---

Figure 10.1. Example of a Values Statement.

The Salvation Army remains an Evangelistic mission with an Evangelical vision. Our core values have shaped our vision, our mission, and our ministries.

The Glory and Worship of God
o We respond to God's love as the principal motivation for all we do.
o We focus upon God through prayer, Bible study and worship.
o We are guided by the Scriptures of the Old and New Testaments.

People Matter Most
o We know people matter to God.
o We believe life is sacred and all people have worth.
o We serve without discrimination.

The Redemption of Human Life
o We preach the universal soul saving message of the Gospel.
o We work as spiritual and social change agents.
o We are a healing and wholeness community bringing others into the body of Christ.

The Redeemed Life
o We teach faith and obedience to God's Word.
o We nurture believers in the disciplines of holy living.
o We encourage the use of spiritual gifts for service.

Parnership and Equality of Men and Women in Mission
o We seek equality in leadership opportunities for men and women.
o We reflect in worship, ministry and service the enriching diversity of culture.
o We strive for partnership in ministry for officers, soldiers, advisory board members, employees, and volunteers.

Servant Leadership
o We follow Christ's example of servanthood.
o We enlist others as fellow servants of the Gospel.
o We enable others as for ministry and service.

Excellence and Integrity in Stewardship
o We require strict accounting in the use of our resources.
o We pursue maximum effectiveness and efficiency in all we do.
o We respond to the needs of those we serve.
o We keep faith with those who support us.
o We work with due diligence and timeliness.

Second Coming of Christ
o We anticipate the coming of Christ to complete the works of His Church.
o We labor to:
Get people saved—Salvation
Keep people saved—Holiness
Get other people saved—Discipleship

Source: *Salvation Army, n.d., p. 7.*

up with their organization's core values. Anything less breeds cynicism and low morale.

There are many benefits that come to the organization that has a clear and well-adhered-to values statement. Those common problems of every organization—stalled programs, unmade decisions, and rancorous meetings—often result from the lack of clear core values. Without clear values, board members and staff alike are unclear about what is important. Corporate culture takes over, and those who can talk the loudest can often pull an organization off course—all because leaders were unclear about what was truly valued. One way to solve these problems is to unite people behind an inspiring values statement.

In contrast, articulated values:

- Bind diverse people together in community.
- Keep work efforts on course even when day-to-day direction is impossible.
- Motivate and sustain positive behavior when times are tough.
- Provide continuity when priorities and demands change rapidly.

As Aubrey Malphurs writes concerning the ultimate benefit of shared values, "If any Christian ministry desires to capture the greater energies and gifts of its people, it must share to some degree their common, core values so that its people, in turn, find common cause with the organization, which lends to biblical community" (1992, p. 25).

A values statement is the foundation for the bright lights of the future. Whether the long-term goal is evangelizing stadium crowds or reaching out to the needy in the local community, the ministry will be driven by its values. And if the values are askew, then the lights of that future will not burn so clearly or brightly.

Mission. Vision. Values. These three concepts make up the core essentials of where an organization wants to go. They are the lights in the distance—the promise and hope of a place where needs are met and dreams fulfilled.

UNDERSTANDING WHERE
YOU ARE NOW

SOCRATES SAID, "Tell me, Euthydemus: have you ever been to Delphi?"

"Yes indeed, twice."

"Did you notice the inscription 'Know yourself' somewhere near the shrine?"

"Yes, I did."

"Did you ignore the inscription, or did you pay attention to it and try to examine what sort of a person you were?" [Xenophon, 1990, pp. 185–186].

Such was the well-known advice given by Socrates: know yourself. The sage of Athens devoted his life to challenging others to look at themselves in a new light. His persistent questions and insights eventually led to a sentence of death. The years since have only verified that message of know yourself. History has shown us the harm done by those who have not been honest with themselves or those around them, and as a result have hurt families or whole nations.

Christianity seconds this idea championed by Socrates four hundred years before Christ. The reformer John Calvin writes, "With good reason the ancient proverb strongly recommended knowledge of self to man" (1960, p. 241). Yet for Calvin the idea of self-knowledge is subtly transformed. A person who has self-knowledge knows that in his or her heart there is a deadly disease—sin. Before God can be rightly known, each person must recognize the need for a savior, and the bankruptcy of his or her own efforts. Calvin recognizes that this is a message that cuts against the grain of human tendencies. The natural pull of the heart is toward self-admiration. People see themselves in a rose-colored mirror and are impressed with their own thoughts and abilities. But that is a deception. Only when a person is starkly honest can growth and change take place.

In the same way, the parachurch organization must strive to meet this same challenge: know yourself. Just as in the lives of individuals, problems and lack of impact in the activities of parachurch organization are often traceable to a lack of self-knowledge. Organizations also seem to be cursed with other unfortunate tendencies found in human beings. They look into a false mirror by refusing to discuss difficult issues, or they go on as if nothing were wrong or changing. All the more reason why parachurch organizations are well served when they ask the second strategic question, Where are we now? It is important that this question be approached with honesty and openness toward truth, which may feel uncomfortable. In asking the question, the organization is following the ancient advice of Socrates and the traditional advice of Christianity. In answering the question, the organization holds a mirror up to its face. It must examine itself carefully. This self-questioning is often done informally, but if an organization truly wants to get below the surface, a structured process delivers more value. This chapter sets down some steps an organization can take to systematically answer this hard question, Where are we now?

To some, this systematic look at present realities may feel irrelevant or like self-serving navel gazing. But that is not true. Because the worldview of the parachurch leader is Christ centered, there is a compelling reason to do what Jesus would do if he were in our place. Honest leaders will readily acknowledge that they do not naturally think of their organizations with "sober judgment," as Romans 12:3 challenges us to do. Furthermore, the Bible also counsels that "by wisdom a house is built, and by understanding it is established; by knowledge the rooms are filled with all precious and pleasant riches" (Proverbs 24:3–4). Such counsel heightens the responsibility of the leader to systematically do a reality check.

This chapter looks at three proven methods for understanding the current reality of an organization:

o Asking honest questions about it

o Taking a look at its strengths and weaknesses, opportunities and threats

o Identifying its address on the organizational life cycle

Asking Honest Questions

A method that asks honest questions implies that the asker is willing to work to acknowledge reality. Answering honest questions means research, and a lack of objective research handicaps many parachurch organizations today. For example, when the Christian Stewardship Association, with the support of the Lilly Endowment, conducted studies on more than 1,500 parachurch organizations, it found that only 20 percent of them had conducted a survey in the past three years to better understand their donors. Thus 1,350 of these organizations were working with little or no knowledge of who was supporting them, no knowledge of their values, interests, life stage, or commitment to the organization. This same research sloth infects other areas of the parachurch organization. Major for-profit firms do not tolerate decision makers who neglect market research data. Parachurch organizations should not tolerate them either. How can an organization claim to serve the needs of its donors or fulfill a mission statement but not take the necessary time and money to know whom it ministers to or those supporting the cause?

Most parachurch leaders do not see failure to survey donors, ministry recipients, volunteers, and members as a lack of stewardship. But it is just that. And this failure demonstrates a certain callousness toward constituents, a kind of arrogance. What could you possibly tell us? is the message these nonsurveying organizations send to the observer. In well-run parachurch ministries, you will find both a fact-finding mind-set and a budget for research. Even where money is scarce, a research mind-set will empower leaders to make twenty-five phone calls to key stakeholders on a particular issue. A lunch every quarter with members of a stakeholder group will yield volumes of helpful insights, especially if there is an agenda of questions to be asked. Lack of funds is no excuse for not getting qualitative input to answer the question, Where are we now?

When research funds are available, a research agenda can be established that allows leaders to drill down deeper into various stakeholder groups. Leaders should survey demographics, strength of spiritual life, attitudes and opinions on issues critical to the organization, and other needs they see or feel. The question is often asked, How often should we be doing research? A reasonable schedule might be as follows:

○ Survey current ministry recipients every two years.

○ Survey current donors every three years.

○ Survey volunteers and staff every three years.

○ Survey potential ministry recipients every three years.

○ Survey relationships with local churches and strategic alliances every five years.

A survey in one mission organization served as a wake-up call. In a mailed survey of current donors, one of the questions asked was how donors would prefer to receive future appeals. The different between the builders (those over fifty-five years old) and the baby boomers and busters were stark and significant. Direct mail, phone calls, even visits from mission representatives were all strongly endorsed by the builders. But the boomers and busters preferred direct mail much less, no phone calls, and certainly no visits. More than the builders, they wanted e-mail and a website, even an 800 number. This information redirected mission thinking to understand that younger donors were not like older donors. To keep its support level into the future, the mission would have to make adjustments in its development strategy.

The following are a few of the questions each organization needs to be continually asking itself.

Are We Living Out Our Values?

An organization's list of, say, "Our 12 Principles" may look great hanging up on the office wall, but do they really reflect the way the organization is run? Perhaps one of the principles states, "Be open to new ideas." But does this mean only new ideas that come from the mind of the president? Perhaps another principle states that women have an equal opportunity to hold the important positions, but in fact few women are in the leadership. Many other contradictions between stated value and actual practice can be imagined, and unfortunately many of these contradictions exist in parachurch organizations across the United States. For a healthy parachurch organization these contradictions must be eliminated.

Once the values of the organization are established, the leadership must be careful to live up to them. If the leadership is not modeling the core values, then it is almost certain that the rest of the workers will not either. Any hypocrisy will be quickly communicated to co-workers even though leaders may not be aware of the signals they are sending. Because the example of leaders is so crucial, leaders must look extra closely at themselves in the mirror of self-examination.

Not just the leaders, but the organization as a whole ought to model the core values. This means that from the person who answers the telephone to the board member at a community function, the values of the organization are firmly in place. This does not mean that a virtual parachurch Gestapo must be invented to ensure that the values are upheld, but it does mean that exceptions to the values are not tolerated and that leadership takes the time to personally observe the different aspects of the ministry. This also means being a good listener to the ideas and frustrations of each stakeholder in the organization.

Is the Mission Being Accomplished?

Each organization must also be sure that each task it adopts is in accordance with its mission statement. A parachurch organization tends to act like a snowball rolling down a hill, always picking up new ministries and new responsibilities. Joseph Stowell (1995), president of Moody Bible Institute, has described how he and the other leaders of this school are guarding their mission: "The question we are asking ourselves after 110 years of doing business was, 'Is it possible that we accumulated a lot of stuff that we are doing that we shouldn't be doing today? What must we shed if we are going to be able to face the future effectively for Jesus Christ? We have a huge conglomerate of ministries: 700 employees, a 64 million budget every year. No nook or cranny will be safe.' We asked ourselves, 'Is this really at the heart of our stated mission?'"

This is an example of the hard questions that each organization must ask.

Is the Vision Becoming a Reality?

The vision statement also must be examined. With the mission statement and the vision statement, the organization has a picture of its desired future ministry. It is as if a map were drawn up, and there at the top is the dot that stands for the organization's goal. Yet as time passes, the organization gets off track and heads down side roads or even roads going in another direction. Just as in the process described by Stowell, each organization must examine itself and see whether it is still heading toward the final goal as defined in the mission and vision statements. The programs and expenses that are not actively moving the organization toward fulfillment of this goal ought to be cut back. This takes a great degree of honesty and can be a painful process, but it is part of the challenge of self-knowledge.

Are We Getting the Results We Want?

Finally, the results of an organization must be faced squarely. Once adequate ways to measure the results of a ministry are achieved, then these results must be examined. This leads to the hardest question of all: Is this ministry accomplishing anything? If the results keep coming back negative, then the organization needs to make changes. Generally this means that a new approach to the ministry must be tried. The members of the organization should spend some time thinking up new, creative ways to implement their vision. Peter Drucker (Peter F. Drucker Foundation for Nonprofit Management, 1993) points out a more dire possibility: if the organization is getting no results, then perhaps there is really no need for the organization. Again, this is a painful possibility, but parachurch leaders must have the honesty to consider the possibility that the need their organization set out to meet no longer exists. And if that is the case, then the parachurch organization is better off either shifting to another ministry or folding altogether.

A willingness to ask these hard questions must become second nature for the parachurch leader. The leader must learn to reinforce the core values and learn to question every activity through the standard set by the mission statement. Asking the questions given here should become a daily mind-set. But organizations also need to set time aside for a more structured process of self-examination. This process consists of the remaining two methods of understanding the current reality of an organization: (1) an analysis of strengths, weaknesses, opportunities, and threats (SWOT); and (2) a look at where the parachurch organization stands in its life cycle.

Looking at Strengths and Weaknesses, Opportunities and Threats

A proven method to answering the question, Where are we now? is the SWOT analysis. The strengths and weaknesses examined in this method refer to internal realities, and the opportunities and threats examined have to do with external possibilities. (Sometimes this type of analysis is also called an *environmental scan*.) This method is effective because it juxtaposes positive qualities with their mirror-image negative qualities. The resulting picture also gives a clear indication of where the organization stands in relation to both internal and external matters. As with all the questions dealt with in this chapter, it takes a good measure of honesty to carry this technique through.

Effective SWOT analysis has two attributes. First, the strategic planning team must have an integrated framework or way to break down the analysis challenge. In large organizations this step is especially crucial. Before the strengths and weaknesses of an organization can even be guessed at, the organization should be broken down into smaller sections that can be examined separately. An ideal tool at the disposal of leaders is the set of key result areas—those areas an organization chooses to measure in the attempt to gauge effectiveness. Each key result area acts as a lens for focusing analysis on itself. The object is to focus assessment so that analytic energy is not wasted. Because any real change will come by improvement on the microlevel, all true self-assessment must start on that level.

The second attribute of an effective SWOT analysis is specificity. If too many generalizations are introduced, so that members of the strategic planning team must talk broad platitudes (for example, "we're growing") or broad critiques (for example, "staff is down"), then creative thought will likely be plugged. Helpful analysis needs to be specific and detailed. It needs to focus on the details of strengths, weaknesses, opportunities, and threats related to a specific result area or aspect of the vision.

When the analysis is done, a vivid snapshot of the organization appears. As strategic thinking moves to the stage of asking the next question, How do we get there? the SWOT factors will play an important part in decisions. The strengths must be augmented and the weaknesses combated; the opportunities must be followed up and the threats must be neutralized. The very execution of a SWOT analysis is helpful to most organizations. But analysis becomes paralysis if leaders stop here. In the following chapter we will look at what to do with the findings of a well-done analysis.

Identifying the Address on the Organizational Life Cycle

Throughout the Industrial Age theorists pictured organizations with a mechanistic model. An organization was thought to work like a giant clock that had to have its correct gears and springs. When problems came to the organization, the approach was to examine the individual pieces of the clock and to replace whatever was broken with a new part. According to this theory, there was no reason why an organization could not continue to prosper ad infinitum.

Today the mechanistic model has fallen away and been replaced by numerous models, one of them being the biological model of organizational growth. Just as a living organism goes through definite stages of life, so an organization goes through predictable stages. We can compare these stages to the stages of human development. Consultant George Bullard (who has built an effective life cycle model for Christian organizations) states that "every parachurch organization has a life cycle. In its simplest terms, this cycle begins when an organization is born, followed by a period of growth, the achievement of adulthood and maturity, a period of aging and often decline, and then either more decline, even death, or renewal" (personal conversation).

Therefore, the third step in self-knowledge for a parachurch organization is to recognize its address on the organizational life cycle. To know this, its leaders must have a good grasp of the its history—when was the organization strong, and when was it weak. The leader ought to have a good grasp on the successes and failures in the organization's past. With this knowledge, leaders can better understand and evaluate the opportunities and choices available to them. By considering the history of a parachurch organization, they can understand where the organization lies on its life cycle. (This historical context will also often form the introduction to the completed strategic plan—the historical setting for the organization sets the stage for any restatement of vision or mission.)

The idea of corporate life cycles was first recognized by Ichak Adizes. He relates that during his work as a consultant to top management, he came across the same types of problems over and over again. "It seemed that I could predict how a certain type of client's boardroom would look before I ever stepped into it" (Adizes, 1988, p. xiii). Once Adizes could grasp the stage of life an organization was going through, the problems it faced were absolutely predictable. This contradicts the old mechanistic view of organizations—the problems that appear are not fixed by simply replacing a part. Instead, each new stage on the organization's arc of growth brings with it new demands and new challenges that must be dealt with and overcome in the same way that a human being must face the new challenges of each stage of life.

Figure 11.1 maps the various stages that an organization typically goes through. Each stage carries an address code that describes its characteristics. There are four separate characteristics—vision, inclusion, programs, and management.

Vision. This is the excitement of a grand idea. It fuels forward momentum and mobilizes people to make significant sacrifices for the sake of the cause. Hope and enthusiasm and excitement reign supreme.

Inclusion. This is the capacity to be in a relationship-building process, during which an organization adds members and donors. It is the ability to enfold and assimilate new people. It is about people identifying with the organization and staying with it.

Programs. These are attempts to provide services and activities. They may include training efforts or ministries.

Management. This is the administrative function of an organization. It includes the decision-making and leadership structures.

In the four-letter codes in Figure 11.1, each of these characteristics is represented by a single letter. When a characteristic is present in a life cycle state in adequate or abundant amounts, it is depicted with an uppercase letter. When little of a characteristic is present, it is shown with a lowercase letter. Note how the four-letter code changes at various stops on the life cycle.

Whereas humans move through the various life stages in accordance with their ages, an organization moves through the stages at its own pace, unhindered by strict chronology. Certain organizations will grow, flourish, and reach their *prime* within ten years. Other organizations may remain in childhood for ten years as they slowly grow and implement

---

Figure 11.1. The Life Cycle and Stages of Organizational Development.

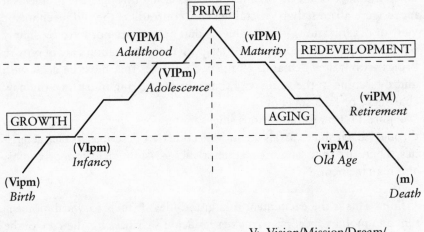

V: Vision/Mission/Dream/
   Energy/Purpose/Leadership
I: Inclusion/Assimilation
   of Members
P: Programs/Services/
   Activities
M: Management/Administration/
   Structure/Resources

Source: *Congregational Passages presentation by George W. Bullard Jr., September 11, 1995. Used by permission.*

their vision. These stages of organizational life are states of mind and being, not necessarily timed steps.

In the beginning there is vision. We can think of this original inspiration for an organization as its *birth*. As seen earlier in the historical sketches of Campus Crusade for Christ and Wycliffe Bible Translators, each organization begins in the mind of a leader or a group of leaders. The four-letter code for this stage is Vipm. Vision is running high, but the other three attributes of an organization are not yet present to any degree. These must wait until the organization is given some concrete shape.

Phase Two brings about a period of growth that moves from *infancy* to *adolescence*. The organization becomes more inclusive as the vision of the founder begins to spread to more people. Donors like what they hear, and the organization begins to gain financial support. These restless and growing organizations have not yet developed a coherent style of management, and they are opportunity driven. Because they are generally living from week to week, they react quickly to new challenges. This opportunistic approach demands a large measure of freedom for all who are part of them. Sometimes parachurch organizations in these stages of rapid growth impose rules and bureaucratic red tape on a system that must be freewheeling if it is to thrive. The parachurch leader must not be frightened by the fast pace of change and the quick turnabouts that a growing organization will go through.

In these early stages of fast growth, there is much pressure on the founder. It is from the mind of the founder that the vision took shape, and it is around the founder that the members of the organization have gathered. If the founder drops out at these early stages or if the founder loses the intensity of the vision, then the whole organization can be in trouble. Adizes points out how immense these pressures on the founder can be: workdays that last twelve to fourteen hours, constant struggling to keep the organization above water, workers who do not have the founder's intense commitment to the original vision, and even family members who do not understand the drive to turn the vision into reality. Each of these pressures chips away at the commitment of the founder, and unless the vision is strong enough, the whole organization can collapse. In this way these early stages of growth are like the refiner's fire that differentiates between true gold and the dross.

The adolescent stage brings on some new problems—as every parent of a thirteen-year-old will testify. In childhood the rapid growth of infancy is stabilized, but adolescence brings on a whole new spurt of growth. The four-letter code for the adolescent stage is VIPm, indicating that vision, inclusion, and programs are strong, but management lags behind. Sometimes the organization at this stage feels as though it has several impulses running through it at the same time, and its movements will seem awkward. The organization is stable and healthy, but the changes are coming too fast for the adolescent management styles to function effectively. The good news at this stage is that the vision is strong, the organization is drawing people to it, and workers are meeting needs with creative programs.

When the turbulence of adolescence is over, *adulthood* begins. At this stage, all four of the indicators are at their full-growth level, and the organization is classified VIPM. The vision is clear and inspiring to all the members of the organization. Many people are included within the organization, programs are running strong, and the management and administrative systems have finally evolved so that they are capable of handling the new size of the organization. The typical problem facing an organization in its prime, says Adizes, is a lack of well-trained workers. The opportunities for growth and programs are evident, but quality people to run those programs can be difficult to find. Some organizations reach this stage remarkably quickly. The Promise Keepers organization grew to adult stature overnight, and in 1997 it was large enough to hold a national gathering in Washington, D.C., that attracted several hundred thousand men. (And just as quickly it went into crisis mode when it shifted from fee- to donation-based financing.) The goal of an organization is to stay at this peak level of performance.

It is difficult to know at what point an organization begins the downward slope of growth, goes "over the hill." Almost always, the first characteristic to go is vision. The organization is then vIPM. Somehow leaders become complacent or distracted and take their eyes off the vision that inspired the organization at the start. The energy level begins to drop off, and there is less creativity and drive from the members of the organization. Parachurch organizations that feel themselves at this stage ought to read carefully the preceding chapter that asks the question, Where are you going? The organization that is on the back slope must somehow reenergize that vision with a fresh restatement of a valid vision or development of a new one.

There are real differences in outlook between the organization that is still in its upward climb and the organization that is heading down the other side of the slope. When an organization is young, success often comes from willingness to take risks and to try new opportunities. As an organization ages, maintenance of the status quo can become the leading goal and risks are often shunned. The young organization is just beginning to build stability and feels the need to prove its worth to potential supporters. The aging organization often has a solid base of support and does little daring that would jeopardize that base.

If the vision is not regained there is an inevitable decline. During this decline each of the other indicators begins to falter as well. Fewer people are included in the organization because there is no longer a vision to inspire new members. As interests ebbs, the programs begin to shrink and even to fail. Finally all that is left is a bureaucratic management that exists solely to perpetuate itself. Shortly after that stage comes the death of an organization.

The years after World War II saw the beginning of many parachurch organizations. Many of them reached their prime many years ago and are now struggling against becoming static or experiencing declining vision. Their capacity to include new donors, volunteers, and ministry recipients has begun to slow down. Often their administrative capacity is strong, but tight structure and controlled policies have choked off other resources. Clearly what is needed is a new vision that would restart the engine of the organization. When an organization develops new vision, it is essentially starting a new life cycle. If this vision is strong enough, it can not only reverse stagnation, but take the organization back to the left side of the growth curve. Suddenly there is a new goal to aim for, and new people and programs spring up around this new direction.

By examining the current status of an organization, it is possible to determine its address, where it is on the curve of life stages. This address puts the problems that are being experienced into a clearer perspective. And it helps leaders anticipate the next stage and its qualities. The chaos that surrounds a young organization is to be expected, and no sharp measures ought to be taken to curb that energy—it is the key to success. But the same chaos is inappropriate in an organization that is nearing adulthood. For an organization to reach its full potential, it must develop an effective management system. It is especially important that aging organizations understand their position and rectify their lack of vision. It takes complete honesty to admit that there is no strong vision, but only that admission allows an organization to find fresh vision and begin the cycle of growth again.

GETTING FROM HERE TO THERE

WHAT DOES IT take to move a parachurch organization from the present into the future? The past two chapters have identified the means to visualize the final destination of the organization and described how to conduct a self-examination. But after these two important steps are completed, organizations still need to implement and monitor a strategy into action. There are four steps to this implementation:

○ Defining strategy

○ Developing strategy

○ Testing strategy

○ Measuring results

After examining each of these steps, the chapter concludes with some challenges to forward progress faced by parachurch organizations.

Defining Strategy

What is a strategy? This was the question of one senior leader from a parachurch organization. This leader had been promoted from the mission field to the home office. He knew what strategy meant in the context of evangelization, now he had been given the task of developing an organizational strategy in North America. And he was lost. To quickly answer this leader's question, we could say that strategy is the guiding philosophy of the organization. But there is a deeper answer: a good strategy tells how the organization is going to use its resources to get from its present position to its preferred future. Strategy answers the most pragmatic question of all, How will we get from where we are to where we want to go?

A visual way to imagine strategy is to picture a trail running across a bare high-altitude landscape. In this world of ice, snow, and rock, the path must be marked by cairns—small piles of stones. Every hundred yards or so considerate hikers will assemble these piles to mark a trail that is difficult to follow. Without these cairns, the hikers would easily lose their way on the pathless landscape.

Most parachurch organizations and their leaders are faced with the same challenge: finding a way across a difficult terrain. The ground underneath their feet is the present; the future stretches out before them. Parts of the path seem obscure, and in the distance the slim trail fades from view entirely. Here and there, faithful cairns provide some guidance. These cairns are the strategies of the parachurch organization. Instead of wandering whichever way seems easiest at the moment, the strategies keep the organization moving step by step toward the final goal.

Often the final goal is mistaken for strategy. The hiker wants to reach the final destination. This is the macro point of view—the big idea. Campus Crusade had a commitment to share the good news of Jesus Christ around the world, and it saw the film *Jesus* as a tool that would facilitate that mission. Around this realization, Campus Crusade shaped its vision: to show the film to as many people as possible in as many languages as possible. Another example of vision comes from the International Bible Society: develop and provide readable texts of the Bible to as many people as possible. These visions are overarching and encompass every facet of their organizations. These are the bright lights of the cities toward which the organizations are traveling.

A vision is unquestionably important, but real action takes place at a lower altitude. This level involves strategies. To reach the final goal, many smaller cairns must be passed along the trail. These strategies break the vision down into manageable and focused steps. Usually the strategies fall into three broad categories: acquisition strategy, in which new territory is gained (for example, gain one hundred new donors per month for the annual fund); reinforcing strategy, in which desirable patterns are strengthened (for example, continue 5 percent new membership growth); and corrective strategy, in which a deficiency is remedied (for example, reverse the trend of declining listener support for a radio program). Such focused strategies organize resources to achieve a specific outcome.

When parachurch organizations find themselves stalled out or lost, it is often because their strategies are unsound or because the vision is sought so intently that the shorter strides of strategy are forgotten. Over the years, scores of visionary people who have begun ministries but who could not develop effective short-term strategies have had to settle for a slower pace, significantly downsize their vision, or even close their doors.

Developing Strategy

A common method for developing strategies is to place them in the format of objectives, goals, and action plans. An ideal plan for a strategy to achieve major organizational goals covers a three-year cycle. Part of a case study that shows how one parachurch organization, the Christian Stewardship Association (CSA), developed a strategy in this goals and objectives format is depicted in Figure 12.1.

Figure 12.1. Example of Setting Strategy as Goals and Objectives.

Some Christian Stewardship Association Strategic Targets (1997, 1998, 1999)

Through studying and reading about other associations and through examining CSA's history, the following eleven areas emerge as strategic result areas that the CSA board and CEO need to regularly monitor in order to be all we can be for Christ's kingdom during our generation. To project the road map of the association in light of the mission and vision, the following strategic targets are identified for the next three years:

Objective One: Education

> Objective: To be the recognized leader and one of the largest providers of development and stewardship educational training opportunities among evangelical Christian ministries.

> Goal 1A1: Realize an attendance of 900–1000 for Stewardship Summit in Kansas City in 1997.
> Goal 1A2: Realize an attendance of 1050 in Orlando in 1998.
> Goal 1A3: Realize an attendance of 1100 in 1999.

Objective Two: Membership

> Objective: To communicate and provide the benefits and services that increase the value of CSA organizational and personal memberships in order to build a growing and satisfied membership base each year.

> 2A Action Plan
> Goal 2A1: Increase membership by 20 percent each year and develop a minimum of twice-a-year communications to members.

> Goal 2A2: Conduct a membership survey/study–needs analysis prior to the March 1997 CSA Board meeting.

Source: *Christian Stewardship Association, 1996, p. 13. Used by permission.*

The mission of the CSA is to influence the world for Jesus Christ by equipping Christian leaders with an understanding of biblical stewardship through education, research, and networking activities. After completing its SWOT analysis, CSA divided its objectives into twelve categories (the number, of course, will vary for different organizations): education, membership, resources, research and grants, stewardship, board relations and development, diversity, advertising relationships, staffing, mailing list development, networking/partnering, and strategic planning.

For each of these areas, a primary objective was established. For example, under the first category, education, the objective was "to be the recognized leader and one of the largest providers of development and stewardship education training opportunities among evangelical Christian ministries." For each of the twelve categories a realistic objective was set.

The second step was to establish measurable goals by which each objective could be realized. For example, to accomplish the education objective, CSA set a goal of having an attendance of nine hundred to one thousand people at its annual conference in Kansas City. For the category of membership, one goal was to increase membership by 20 percent each year. Goals like these are best stated with active verbs and in such terms that it will be possible to measure later whether these goals have been met.

Ideally, there will be a third level to a strategy, in which the staff lists out specific action plans. Each goal will have as many actions plans as are needed to reach the desired result. These action plans will represent the most pragmatic statements of all.

Testing Strategy

Every strategy developed by the parachurch can be tested for its soundness. Before the organization heads for that cairn, it needs to be tested to ensure that it really does take the parachurch organization in the correct direction. The following five points are a grid through which the strategy can be evaluated.

• *Internal consistency.* Is the strategy consistent with itself and its context? Does this strategy conflict with other substrategies of the organization? For example, does a goal for a service also reflect staff growth and a budget to provide the service?

• *Environmental consistency.* A good strategy harmonizes with events taking place in the external environment. For example, a parachurch organization should not leap into the publishing business at a time when the book business is having particular problems. It makes sense to pay attention to what is going on outside the organization—if government funding is being reduced in social services, then it may be a good time for a relief mission to expand.

• *Appropriateness.* A good strategy is a reasonable match for available resources. Along with financial resources, there ought to be sufficient commitment from the members of the organization. If a small crisis pregnancy center serves a small town but desires to expand statewide, that vision must align with the desires of the staff and volunteers in the organization.

• *Risk acceptability.* All strategies have a certain amount of risk involved with them—to get to that cairn a certain amount of rough trail must always be passed. But good strategy brings with it a reasonable risk. Developing strategy never ought to feel like gambling. Faith stretching is acceptable, but an unrealistic capital campaign goal that is well beyond the recommended amount should not be attempted.

• *Appropriate time line.* Effective strategy articulates what goals need to be accomplished and sets a reasonably paced time line for this work. Too little time allotted to reach a goal sets workers up to fail.

As author of these criteria, Phillip V. Lewis points out that "although these criteria do not guarantee success, they are valuable for giving leaders the time and room to maneuver, and these questions also provide many decision-making opportunities" (1996, p. 194).

Measuring Results

Results are the visible fruit of an organization's efforts, and as such are one of the primary indicators of an organization's impact. Once an organization has moved through a year of reaching goals, then it is important to measure the results. Consider for a moment what would happen if an organization had no accurate means to measure the results of its ministry. The organization could have hundreds of strategies and plans, but would have no hard evidence that all its labors were truly accomplishing anything.

In a for-profit corporation, performance is almost always measured by the bottom line: money. It is not quite so cut and dried for a parachurch organization to measure the results of its work. Many parachurch leaders even shy away from attempting to quantify results. Peter Drucker recounts a frequently asked question from churches: "How do you measure results when we know our rewards are in heaven?" (Peter F. Drucker Foundation for Nonprofit Management, 1993, p. 40). The question brings out an important truth. Parachurch organizations are not looking for the same kind of results that secular organizations are after. Yet by carefully analyzing the results of their work, they can gain insight about the methods and practices that are most effective, that advance God's kingdom most. The Salvation Army is a good example of this kind of attention to program results. It knows the percentage of alcoholics who are restored to health, and the percentage of criminals who are rehabilitated through their efforts (Peter F. Drucker Foundation for Nonprofit Management, 1993). Knowing this information allows the organization to use its resources more wisely. Ignoring this information is a sign of poor stewardship over the gifts that God has provided.

Both quantitative and qualitative measurements are needed for an organization to correctly gauge its impact. *Quantitative* measurement deals primarily with numbers and statistics. It is important for an evangelist to know how many people have been coming forward to receive Christ at the nightly meetings. It is important for a rescue mission to know how many meals are being served. This type of information is usually the easiest to get; it involves simply counting heads and tabulating the results.

Really helpful quantitative measurement goes deeper than this. The organization needs to know more than raw numbers; it needs to know the effects of its efforts. For example, Campus Crusade during the 1970s made a number of attempts at *saturation* evangelism. The organization literally saturated a campus or an entire city with the Gospel. The numbers for such an effort were extraordinary: millions heard the Gospel, thousands responded. The head counts could look great, but without measurable results there is no way to know the true effectiveness of the strategy. The parachurch organization must find ways to quantify the real impact of its work.

Qualitative measurement involves asking more detailed questions, through interviews or other methods, of those who responded or did not respond to the organization's efforts. The information garnered from this approach will be quite different from the numbers that come from the quantitative approach. Those involved with a radio ministry, for example, need to know not just the number of people who listen to a broadcast but also people's specific reactions. They need to take the time to ask listeners what impact particular programs are having on their lives. Concrete responses allow the organization to adjust its program so that its mission is accomplished with the intended audience.

Because each parachurch organization is different, the results that each measures will also be different. At some point the leaders of the organization must determine what the key result areas are for their organization. What will they monitor? What health indicators or other measurements of impact will be systematically observed? This list of *things we have to measure* is most useful when it represents the breadth of an organization ministry. The criterion for selecting things to measure is basic: Where must you have performance because without it the organization's vitality and even life would be threatened?

The old adage works well, "Measure what's important, and what's measured will become important." When an organization is clear about the results it seeks to achieve, it is well positioned to turn its vision into reality. Not knowing the organization's impact is a definite liability. How can leadership know where to put pressure or what to monitor if it does not look at the organization through the eyes of clear results? By focusing on key result areas, the parachurch organization brings a significant level of stewardship and accountability to the organization.

Facing the Challenges of Forward Progress

Every parachurch organization struggles to turn resources into desired outcomes. It is never an easy matter to turn the dreams of an organization into a reality, but there are at least seven challenges that make it difficult for the parachurch organization to do this.

The first challenge for most parachurch organizations is that they must get by on thin resources. More than any other force, lack of money impedes most parachurch organizations from achieving what they desire. Thin resources have the tendency to gut the parachurch leader of courage and a willingness to take risks. For the parachurch, even the most basic advances require time-consuming fundraising. For example, Turning Point Ministries, an organization that trains people in local churches to set up small-group systems to address life-controlling problems, hoped to add a video training system to augment their live training sessions. It researched this possibility and found that to produce and market a video training product would require over $400,000. Turning Point is not in a position to visit a local bank and obtain a loan for the amount needed; instead, it must work vigorously to identify foundations and donors who believe in its cause. What would take only a few hours in the for-profit world takes a parachurch organization days or even months of work. If the parachurch is going to advance its dreams, it must find ways to get resources, and it must be acclimated to a sometimes slow pace of progress.

A second challenge faced by parachurch organizations is a disease called *founders fever*—seen when the founder refuses to relinquish control of an organization to the next generation of leaders. Here are some major symptoms of this disease, which can strike seemingly healthy parachurch organizations:

○ Unwillingness of founder to let go of the reins

○ Continued meddling (even subterfuge) by founder after he or she leaves

○ Fear-based decisions by leadership

○ No leader development strategy in place

○ Loyalty to methods that were successful in the past

○ Fear of speaking within earshot of the founder about needed changes

Most parachurch organizations are in ministry for the long haul, and they set their goals into the future. If a parachurch organization is around for a few decades, sooner or later it must face a leadership transition. Unfortunately this transition is not always smooth, and the founders may have trouble letting go of the organization that they started. Such transition crises are a drag on forward movement, impeding the progress of the parachurch organization.

A third challenge is a tendency toward unarticulated strategy. Parachurch organizations often fail to give each of their workers a sense of the expectations for their work. The large organization must have cairns that mark its path, but each individual also needs definite strategic markers that show forward progress. In one mission organization, regional staff who were responsible for raising funds, recruiting missionaries, and garnering prayer support were working with no job or role description, no action plan, and no productivity targets. As could be expected, these workers had no real understanding of where they fit into the larger strategy of the organization. Such confusion can be avoided if the leadership sets up clear markers for each person in the organization.

A fourth challenge faced by many parachurch organizations is lack of alignment. What it means to be in alignment is captured in the phrase *contending as one*. When an organization is in alignment, every resource, program, and structure within the organization is brought into harmony with its overarching goals. As time goes by, leaders can find themselves simply managing large systems and not working for the larger strategy of the organization. When there is a lack of alignment, different parts of the organization are following different trails and looking for different cairns.

A fifth challenge that keeps a parachurch organization from meeting its strategic goals is ineffective structures. At the very smallest level, the parachurch organization feels like a family-run store or a small business. But as the workforce climbs to more than fifteen people, structure becomes an issue. Often the parachurch organization has had no professional guidance in developing its structure. People are added, removed, and placed in positions according to common sense or simple availability. This ad hoc structure does not allow the organization maximum impact. Few organizations value outside counsel and perspectives for addressing structural weaknesses; few even understand their need for this outside assistance.

A sixth challenge is that of context. The parachurch organization often finds itself in an environment that makes forward progress difficult. Often the organization is physically surrounded by such overwhelming needs that it finds executing a strategy difficult. A parachurch organization committed to minister in an inner-city block that is dominated by crack houses would face this challenge of context. The environment itself would militate against strategic progress, with its uncaring landlords, apathetic or discouraged neighbors, and gang members. In this hostile environment it would be difficult to set up strategic cairns, and the path between these cairns would be difficult to pass. Another aspect of context is the larger reality of the present culture. The modern world is not always a friendly environment for those motivated by religious faith. Popular culture continues to marginalize religious faith and the impact of religious organizations. This means that many parachurch organizations, especially those that fall along the conservative side of the spectrum, must operate in a resistant environment.

A seventh challenge to parachurch strategy is an unhealthy or dysfunctional culture within the organization. The varieties of dysfunctional cultures are myriad. Leaders may have gotten into the habit of freezing frontline workers out of key discussions. The place may be inhabited with cranky, overextended workers. Weak staffing and recruiting over the years may have filled the organization with people who are not growing. Pay may have been too low for too long. These situations come together and conspire to create a work climate in which change is difficult.

In this case the leaders of the organization must back up and address the problems in the climate before implementing a new and more challenging strategy. The goal is to develop, as Marvin R. Weisbord puts it, a *productive workplace.* "Productive workplaces are those where people learn and grow as they cooperate to improve an organization's performance. The 'bottom line,' in this way of looking at things, is dignity, meaning and community in work" (1987, p. xiv).

Sometimes the culture is averse to taking risks. Generally, younger organizations are more flexible and willing to take risks. But as organizations mature, dreams and risk taking atrophy. When this happens, the climate tightens. If leaders of mature organizations want to move out into new areas and launch acquisition strategies, they will have to limber up their risk-taking muscle either by shocking it with a stretching initiative or by slowly working up to a higher level.

The path traveled by parachurch organizations stretches into the next century. The parachurch has grown by leaps and bounds over the past fifty years, and the prospects of further growth seem bright. The next century is open to every organization that can articulate a compelling vision and move strategically to realize that vision. But this open future is not guaranteed to any organization. For both small and large organizations the continuing challenge is to set up the strategic cairns that line the future path and to keep the organization moving down that path—passing those cairns one by one until it reaches the goal.

PART FOUR

WHERE IS THE PARACHURCH HEADED?

THIS LAST SECTION looks at the future of the parachurch as it confronts the challenges to come. These challenges include building a Christian foundation for parachurch finances, developing a partnership with the broader church, and finally, navigating the changes of the future. How well a parachurch organization will continue to prosper will be determined by its answers to these questions:

- How should a Christian organization approach the thorny issue of finances?
- What will it take for the church and parachurch organization to complement each other?
- Will the parachurch organization find strong answers to the challenges of the future?

13

FINANCING TOMORROW'S PARACHURCH

"LUNCH LADY, YOU save our lives!" proclaimed the homeless man, as he took a sack lunch from the hands of Beverly Graham. Thousands of the most down and out of Seattle's underclass—alcoholics, drug addicts, mentally and physically disabled—would second those words!

During its first seven years (from 1990 to 1997), Graham's enterprise, Sack Lunch, prepared and distributed more than 180,000 lunches and 400,000 sandwiches. The inspiration for her solo crusade came when Graham, a professional singer, was performing at clubs in downtown Seattle's Pioneer Square in 1989. She walked past homeless men and women digging through trash for food and sleeping on heat vents. Blankets, sleeping bags, and socks were pulled from her closet and handed out to the needy. But that did not seem to be enough. Soon she was putting together sandwiches in her home kitchen, making sack lunches, and regularly delivering them to the needy on skid row.

It was a one-person operation until retirees Jim and Fran Mather offered to help and moved the food preparation into their church. "She's a saint," Jim Mather said. "She just has proven to all of us that love is what God asked us to give." In no time, the effort swallowed up $50,000 of Graham's savings. She and her husband took out a second mortgage on their house. To broaden their base of financial support, they obtained nonprofit status and asked others to support the ministry of Sack Lunch (Modie, 1997, p. A11).

Like Sack Lunch, most parachurch organizations begin small, with a vision and a passion to meet human needs; then they quickly move to the reality of financing the effort. In the early years of an organization, this involves a tremendous amount of personal sacrifice and faith. Dawson Trotman, founder of what became Navigators, mortgaged his house and gave everything he had to ministry. Frequently, Trotman lived day to day, constantly sacrificing (Skinner, 1974). Another example is Bill Bright, who sold his specialty food business to begin Campus Crusade for Christ (Zoba, 1997).

When Billy Graham's lifetime associate Cliff Barrows recalls the early years of Graham's ministry in the 1940s, he tells about continually trusting God to provide financially—waiting on the Lord, praying, and looking for opportunities. The members of this young evangelistic team would leave their families to travel around the country and live from the money given through love offerings collected at the crusades. More than once they considered mortgaging their homes. On several occasions, they contemplated cutting trips short as the money got low; invariably they would kneel in prayer to ask for God's provision. Those involved in these crusades can tell story after story of how God met financial needs (Pollock, 1979). Many missionaries and Christian workers share this experience of relying on God for their individual support.

Mission Aviation Fellowship cofounder Jim Truxton recalls that MAF considered itself a faith mission—which meant trusting God completely for all support. After World War II it did not make direct appeals for money but put ads in the *Sunday School Times* and *Stars and Stripes* informing people about its ministry (Buss, 1995, p. 22). One of the early supporters of this work was a Navy pilot and committed Christian who read the informative ad in *Stars and Stripes* and started tithing to MAF because he believed in the mission of the ministry.

It is claimed that money makes the world go around—this may be an overstatement, but it is certainly true that money is essential to every parachurch organization. As Chapter Three points out, the ability of parachurch organizations to seek financial resources independently of the traditional church is a significant factor in the prospering of the parachurch. Past growth and current prosperity have been reliant on well-financed operations. As the parachurch looks to the future, its continued prosperity is dependent on successfully finding ways to raise the money to fund programs and put vision into practice.

The parachurch has a voracious appetite for funds. Church growth expert David Barrett estimates that, worldwide, parachurch budgets are growing faster than church budgets. He estimates that in 1996, parachurch organizations had outgrown churches in total income with $100 billion to the churches' $94 billion, and that by the year 2,000, the figures would be $120 billion for parachurches and $100 billion for churches. He further estimates that in 2025, parachurch budgets will exceed $570 billion, almost double what is given to churches (Barrett, 1997, p. 24). So far parachurch organizations have been able to circumvent the offering plate by appealing directly to Christians for financial support of each ministry—and these appeals have largely been successful. But the amount of funds that must be raised to continue to support all the parachurch visions make it imperative that a strong philosophy of finances be developed. This philosophy is relevant not just for large organizations with large donor bases but also for individuals who have to raise their own support from a much smaller base of donors.

This chapter discusses the enormous challenge of financing the prospering parachurch into the future. It explores:

o The cultural context for financial growth
o The good news and bad news about parachurch financing
o The Christian worldview of money
o A more excellent way to raise money
o The future of parachurch financing

The Cultural Context for Financing Growth

The dramatic growth of the parachurch has benefited from a variety of dramatic shifts in our culture. One shift that has helped feed the growth of the parachurch is materialism. We live in a culture that worships at the shrine of four related idols: pleasure, wealth, professional status, and physical appearance. We are a culture of convenience rather than duty, centered on avoidance of personal pain rather than seeking to relieve the burdens of others. Our culture places the quest for the good life above knowing God.

Robert Wuthnow's three-year study on religious and economic values found that 89 percent of the respondents felt "our society is much too materialistic." Seventy four percent said materialism is a serious social problem, and 71 percent said society would be better off if less emphasis were placed on money (1993, p. 238). Wuthnow further points out that whereas religious tradition provided earlier generations with moral values to curb the pursuit of money, the evidence today suggests that faith makes little difference in the ways people actually conduct their financial affairs (p. 239).

For the parachurch this materialism is a two-edged sword. On the one side, potential givers are pulled into the materialism trap, and this negatively affects their giving. On the other side, materialism is perceived as an evil and becomes an enemy for the parachurch to fight, and this strengthens fundraising.

Related to the growth of materialism is the rapid secularization of our culture over the last half of the century. For the parachurch, secularization has become a rallying cry, another enemy to fight. Concerned Christians are willing to support parachurch groups committed to hold the line on secularism. The secularization process has been going on for over two hundred years but since World War II has advanced especially rapidly—as evidenced by the popular media, an educational system that ignores religious commitment, and a political climate that locks religion out of the debate.

Another shift that has affected the financing of the parachurch is the general move from a "missionary basis of operation to a business basis." Peter J. Wosh (1994, p. 261) chronicled this shift in a study for the American Bible Society (ABS) in order to illuminate a fundamental change that many parachurch institutions have experienced. Like ABS, they have moved from serving as missionary and moral reform agencies to functioning as national, nonprofit, corporate bureaucracies that pursue financing at a level and magnitude comparable to and often outdistancing secular nonprofits. The main tool that has allowed parachurches to adapt secular business principles and fundraising techniques is technological change.

Able to use nonprofit postage rates and to develop independent mailing lists, parachurch organizations are often at the forefront of fundraising. Computers allowed mechanical Addressograph lists to be converted to electronic sortable lists in the 1970s, and by the 1980s parachurch organizations were using all the most advanced technology to raise money. According to Tom McCabe of Killian McCabe and Associates in Dallas, Texas, who has spent his entire career working with direct-response fundraising for nonprofits, "Once the eighties hit, personalized mailings were commonplace—phonathons, the use of television and sophisticated direct mail segmentation, and as many as fourteen mailings a year to a list were seen in the parachurch marketplace" (interview by the authors, Jan. 1997).

At the forefront of parachurch prospering was the rapid increase in the ability of parachurch organizations to raise money independently of the traditional church. No longer did they have to go to the churches to get support from the layperson. Tim Stafford writes, "This growth in parachurch giving is at least partly a return to nineteenth century giving patterns, when giving was more independent of denominations and unified budgets" (1997, p. 22). At that time agents visited churches to solicit funds. Current growth is rapidly funneling resources away from the church, and as Stafford suggests, "the church is being submerged by a new species of institutions" (p. 23).

With all the emphasis on the separation of church and state, most people do not expect parachurch organizations to be the recipients of government money, and those parachurch organizations that receive government aid do not particularly want their individual donors to know about that support. Certain segments of the parachurch (particularly social services and relief and development organizations) are most likely to serve as a conduit for government moneys: for example, both World Vision International (relief and development) and Baltimore Catholic Youth Services (social services) receive government funds. The Lyndon Johnson years opened up social services funding, and the Reagan and Bush years funneled such funding through the states and nonprofits, including many parachurch organizations, in order to downsize government. The Clinton years have continued this trend.

These issues and events provide the context for the prospering parachurch. In addition, two shifts in the traditional church are related and noteworthy. First, there has been a steady decline in giving to the church and to denominations, as John Ronsvalle and Sylvia Ronsvalle (1996) have thoroughly documented. A second shift has been the sharp decline in the teaching about money and possessions in the churches. The study report *The Reluctant Steward* says, "Today's pastors are, at best, reluctant stewards of their church's human, physical, and financial resources . . . and today's seminaries, also by their own admission, are extremely reluctant to take the lead in helping pastors and other church leaders learn how to become better stewards" (Conway, 1992, p. 5). As a result the church has failed to influence the culture toward the compassionate use of wealth.

When it comes to giving, people in today's culture (including Christians) have moved from the biblical definition of money (seen in terms of giving out of charity, love, and grace) to a human-centered definition of money (seen in terms of giving in order to get something back). The next section discusses the consequences of this shift.

The Good News and Bad News About Parachurch Financing

The good news about parachurch donors is that they are considered as generous as any in the world. A comparison of Evangelicals to other large groups proves this point: Evangelicals give about 4.8 percent of their income to charitable causes, mainline Protestants 2.8 percent, Roman Catholics 1.5 percent, and the general population less than 1 percent (Hart, 1990, p. 54). The bad news is that they make little real sacrifice, and by biblical standards they have a long way to go (Stafford, 1997). Donors care about their communities, espouse wholesome values, feel responsible to the poor, and show their concern by their giving and volunteering, but their giving does not come close to the biblical standard of 10 percent of their income—rarely will giving interfere with their pursuit of "the good life."

Russell Chandler estimates that if Christians would raise their giving to the biblical standard, it would more than double what is given to religion. In *Racing Toward 2001: The Forces Shaping America's Religious Future,* Chandler states, "If church members were to boost their giving to an average of ten percent of their income (the tithe), the additional funds could eliminate the worst of world poverty . . . plus another $17 billion for domestic need—all while maintaining church activities at current levels" (1992, p. 220).

As our culture has defined its values without thought of God, so it has defined its giving without thought of God. Following the lead of the broader culture, many Christians have become uncomfortable with discussions of how their faith should affect their finances. The fear of hearing sermons on money is the chief excuse they give for not attending church and for not bringing guests. It is a topic pastors avoid like the plague.

The solution to the problem is not more sophisticated fundraising techniques. In fact, research shows that focus on technique has a negative long-term effect. Rather the solution is a holistic approach that starts with the heart attitude of the donors and their realization that their giving is first and foremost about their relationship to God. This heart change can be encouraged through the teaching of the seminaries, pastors, and parachurch ministries.

Robert Payton, former president of the Center on Philanthropy, wrote in *The Responsibility of Wealth,* "The strength of American philanthropy is based upon its religious origins and values and traditions." He goes on to say, "[Giving] as we know it today may not survive a serious deterioration of its religious values" (1992, p. 139).

Virginia A. Hodgkinson, vice president of research at the Independent Sector and executive director at the National Center for Charitable Statistics, addressed the future of individual giving and volunteering with a strong indictment that the reason for a decrease in giving to religious causes "may lie in the decline of transmitting the meaning of stewardship to the current generation and the lack of clergy education in stewardship typified by the fact that courses in stewardship are no longer taught in theological schools" (1990, p. 302). She also states that "there does not seem to be a secular moral tradition that has the influence to generate such generous behavior among large segments of the population" (p. 306). The decline in the value of stewardship does not mean a drop just in religious giving, all secular nonprofits and charitable groups are affected as well. Independent Sector research finds that 73 percent of all contributions given to charities other than religion come from the group that supports religion and claims religious membership and involvement (Yankelovich, Skelly, and White, Inc., 1986).

An obvious first question is, why talk about faith and finances now? Giving is at an all-time high, so why not just leave it alone? As long as the money is coming in, why bother with the philosophy behind the giving. The answer is that there is a vital link between faith and finances. There is no issue more relevant to the spiritual growth of Christians than how they deal with money. Jesus taught that what Christians do with their possessions is an accurate reading of the climate of their souls.

The Christian Worldview of Money

Don Chase lives in New England. He is a retired corporate executive and investor, a Christian who has given to parachurch organizations for many years. Don and his wife, Barbara, are constantly inundated with requests for financial support. For more than twenty years Don struggled with the concept of Christian stewardship. He agonized over how much to give, where to give, and what God's expectations were of him. In the early eighties, two young men he was discipling began asking him hard questions about the role of stewardship in the Christian life.

The three of them started digging into scripture, the Old and New Testaments, trying to find peace. The light came on after they studied Mark 12:44, the story of the widow's mite. Jesus knew that the rich gave out of abundance but that the widow gave up ownership: "But she out of poverty has put in everything she had, all she had to live on." Don saw that the amount of the gift is not important, but the heart attitude is. The value system of the giver is what counts. Giving is about the giver's relationship to God.

Don recounts, "I had been miserable. I thought I was the owner of my wealth. But God was really the owner. God wanted me to simply steward what he owned," as in Matthew's account of the parable of the talents (Matthew 25). Don says, "The point is not that the more I give to the Lord the more the Lord will give me, but the better steward or manager I am, the greater the multiplication of gain. As my increase becomes greater, God also expects more of me." For Don it was a freeing experience to discover that all his money, time, and abilities belong to the Lord in the first place. His task was simply to be the steward of the gifts God had given him (McKay, 1997, p. 18).

Don and Barbara Chase are but one couple out of millions who support the parachurch. Like the Chases, most parachurch donors have their struggles and individual stories to tell about their giving. If Christ is not first with their money, then he is probably not first in their lives—giving demonstrates materially where people are spiritually. For believers, their checkbooks are better reflections of their spiritual condition than the underlining in their Bibles.

Money is in primary competition with Christ for the lordship of believers' lives. But as Luke 16:11 suggests, if believers are not faithful and wise stewards of their worldly wealth, why would God trust them with true riches? Ultimately all believers will stand before God and be asked to account for how they handle their money. Scripture instructs that if we waste our possessions, we will be reproved when it comes time to give account for our lives.

As we have seen in earlier chapters, the parachurch organization is built on a Christian mission statement and approaches its ministry with a Christian worldview. Likewise, the financing of the parachurch is founded on a godly perspective on giving. This means a worldview that acknowledges that God has provided all resources, that God has given believers the responsibility to manage these resources as stewards, and that God will ultimately hold believers accountable for how they use his resources.

As the Chases learned, having a Christian worldview means believing that one is created in the image of God for the purpose of serving God—not oneself. Believers are God's people. Their resources are not their own. The world does not truly own any money or property because, as the Bible teaches, God is the true owner and source of all resources. From this perspective, giving opportunities bestow upon believers the privilege of distributing what God has given them.

The natural tendency is to imagine that believers give to help parachurch organizations pay their bills—or to pay God's bills! Or, more cynically, giving is thought of as the way people get the organizations off their backs. However, the primary purpose of giving is to teach believers always to put God first in their lives, and to help them grow more like Christ. They prove their faithfulness to God by how they handle their finances. As Deuteronomy 14:22–23 instructs: "Set apart a tithe of all the yield of your seed that is brought in yearly from the field . . . so that you may learn to fear the LORD your God always."

Because finances are first and foremost about believers' relationship to God, Christians ought to view giving as being for their own benefit. Stewardship is God's way of raising people, not an organization's way of raising money. To help believers become the people he wants them to be, God is working through them, helping them learn how to give.

Many may remember the television show *Candid Camera* (a forerunner to *America's Funniest Home Videos*), where people were filmed in difficult situations, not knowing that they were on camera. One time, the producers placed money in an envelope on the sidewalk and televised what people did. Some looked surprised and tried to find whom the money belonged to; others coyly pushed it in their pocket and quickly left. Similarly, each day God slips money into the pockets of believers. It may come from employment or from an allowance or a gift; but, like the *Candid Camera* producers, God steps back and says, "Let's see how they respond: 'more money for me' or 'more money for God's ministry'?"

To have fellowship with God, believers must put God first and reverence him. Financial giving starts believers on the road to being more and more like Christ. In Malachi 3:8, God says: "Will anyone rob God? Yet you are robbing me! But you say, 'How are we robbing you?' In your tithes and offerings!"

The reality of today's Christian world is that God is being robbed. On the one hand believers are robbing themselves and God if they do not consider their responsibility of stewardship. On the other hand they can be doubly blessed, both here on earth and in heaven, if they follow God's philosophy of giving.

A More Excellent Way to Raise Money

If the primary purpose of a Christian's giving is to worship God and develop an intimate relationship with God, then the top priority of parachurch fundraisers is to educate their constituents to give from the biblical perspective of stewardship. Because the traditional church's role is decreasing and the parachurch's role is increasing in terms of giving, the parachurch now has an added educational responsibility. They can fulfill this responsibility by placing donors' relationship to God before their relationship to the parachurch organization. When parachurch fundraisers follow this approach, they will implement all telephone calls, appeal letters, and conversations from the perspective of helping Christians put God first in their lives, rather than just support an organization.

Figure 13.1 depicts both the *vertical* relationship of the believer with God and the *horizontal* relationship of the believer with others. Most fundraising and giving tends to operate horizontally. It is the vertical relationship that ought to have the primary value. God asks every believer to

Figure 13.1. Helping Christians Put God First in Their Lives.

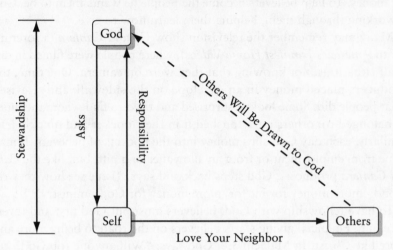

be a steward of all his or her possessions, a vertical relationship, and the believer is then responsible to use those possessions in his or her horizontal relationship with other people. In this model the primary motive for giving is to please God, but a natural by-product of this motive is giving to others so that they in turn will be drawn to God.

There is not much emphasis on the vertical relationship in today's parachurch fundraising practices. As parachurch organizations have put their fundraising on a business basis, they have often left God out by focusing more on how to get money for themselves than on helping donors develop their relationship to God through giving. Christian and particularly parachurch fundraising, in the pressure to meet bottom-line needs, has too often adopted the values of the world: stressing immediate benefits to the giver, providing premiums, being as emotional as possible, and playing along with self-serving concerns. Fundraising from a stewardship perspective that focuses on the vertical relationship of God and donor is seldom found.

Most Christian donors just feed the system when they give out of guilt or from a sense of obligation rather than from a sensitivity to God's spirit in their lives. Many feel obligated to give to every appeal. Someone has to stop the cycle. Think what would happen if believers wrote to organizations and revolted against their manipulative methods. Think what would happen if a parachurch CEO were willing to risk the possibility of less income in order to bring the organization in line scripturally? What if a fundraiser were willing to change the fundraising approach to encourage stewardship-motivated giving?

The parachurch organization that places the donor's relationship to God above getting money for its ministry must start by declaring this position to its constituents. Then it must look at its own fundraising practices to examine whether its materials and efforts are encouraging a focus on God. Prayer becomes an important part of the process as fundraisers seek God's wisdom and pray that God will be the one moving in the hearts of donors—not the pull of benefits, recognition, or guilt.

When hosting banquets, sending direct mail, placing telephone calls, and visiting prospective donors, the parachurch fundraiser places first the goal of helping the donors in their relationship to God. Appeals become vehicles of education and provide donors with the opportunity to give to God. The dynamics are multifaceted and cyclical. Educators, pastors, seminaries, and colleges all must start by teaching these principles. Then donors must follow suit by giving from this perspective.

If a parachurch organization is willing to step out and approach its financing from a biblical perspective and change its fundraising approaches, its first step is to educate and disciple others. According to George Barna, eight out of ten Christians do not give at the 10 percent minimum level, do not believe they could give at that level, and do not have the practical budgeting tools that would enable them to tithe (1994, p. 56). As the notion of stewardship has withered over the years, so has teaching about it. The need is great to educate Christians that generous giving is possible.

The principle of sowing and reaping can be brought into sharp focus through education. Jesus did not say, "Go, collect money!" but, "Go, teach, make disciples." Scripture asks for a commitment to God and to his truth. It does not appeal to reason or pragmatism but pleads for a growing relationship with Jesus Christ through repentance and forgiveness and a life lived wholly for God. The stewardship that grows from this philosophy is as much a relationship as an action.

Stewardship starts with believers, their families, and their Sunday schools. They must challenge their churches, seminaries, and Christian schools to get stewardship back in the curriculum and into the heads and hearts of Christian believers. If this holistic, God-centered approach is not achieved, the parachurch financing challenge may be very difficult in the future.

The Future of Parachurch Financing

A parachurch organization that relies today on giving derived from the values of those over fifty-five years old will eventually be in a crisis. The goals and plans that bring a response when shown to an older generation of Americans will likely find few takers if presented in the same way to the current younger generation. The evidence for this is striking. Chapter Eleven mentioned a survey in a mission organization that asked donors to identify their preferences when it came to receiving future appeals for funds. Figure 13.2 illustrates some specific findings from that survey. Note the striking differences between those under fifty-five and those over fifty-five years of age. Can parachurch organizations continue to use their existing fundraising machinery and survive? Not likely, unless they have developed effective ways to involve younger donors, volunteers, and staff.

Few parachurch organizations are actively working to replace aging donors with younger ones. Fully 90 percent of organizations that participated in a study indicated that they had never done a survey of their mailing lists. Two-thirds of the respondents said that they had mixed feelings or were dissatisfied with their organization's ability to replace aging donors. Astute parachurch leaders must view their lack of understanding about donors with alarm (Willmer, 1996, p. 12).

The key to attracting young donors is building relationships with them. As we move into the twenty-first century, the demand for high-value experiences and relationships with organizations is getting stronger. Younger stakeholders and donors do not have the loyalty, patience, or time for relationships with organizations they deem as unproductive or as not adding

Figure 13.2. Changing Donor Preferences.

I Would Prefer	Total	Age of Respondent		
		<35	35–54	>54
Printed material through the mail	68%	46%	68%	72%
Printed proposals on specific projects	40	27	38	44
A videocassette mailed to me	25	25	30	21
800 # for getting information about projects	23	32	27	19
A visit from a representative	15	5	12	18
A www (Internet) site	14	43	23	3
E-mail	12	39	16	4
A telephone call from the mission	3	0	4	3

Source: *Data from research conducted for the Foreign Mission Organization by David Schmidt & Associates, 1997. Used by permission.*

real value to God's kingdom. They are intolerant of organizations with no real commitment to maintain a vital relationship with donors and supporters. Parachurch leaders will have to be extremely focused and intentional in learning to build relationships with younger supporters of the ministry. Among other things, they must communicate with these young people through their preferred media.

The strong cultural and religious shifts of today are paving the way for a different future. Religion and religious giving—and the parachurch—will probably look very different in the years to come. The eventual answers to the following questions will determine whether parachurch giving will be a boom or a bust.

The United States today might be called a post-Christian nation. What will be the giving consequences of this change? What will be the role of religion in individual and corporate lives? Will materialism become the predominant religious faith? Will government policy encourage or discourage religious giving? In addition: Will the changing nature of churches affect giving? What will be the impact of the considerable ethnic and demographic shifts that are occurring? Is the market now saturated for donors? Is spiritual awakening imminent?

The jury is still out on most of these questions; yet each answer will have a tremendous influence on the future of parachurch financing. It has been asked whether the parachurch can survive its own success? The answer is yes, if its donors are drawn to give from a godly perspective.

14

ENHANCING THE PARTNERSHIP
BETWEEN CHURCH
AND PARACHURCH

MANY PARENTS HAVE had the experience of traveling by car for a family vacation. In the front seats, Father and Mother sit quietly, but the backseat often turns into a cauldron of disagreement. Little Johnny and Jane bicker and argue until it seems that the backseat is going to explode. All parents have their own way of dealing with this problem: perhaps Mother sits in the back with them, perhaps Johnny and Jane are threatened with a punishment, perhaps Father pulls the car off the road until peace settles in the war zone. The parental reaction that would be foolish is to overreact to these petty squabbles and decide that what the siblings need is a battery of professional counseling sessions. Such problems are the natural result of traveling with children who are energetic and independent. The battle raging in the backseat is a sign of life and health.

The relationship between the church and parachurch can be compared to this backseat rivalry on a family vacation. The traditional church is the older sibling and is used to getting all the attention. Its baby sibling, the parachurch, once lay compliantly in the child seat. As has been traced in previous chapters, however, in recent years the parachurch has come into its own until it now seems every bit as strong and independent as the traditional church. The church and parachurch sit in the backseat of this historical vehicle and argue over who gets what, and who is most favored. But just as with real children, the fighting is a sign of life. There are tensions between the church and parachurch precisely because each is strong and has its own mind and will. The challenge to Christian leaders is to channel some of this energy into positive tasks and partnership and see to it that this squabbling does not degenerate into serious dysfunction.

This chapter first attempts to analyze the tensions that have come to mark the relationship between church and parachurch, and then it puts forward some steps that can be taken to minimize these tensions.

"You Strip-Mine Our Wallets"

No one complains that the parachurch is taking up prayer time that ought to be devoted to the church. To imagine a pastor haranguing a congregation for too much prayer time given to parachurch organizations is ludicrous. Even though every Christian ministry gives at least lip service to the importance of prayer, the issue simply does not stir up passion. But there is one subject that will nearly always raise the temperature in the room: finances. Jealousy or suspicion over funds is certainly the top tension between the church and parachurch. Prayer time can be divided amicably, but when it comes to money, there are no jokes.

As with most problems, both sides contribute to the tension. The part each side plays becomes most clear when the question of access is examined. Many parachurch organizations desire to present their ministry and needs directly to a large congregation. In the past this has been the way that many parachurch organizations have gained support. But as the parachurch has become more powerful, local churches have become more wary of letting these organizations do their fundraising at the church's expense. The feeling is that parachurch organizations practice strip-mining when they visit churches. They walk in, oblivious to the needs of the church, and attempt to mine the resources for their own benefit. The parachurch has developed standard rhetoric that sounds good: "We are here to serve with you"; "We are partners." But churches have become more savvy. To combat these invasive efforts many local churches have closed their doors to parachurch ministries, unless they are obviously helpful to the church (a Christian summer camp for youth, for example). Increasingly, churches are looking for real win-win relationships—not just win-win rhetoric.

The closed doors have not daunted parachurch ministries. They have found ways to get around them and gain direct access to Christians. Modern technology has been the key to parachurch fundraising methods. Taking their cue from secular organizations, parachurch organizations have put together large mailing lists of those who might support a Christian ministry. These mailing lists are commodities that may be bought and sold by organizations looking to raise funds. In addition to conducting mass mailings, organizations can advertise on Christian television or radio. Newspaper ads and stories are also a way to get exposure and publicity.

These new methods have evolved into a virtual fundraising art form. It is now commonplace for parachurch organizations to bypass the church entirely and take their fundraising appeals directly to Christians.

This development naturally does not sit well with many church leaders. Large and prospering churches can shrug it off, but churches barely able to meet their needs can grow resentful of parachurch organizations that maneuver for funds. Church leaders have little recourse to put a stop to this, but through direct teaching they are able to have a limited impact on this trend. The idea of *storehouse* giving is one example of local churches' attempt to regain lost ground. This idea, based on Malachi 3:10, "Bring the full tithe into the storehouse," makes the local church the distributor of all money for ministries. In other words, the church functions as the central distributor, or storehouse, giving money to ministries that the church leadership and members decide upon. If storehouse giving were strictly followed, it would certainly short-circuit the fundraising appeals of many parachurch organizations. Such strictures are unlikely to ever be widespread, and now have little impact, but the fact that ideas such as storehouse giving are being voiced demonstrates that there is resentment among church leaders over money-seeking parachurch organizations. The parachurch continues to pursue its fundraising with little sensitivity to the needs of the local church, and the local church fights back by trying to bar the door to parachurch organizations.

There is a third factor that exacerbates the problem still further. The Christians who are caught in the midst of these battles are receiving less and less teaching on how money is to be used by a Christian. As described in the previous chapter, the biblical concept of stewardship has been ignored by the traditional church. Most Christians have grown accustomed to listening to appeals for money. Whether the appeals are made from the pulpit of the church, over radio, or through a direct-mail campaign, the basic message is easy to follow: "We need money or else this ministry will not function; please send what you can." The appeal often works, and ministries stay afloat financially, but they make little attempt to teach Christians about the way their money and resources ought to be used. This lack exists on all levels, from the local church to the seminaries that train leaders.

In the rush to get funds, the concept of stewardship has been left behind. It was not so long ago that stewardship was an active theme in Christian teaching. A fine example of the importance of stewardship can be gained from a look at the Keswick Convention. This annual meeting met for the one purpose of deepening spiritual life through teaching on the *abundant life* available to all Christians. Well-known preachers and teachers such as

Donald Barnhouse and W. Graham Scroggie are among those who have spoken at this influential meeting. At the 1892 convention, a teacher named Hubert Brooke gave a series of messages, one of which in particular exemplified the importance of stewardship. He said: "We are all stewards—we cannot avoid that—of the manifold grace of God. What, in different forms, is underlying every pleading word spoken here, is that you will begin to be honest stewards. If every believing soul here became from this day an honest steward, we should have nothing more to tell you. . . . Recognize that for the use of every single thing you have, you are responsible to God" (Stevenson, 1963, pp. 38–39).

For the spiritual leaders at these meetings, there was a deep connection between personal piety and the way one's possessions were used. A person's resources were a sacred trust given by God that must be used wisely. However, in the crush to raise money, these foundational principles have been forgotten. Christians who are able to give often do not do so because of firm beliefs about the place of money in the Christian life. Instead they give out of a sense of guilt or to help a ministry avoid an impending crisis. A lack of sound teaching on stewardship leaves the average Christian blown this way and that under every forceful appeal for money. This fickleness heightens the already high tension between the church and parachurch over financial issues.

"You Take Our Workers"

A second major source of tension between the parachurch and church is personnel. Many Christians may be surprised to hear that this is a source of tension. They may remember a young person from their church who served with a parachurch organization overseas and the way congregation members gave that person their full support. In many churches, when a talented young person decides to join a parachurch organization, it is a time for rejoicing, not for jealousy. In churches that have large numbers of educated young people, it is easy to be glad for those who opt to work with a parachurch organization. But for a smaller church or for a national church overseas, it can be devastating to lose promising leaders to parachurch organizations.

Jack Graves tells the story of one young man who, "according to his doctoral adviser at a leading evangelical theological seminary, . . . was one of the best students the adviser had ever had from Africa. Because he was fluent in French, English, and Kiswahili he was being pursued by three of Africa's graduate evangelical seminaries. So my sadness at learning that he would not be returning to Africa was only exceeded by the frustration of learning why not. He explained that he had just accepted a job with an American mission agency to represent their work in Africa" (1992, p. 154). And this is no isolated story. Time and time again Third World countries lose their best and brightest to parachurch organizations. Graves calls this the *theological brain drain*. When a parachurch ministry launches a program in Africa or Asia, it looks for national leaders to head the program. These national leaders are often recruited from the national churches, which desperately need strong leaders and theologians. The same thing happens in the United States, albeit on a lesser scale. Small churches and denominations lose their most promising young people or pastors to parachurch organizations.

This problem cannot simply be laid at the feet of insensitive parachurch organizations. There are many factors within the church that make working for a parachurch organization attractive. However, just as with tension over finances, when dealing with personnel issues, both the church and parachurch need to examine their own practices critically. Often it is not so much a case of the parachurch stealing leaders as it is of the church repelling leaders. The pay scale differs drastically between large parachurch organizations and the salaries paid by most churches. Sometimes this is because churches can simply not afford to pay the pastor or youth leader an appropriate amount, but just as many times, the congregation or the denomination does not have the vision or will to pay the salary that the leader deserves. Because the monetary support is not present, when the opportunity comes to work for a well-funded parachurch organization, it is a hard offer to resist.

But the issue goes deeper than salary comparisons. The traditional church—on the denominational level and the local church level—has not welcomed those who have vision. In the earlier chapters on the history of the parachurch, there were numerous examples of leaders who were not accommodated by the established church of their day. From Robert Raikes, who wanted to educate children through Sunday school, to Cameron Townsend, who had a vision to translate the scripture into every tongue, the church has not accepted visionary leaders. The only option left for these leaders was to blaze a path on their own, and a parachurch organization generally coalesced around their visions. Rejection by the church is the reason for the existence of many parachurch organizations.

So again we find that neither the church or parachurch is entirely at fault. The tension is created by faults on both sides. The parachurch in its zeal to expand is guilty of taking valuable leaders from the local churches, and the local church is at fault for not providing an environment in which leaders flourish.

"We Can't Compete"

During a recent Sunday morning service in Southern California, a young woman spoke to a small church about her summer experience. She had gone to Ireland for two months on a short-term mission with a large parachurch organization. Her face was aglow as she described the new friends she had made and the work she had done with Irish churches. The members of the congregation listened attentively and smiled at her exuberance. Many of them had given her money, enabling her to pay for this trip to Ireland, and they were proud that this young woman from their church had represented them overseas. When the girl finished with her descriptions of visiting colorful Irish villages and of sharing her faith with Irish children, she gave the requisite thank-you's and took a seat. Then the pastor stood up to make the announcements. The young pastor mustered up excitement to tell his congregation about the midweek prayer service and Bible study. Then he reminded the congregation of the work day planned on Saturday. All the men and women were invited to come and fellowship as some rooms were painted and tidied. The contrast could not have been greater between the energizing programs of parachurch work and the routine work that is part of being involved with the church.

This contrast is the third tension that exists between the church and parachurch. By its very nature the parachurch runs special events, whereas the church must worry about the upkeep of an aging building or its weekly prayer meetings. Once again, the tension is not the fault of one side or the other. The church tends toward unnecessary envy of the programs of the parachurch, whereas the parachurch at times shows ambition beyond what is needed.

There are two ways that this tension especially manifests itself. The first is in the area of publicity. The skyrocket success of an organization such as Promise Keepers garners national media attention. This publicity is not a new phenomenon—the campaigns of Billy Graham have always been well publicized by the media. Successful parachurch organizations quickly become adept at using the media to their own advantage. There is nothing wrong with being skilled at getting publicity; the problem comes when the local church is bypassed in the process. Ambition starts to assert itself when no thought is given to the place of the church in a ministry.

The second way that programs cause tension is that the parachurch sometimes accomplishes something that the church would like to be able to do. For example, when a disaster strikes a city, the first religious organizations on the scene are generally parachurch organizations. Even if the disaster takes place right across the street from a church, it simply takes too long for the church to get itself moving. As the church makes phone calls and tries to mobilize its members, the parachurch organizations have already arrived and are doing the work. This quick reaction time is built into the structure of the parachurch for two reasons. First, each organization is focused on a specialization, its workers are able to move fast and effectively in that field. Second, the parachurch is often able to choose selectively who will be involved in its ministry. The church must try to involve all its people in a ministry. This naturally results in less efficiency overall from workers and slows down the church. For these same reasons, parachurch organizations can put on programs that seem much more exciting and cutting edge than the programs of the local church. This often causes envy on the part of local church leaders, who are simply unable to compete with these programs.

The practices of Billy Graham and the Billy Graham Evangelistic Association offer an example of how to avoid the tensions that naturally arise when a parachurch organization takes away so much attention from the church or when parachurch programs seem to outshine church programs. From the beginning of his ministry, Graham has tried to involve local churches in his crusades. Even before he became nationally known, he was following principles that allowed him to work closely with churches. For example, he writes about an early campaign in Augusta, Georgia: "The first [principle] was to work for as broad church involvement as possible. Our citywide Campaign in Augusta was officially sponsored by the city's ministerial association—a sort of council of churches. Such extensive sponsorship never happened before; in all previous cities, a few churches, or in some cases only one church invited us to hold meetings. In Augusta we had all-out support from virtually the entire Christian community" (1997, p. 125).

Although this policy has often stirred up controversy, Graham has always striven to get the full support of the churches in the cities he visits. By doing this he makes a statement: this program is not about publicizing Billy Graham, it is about furthering the work of Christ. Too often for other parachurch organizations this is not the case, and they appears to care more about publicizing themselves than about any kind of real partnership. Again, ambition then begins to mark the work of the parachurch.

If the church and parachurch are to resolve their deep-set tensions, they must adopt the approach exemplified by Billy Graham. This means a whole new way of understanding the church in relation to the parachurch: not as fighting siblings but as partners in the work of Christ, each with its own kingdom of jobs. On the one hand the parachurch is not the local church. It was not ordained by God to do the work of the local church—

to create a worshiping community or to celebrate the sacraments. The parachurch has occasionally impinged on these duties of the local church. On the other hand the local church has been slow to recognize the tremendous growth of the parachurch and its impact outside the walls of the church. Clearly, God has desired that the parachurch be an important player in the spiritual awakening of our culture. The next section sketches out how the parachurch and church can come to an understanding of their different roles and the steps that can be taken to make partnership a reality.

Part of the Family

Charles Hodge's massive *Systematic Theology* was first published in 1872. Through the course of three volumes, he attempts to deal with all the major heads of Christian doctrine, from a basic defense of Theism to a survey of eschatology. Naturally, Hodge also spends time discussing how the church fits into God's plan. He takes the common Protestant view that the Church is the invisible body made up of those who truly have faith in Christ. Meanwhile, the visible, local church is a "divine institution," and as such it is incumbent on every believer to be joined to this visible church (1989, p. 360). But what is truly memorable is Hodge's studied neglect of the existence of Christian institutions that do not fit into his notions of a traditional church. Writing in a time that was rife with evangelists and missionary organizations, Hodge could see the church only as it was manifest in denominations.

This neglect has been only too common in the worlds of theology and academia. The recent book *All God's Children: A Theology of the Church,* by David L. Smith, continues this scholarly myopia (1996). Through 423 pages every aspect of the church is examined, from its history to its theory, yet parachurch organizations barely muster a mention. The need for the church to address poverty and to make disciples is mentioned, but not the fact that the Church—the body of Christ—is often doing these things through the work of parachurch organizations.

It seems strange that in the midst of a religious landscape in which many parachurches surpass many denominations in total budget and often in influence, there is so little scholarly attention given to the parachurch. Theological books and seminaries treat the parachurch with all the importance of a youth soccer league. As a result of this neglect, there is confusion as to the place of the parachurch in the context of the Church. Although the topic is hardly mentioned in books, most leaders have set opinions of the place of the parachurch. Some see the parachurch as at best a usurping nuisance, and others see the parachurch as the savior of inactive denominations that refuse to carry on the work of the Lord. Both these views are off balance and need to be modified by respect for the newer institutional expression of Christianity.

This respect must grow from a new consensus on the place of the parachurch. To put it simply, we are all part of the kingdom of God. There will always be disagreement as to the exact relationship of church and parachurch. Depending on individuals' church affiliations, they will place different emphases on the importance of the visible church and the importance of certain denominational distinctives. Not in this chapter, and not even in a series of books, would it be possible to settle all these ecclesiological issues. Moreover, in the end, solving those questions is not important. What is important is that the parachurch be recognized as doing part of the work of God and being part of the family.

The Great Commission to tell all people the good news of Christ was a command to all believers. The parachurch has been in the forefront of fulfilling that command. Part of the mission of the Church universal is to minister to the poor. Once again the parachurch has ably demonstrated its commitment to this goal. In every way, the parachurch has demonstrated itself to be part of God's work, and others who analyze the church will have to work harder to begin to include the parachurch in their schemes.

The parachurch, too, must understand the primacy of the church in the day-to-day spiritual lives of most Christians. There is a need for the local church to carry on the ordinances of baptism and the Lord's Supper and to provide a place for Christians to fellowship and worship on a regular basis. The Bible also specifies a number of offices that are to be included in the local church, such as pastor, elder, and deacon. Clearly the traditional church is a large part of God's great plan. Those in the parachurch must accept the special place of the church.

There is a definite place for the traditional church, yet the Bible leaves plenty of leeway as to the organizational face of Christian work. Kevin Giles, after a thorough examination of the church in the New Testament, comes to the conclusion that it has no single "correct" structure. He writes that "in the New Testament we see variation and development in the theological understanding of the church" (1995, p. 183). There is plenty of room for organizational creativity among Christians, and the parachurch is an institution that is uniquely fitted to the modern age. God is perfectly able to work outside the traditional church structures, and the parachurch is an example of this divine *extra-ecclesial* work.

The Need for Synergy and Balance

Once a mutual understanding between the church and parachurch is opened up, there is an opportunity for a new relationship. This new relationship can be summarized with two words: *synergy* and *balance*.

These two words can be illustrated if we recall once again the brother and sister fighting in the backseat of the car. The energy and the friction between these two siblings is natural. The challenge for the parents is to redirect that energy and fierce will into a channel that is more fruitful. One way to do this is to start the two children working together on a fun project—perhaps a game. This is easier said than done in the case of warring children, but if it is successful, the children will use their combined energy to accomplish something. That is the challenge for the church and parachurch. Too much energy is lost in their battles. What is needed is working together—synergy (*syn* means "together", and *ergy*, "work"). Synergy comes about when the two parties recognize that they have a common project: building the kingdom of God. When the importance of this is grasped, the battling may stop, and the two may finally pool their energies for the sake of God's work.

The second goal is balance. The church and the parachurch must see each other as complementary organizations. Each has a unique role. This is another issue that the fighting siblings illustrate. One of the biggest causes of sibling rivalry is jealousy over the attentions of the parents. One child suspects that somehow the other is getting favored treatment. Most of the common tensions that exist between church and parachurch grow out of this jealousy. One side thinks the other is getting a bigger share of attention. But if parachurch and church come to see that each has an important place in God's kingdom, then finally there can be balance. When each side feels secure in its place, then the way is opened up for more effective work. The following four steps might establish this partnership.

Make Partnership a Deeply Held Value

Many parachurch leaders use the language of partnership—especially when they need help from the church. But far too often these sentiments are just rhetoric, and the actions of the leaders give a drastically different message. The new understanding, delineated in the previous part of this chapter, sets out the church and parachurch as equal partners, each with its own special place in the kingdom of God.

Leaders in both the church and parachurch must find tangible ways to show that *partnership* is not just a nice word. To be effective, this task must be approached systematically. There are many ways it can be carried out, depending on the local situation and size of the church or parachurch, but unless a determined effort is made, partnership will remain just a word.

In June of 1980, the Lausanne Conference for World Evangelization met to discuss the need for cooperation between church and parachurch. Those who gathered discussed many ways to increase cooperation, but the most urgent need was for dialogue (*Co-Operating in World Evangelization*, 1983, p. 17). Twenty years later, dialogue is still needed if partnership is to be a reality.

There are many ways for this dialogue can occur. Rather than just complain about parachurch organizations, local churches ought to initiate dialogues with them in their local areas. In nearly every part of the country, there are rescue missions, evangelistic organizations, mission agencies, music ministries, and teen pregnancy outreaches. Many of these smaller organizations are searching for ways to establish ties to churches, but for the most part they have been rebuffed. Church leaders ought to get a handle on the different parachurch ministries and look for ways that the church can be involved with them. If the young adults in the church are starting a program to evangelize in a local park, then perhaps it would be possible to team up with a local outreach ministry. If the church wants to do something for the poor in its area, then perhaps it can team up with the local rescue mission. There are many ways that the church can partner with the parachurch. Once there is a commitment to start a dialogue and to partner with the parachurch, the opportunities will quickly present themselves.

The leaders of the parachurch must do their own part in the pursuit of partnership. They must honestly examine their ministries and ask, Is our work partnering with the local churches, or is it marked more by competition and independence? If active partnership is not apparent in a ministry, then it is time to consider some fresh ways to involve the local church. Efforts can be made to acquaint local congregations with the ministry of the organization, or perhaps a program can be arranged that allows the youth groups of local churches to be involved with the ministry.

In order to partner with the church, parachurch organizations must win the confidence of church leaders. They must demonstrate by their actions that the ministry is not out to cut into small local churches. This means toning down any harsh rhetoric about the failings of the church and discouraging publicity that concentrates on the glory and accomplishments of the organization itself.

Teach the Fully Devoted Christian Life

In Ephesians, we learn that Christ dispensed gifts to his Church. Some members were appointed as apostles, some prophets, some evangelists, some pastors and teachers (4:11). The reason for these gifts was so that the body of Christ might be built up, and believers given the knowledge to fend off crafty human doctrines. Both the traditional church and parachurch have received workers who have these gifts from God, and therefore both are responsible for the teaching of God's people. Many of the tensions between church and parachurch exist because there is not adequate teaching as to the nature of the kingdom of God or the Christian life.

As we have already noted, people lack understanding of the nature of the body of Christ. Church leaders have trouble accepting as equal partners organizations that do not dispense the sacraments or preach the Bible. At the extreme, church leaders recognize as valid only organizations that are directly tied to their own denomination. This narrow thinking as to the body of Christ causes confusion and heightens the tensions between church and parachurch.

This kind of body sectionalism is reminiscent of the controversy addressed by Paul in 1 Corinthians. In speaking of the different gifts given to different believers, Paul chastises those who see their own gifts as most important: "Indeed, the body does not consist of one member but of many. If the foot would say, 'Because I am not a hand, I do not belong to the body,' that would not make it any less part of the body. . . . As it is, there are many members, yet one body" (12:14–15, 20). Those who work within the parachurch believe in the same God, the same Lord, and the same Spirit, and they have the same faith; it is clear that these people are part of the larger body of Christ. As members of this body, they ought to have their work and their place recognized by the traditional church. If believers all over the world who worship at a local church were to hear this message and grasp its importance, the tensions between church and parachurch would be eased significantly.

The idea of storehouse giving also illustrates a failure of the church to adequately teach its members about the Christian life. Storehouse giving has an allure because it shifts the responsibility for good stewardship away from individuals and onto the leaders of the local church. Such an arrangement makes the life of the individual Christian easier and increases the centralized power of church leaders. But these are not goals that the New Testament recognizes. The leaders of the church ought instead to equip the individual members of the church to make good decisions for themselves. This means teaching basic principles of giving and explaining how individuals can give responsibly.

Before this philosophy can be implemented, leaders of the church must understand that they have nothing to fear from individual responsibility. When the principles of stewardship are understood, the people will continue to give generously to the church but will also be able to make wise choices of the outside organizations they ought to support. Acting by the principles of stewardship, believers would know not to send money to the organizations that simply put together the most spectacular ministry or that moan loudest about their need for emergency money. Instead they will prayerfully consider what issue God would have them work on with well-placed financial gifts. This individual stewardship is a gift that each Christian ought to enjoy and to use to deepen his or her own spiritual life.

Establish Personal Accountability

It has been almost ten years since the televangelist scandals rocked the Evangelical world. Popular preachers such as Jim Bakker and Jimmy Swaggart were shown to be deeply involved in immorality. The wealthy lifestyles of many other televangelists came under scrutiny as well. These scandals caused many Americans to lose trust in religious leaders and left them wondering how these deep problems could have gone unchecked. The revelations about the personal lives of these ministers put the spotlight on the lack of accountability in many parachurch organizations. When a person is surrounded by money and by people who are eager to please, and when there is no church body to which the person is accountable, it becomes very easy to slide down the slippery slope of sin. Thus a third step needs to be taken to bring about partnership: an increase in accountability.

Denominations are generally set up to provide built-in accountability. Pastoral work in the local church does not bring with it the tempting money and fame of television ministry, and often pastors or priests must constantly interact with peers. If there is a complaint or if someone senses that something has gone wrong in the minister's life, then there are reasonably clear channels by which the minister can be held accountable.

The very nature of the parachurch leaves it open to the problems that beset televangelists. Most parachurch organizations form around a highly independent and driven leader and are successful because they have gone about ministry in their own way. In many parachurch organizations, accountability is negligible, and this leaves them more open to damaging scandals, financial or moral. This lack of accountability is a prime reason for the distrust that the church feels toward the parachurch. Church leaders see publicity-hungry and money-grubbing parachurch leaders as a threat and are unwilling to partner with them. The parachurch must find ways to put at ease these worries, and the best plan for doing this is to voluntarily set up accountability structures. Organizations such as the Evangelical Council for Financial Accountability (ECFA) are one way parachurch organizations can police themselves. The ECFA's mission statement, for example, states, "To help Christ-centered evangelical nonprofit organizations earn the public's trust through their ethical practices and financial accountability" (Evangelical Council for Financial Accountability, 1996, p. iii). Voluntary membership in an organization such as the ECFA means that a parachurch organization is complying with certain ethical standards. Parachurch organizations that will not allow others to look into their finances should be viewed with a measure of suspicion, even though there may be legitimate reasons for this secrecy.

But more than financial accountability is needed. It is also imperative that there be some kind of spiritual accountability. An ideal way for the parachurch to get spiritual accountability is to work at having strong relationships with local churches. Seeking this kind of accountability is one of the best ways to enter into real partnership with the traditional church.

This spiritual accountability comes on two levels, personal and corporate (*Co-Operating in World Evangelization,* 1983, pp. 32–34). On the personal level it is important that each parachurch organization require that its members be active members in a local church. This requirement places each member of the parachurch under a spiritual authority in both moral and theological matters. Such a requirement also builds trust with the local churches, as they see that the parachurch is serious about being a help to the local church. Accountability on the corporate level is trickier to establish. Some organizations have found it helpful to include representatives from the local church on their boards. This allows the local church to have an official say in the actions of the parachurch. Other parachurch organizations have voluntarily offered to report to the Evangelical churches in their area, asking for their input and thought on the parachurch ministry. There are many ways for the parachurch to establish accountability, but if the parachurch and the church are ever to enter into true partnership, it is essential that parachurch organizations find effective ways to keep themselves accountable.

Develop Role Clarity

Within any kind of a relationship, from relationships between family members to relationships between organizations, role clarity is an important part of harmonious work. Within a family this is especially clear. The father and mother must understand between themselves what their responsibilities are. The children also must know what type of behavior is expected of them and how they fit into the family. One sign of a dysfunctional family is that the understood roles have become confused—perhaps the father is largely absent, and that throws family relationships out of whack. Relationships between churches and parachurches depend also on role clarity.

When tensions between the church and parachurch build up over programs, it is largely a case of the two sides not understanding their proper roles. When the church envies the parachurch, many times it is a result of not seeing that the parachurch is called to specialized ministries. By the very nature of these specialized ministries, they will garner more excitement than the weekly programs of the church. Conversely, the parachurch will often castigate the church for not being on the front lines of evangelism and social programs. But this criticism is often unfair. The church, in its generalist and inclusive role, is not able to react as quickly or focus its energies on a single problem in the way that the parachurch can. A good number of the current tensions could be abated if the differing roles were recognized and appreciated.

As with the other steps, the key to role clarity is dialogue. Leaders from the church and parachurch need to be in contact with each other. The expectations of both sides must be frankly stated and discussed. Financial issues must also be touched on, so that each side can come to understand the other side's financial concerns and needs. As talk proceeds, church and parachurch will begin to see that those they considered their competitors actually are fellow workers.

The Ideal Relationship

It is a truism that as long as the church and parachurch are composed of fallen men and women, the organizations and their actions will be less than perfect. Careers and dreams are on the line for leaders, and it is difficult to subjugate human desires to the needs of the kingdom of God. We should be wary of any attempts to completely smooth out the relationship between church and parachurch.

But although we may never see a perfect church-parachurch relationship, we are still justified in asking what the ideal would look like. This ideal must be the goal to which Christian leaders are striving. In the preamble to *Co-Operating in World Evangelization, A Handbook on Church/Para-Church Relationships* (1983, p. 8), John Stott tries to pinpoint this ideal relationship. He begins his short examination with a verse from Philippians: "Only, live your life in a manner worthy of the gospel of Christ, so that, whether I come and see you or am absent and hear about you, I will know that you are standing firm in one spirit, striving side by side with one mind for the faith of the gospel" (1:27).

Although Paul did not have parachurch-church relationships in mind, there are several ideals here for which both churches and parachurch organizations can strive. This is Paul's call for responsibility to believers in Philippi. He tacitly acknowledges that they will not always have an apostle to watch over them, and that it is up to them to conduct themselves and their ministry in a manner worthy of the Gospel of Christ. Paul does not provide leaders with a list of rules for getting along, but each is expected to exercise his or her own Christian freedom in ways that are honoring to God.

In the final two clauses of the verse, we find two crucial components of our ideal. First, people are to stand "firm in one spirit," and second, they are to strive "side by side with one mind." As emphasized in this chapter, church and parachurch are each part of God's plan for taking the Gospel to all people. There is one God and one Lord and one Spirit, and leaders from church and parachurch have believed in one Gospel. Above everything else there ought to be a unity of mind that characterizes this tricky relationship. But this unity of mind does not mean that ministries must be joined together or that all differences must cease to exist. Instead they are to strive "side by side with one mind." In this understanding of the ideal, church and parachurch are allowed to keep their own distinctive ministries, but they are not to see themselves as competitors. Both are striving for the same goal, and both are working for the same kingdom. And this is the ideal relationship: unity of mind, but accepted differences in ministry.

15

CHALLENGES TO THE
PARACHURCH'S FUTURE

THE FUTURE IS always an alluring topic. The looming millennium has only intensified the speculation as to what the future holds. Books such as the *500-Year Delta*, by Jim Taylor and Watts Wacker, foresee a chaotic future approaching. Among Taylor and Wacker's predictions are that multinational corporations will soon have their own embassies and that 30 percent of the U.S. workforce will be engaged in helping the elderly. These types of predictions sound possible, but at times the authors fall into the same quagmire as other futurologists: they make wild guesses. Not-so-probable guesses about what will occur in the next five hundred weeks include "consciousness will be downloadable" and "being unknown will be a status symbol" (Taylor and Wacker, 1997, pp. 270–271). Given the limits of science and the stability of human nature, such guesses will never prove true. Futurologists of the past could do no better and to read about their projected science fiction–like cities is now a way to spend an entertaining afternoon.

Amid all the speculation about the future, what is certain is that the cadence of change has increased. That has been true throughout human history, but each passing decade now seems to bring with it a doubling of the speed of change. Parachurch organizations are affected by change as much as any business or government, and it is imperative that they have an understanding of the basic challenges that the future holds so they can adjust. As this book has developed, the parachurch has prospered because it has taken advantage of the cultural forces at work in contemporary society. But those same forces can slow the work of the parachurch if leaders fail to make adjustments—no one has the future guaranteed. This final chapter is an attempt to provide parachurch organizations with some ways to think about the broad challenges facing the parachurch world. There are four main challenges:

o The challenge of a multicultural world

o The challenge of a postmodern world

o The challenge of a changing religious scene

o The challenge of new leadership

By addressing these four challenges the parachurch will be well equipped to stand strong as the waves of the future break around it.

The Challenge of a Multicultural World

Old pictures of parachurch staff and leaders look remarkably similar. They feature a group of white men sitting around a large table or standing in front of a new building. But those homogeneous pictures are changing as women and ethnic groups play a larger part. As we venture into the coming century, the dominance of people whose roots lie in Europe is fading. What is arising is a nation made up of many minorities, each keeping its cultural heritage to some extent. This demographic shift is causing many tensions—racial, cultural, and religious—which threaten to erupt into violence on occasion and which give steam to political controversy. What is not often recognized is the challenge that these changes pose to the running of a parachurch organization.

Many parachurch organizations are still operating according to the old demographics. Perhaps they have their headquarters in a small city where the demographic changes are not so evident, or perhaps they operate in the center of a large city and simply ignore the changes taking place around them. As seen in the third chapter of this book, the parachurch prospered because it found common bonds to unite a fragmented American religious landscape. In a way that no denomination could do, parachurch organizations united people under the simple Gospel message and built united centers out of disparate groups. National parachurch groups have prospered because they have had a message that appealed to a broad band of people living throughout the United States. Today new divisions in society are challenging the ability of the parachurch to reach a large portion of the U.S. population. The parachurch organizations that are not able to reach today's multicultural audience face the danger of becoming irrelevant to the various needs of that audience. As the years pass and changes mount, they will find themselves appealing to an ever narrower constituency. Parachurch organizations that today have a national audience will find themselves speaking to only a fraction of a nation. The parachurch must change as the kingdom changes.

So far, large parachurch organizations have been partially shielded from the changes. The old constituency still holds most of the power and wealth and still gives strong support to the parachurch. But on the local level the changes are immediately apparent. To examine these changes that will soon face even the largest of parachurch organizations, we can follow a case study of the Los Angeles First Church of the Nazarene (Benefiel, 1996). The steps that this large church took to meet the challenges of multiculturalism serve as a map for the steps a parachurch organization will have to take.

This church is located close to downtown Los Angeles, and is literally the first church of the Nazarene, being the mother church of its Nazarene denomination. It was founded in 1895, in the heart of a city that has changed with every passing decade. The congregation had relocated twice in its hundred years of existence, once in the late 1930s and again in the late 1940s. In the 1960s, the congregation built a large sanctuary and expected to stay at this location indefinitely, serving a middle-to-upper-middle-class white neighborhood. But Los Angeles stays still for no one, and almost as soon as the building was complete, demographic change began to erode the congregation's traditional foundations. The percentage of non-Hispanic whites within a mile of the church declined steadily: from 80 percent in 1960 to 45 percent in 1970, and then it fell even further—to 25 percent in 1980 and finally to only 10 percent in 1990. Longtime members began to attend churches that were closer to home, and the attendance began to drop dangerously. The church leadership was faced with a choice: should the church relocate to be closer to its accustomed constituency, or should it find a way to flourish amid its changing environment? All parachurch organizations, even the very large ones, will soon face a similar choice, and the options open to the Nazarene church are instructive to every parachurch organization.

In his case study of this church, Benefiel sketches out five strategies often used by organizations facing a strong demographic change. The first strategy is to *hold out*. It involves an attitude of denial toward change: "Maybe things will get better in a year or two." The hope is that the current level of ministry can be maintained indefinitely. The second strategy is more defensive minded: *keep out*. With this common strategy, the organization begins to take on a siege mentality. Its energies are spent erecting and maintaining walls that keep people outside. The third strategy is to *move out*. Again, this is only a temporary solution to the problem. As the earlier relocations of the organization in the case study show, there is no way to evade the creeping demographic changes of this culture. If an organization moves a little further away from its present site, it will be only a matter of years until the same problems are faced once again. The fourth strategy is to *close out*. This is an admission of defeat. The leadership then clearly states that the organization has been swallowed by the changes in the society. The fifth strategy, and perhaps the only one that is viable in the long term, is to *reach out*. This approach sees the demographic changes but, instead of reacting negatively, decides to find a way to minister effectively in the changed environment.

With the help of a farsighted leadership the Los Angeles First Church of the Nazarene was able to make this last transition, becoming a church that served the needs of its multicultural neighborhood. Four ethnic congregations were started, yet a strong sense of inner unity was encouraged also. These were not four churches within one building, but four interrelated congregations that made up one church. By finding a way to turn the external threat of demographic change into a strength, the church has modeled an approach that many parachurch organizations would do well to imitate in the coming century of change.

Instead of serving a national community divided only by superficial differences, the parachurch now finds itself serving a fragmented nation divided into hundreds and even thousands of subcommunities. This fragmentation grows each year. The challenge for the parachurch is to refrain from giving in to tribalism and to acknowledge and affirm differences. At the same time, the parachurch must present a set of core values that will bind diverse people into a community of faith. The options that are open to each parachurch organization are essentially the same as the ones that faced the Nazarene church. Either ignore the change, run away from it, or actively seek to embrace it and to include other ethnic and racial groups within the organization's bounds. In the end, to reach out is the only option a parachurch organization can choose if it expects to prosper in the next century.

Just how the parachurch can reach out to different ethnic groups is a question for which there are no easy answers. But there are at least two ways that each parachurch organization can begin to move into the new multicultural reality. The first way is deceptively simple: include in the organization people who have different cultural backgrounds. Some organizations seem to work on the unspoken principle that such changes will happen automatically and without effort. But this has not proven true. Continued relevance demands that definite steps be taken to ensure that various ethnic groups feel comfortable and accepted with the message and leaders of the organization.

The second way parachurch organizations can take to become more inclusive is to learn to speak other "languages." This does not necessarily mean writing bilingual tracts, but it does mean making a continued effort to produce materials that can connect with different groups. In the secular business world, new product advertising is tailored to speak to the needs of a particular group of people. Different ads may be used to meet the cultural backgrounds of various groups of people. The parachurch is involved in doing something far more significant than selling a new brand of soap, but the concept of tailoring a message to different communities is vital. If the parachurch neglects to find new ways to communicate its eternal message, then it will forfeit its place of importance.

The Challenge of a Postmodern World

We are living in what is best understood as an in-between time—the age of modernity winds down as postmodernism emerges. There are several hallmarks to the ideas that go under this rubric. Two have special bearing on religious beliefs: disbelief in objective truth and a deep sense that morality is relative. Today's high school or college students are unlikely to believe that there are any universal ideas or truths. Students are likely to have been bombarded with the conflicting claims of many different religions and to have determined that all truth is relative. It is rare to find an individual who will declare for any belief: "I think this is true and others false." This implicit denial of universal truth has repercussions in the moral realm. If all religions are equally valid, then their lifestyles and morals must also be equal. The effect of this denial of truth and moral relativism is twofold. The first effect is an eclectic approach to life. The ideas and morals that fit the individual's personal taste are adopted. The second effect is that if all truth is relative, then tolerance should prevail, and proselytizing one's faith is viewed as bad manners.

A second characteristic of the current generation is a deeply ingrained cynicism. The boomers swept into the national consciousness on a tide of optimism and idealism. The times were changing, and the new would replace the old. Lyndon Johnson was president, and his social programs promised to eliminate poverty. But the dream proved illusory. Those coming of age in the nineties can see the wreckage of this idealism, and they steer clear of it. They ask, "Why be involved in politics? All politicians are in the pocket of rich corporations anyway." Even that refuge of idealism, higher education, is no longer the place to find personal fulfillment but simply the place to go when a person wants a good job. When religion is mentioned, people in this younger generation ask, Doesn't the church just want money from me? This makes it hard to get them into a church building or to listen to a religious speaker.

The third characteristic of this generation is that its members are *technoliterate*. The gadgets available to the sixties generation pale in comparison to those at the fingertips of most young people in the nineties. The most obvious technological advance has been in the world of computers. It is difficult to get through college, with its constant demand for typed papers, without a working knowledge of computers. And few young people are ignorant of the Internet and the information accessible through the World Wide Web. Besides computers, there are now pagers, answering machines, color photocopiers, audio CDs, and VCRs. This generation is the first to arrive at adulthood with this wave of electronic technology.

These three characteristics (denial of truth, cynicism, and technoliteracy) will challenge everyone in parachurch leadership to develop a unique approach to ministry for this generation. It takes a high level of discernment to determine which differences are simply age related and which ones are permanent. For example, the taste for loud and obnoxious music seems to subside as youths advance in years. So to gear a ministry to loud music will backfire in the end because those young tastes will change. But other generation X characteristics are unlikely to disappear, and unless the challenges are met, Christian organizations will someday look around and realize that they are no longer meeting the needs of a culture dominated by this generation.

Organizations can meet the challenges of this generation by refusing to meet their cynical expectations. Instead of presenting ideas that flatly condemn all religions other than their own and all religious differences, Christian leaders must admit there are points at which the different religions have something important to say, even as they insist that at the heart of Christianity is unique truth. Instead of meeting young people's expectations that Christians leaders are after money or that church is just an escape from real life, Christian leaders need to prove this is not so and demonstrate how there is reason to be guardedly idealistic about the church. Instead of running away from technology, Christian leaders must use it as a tool to reach people for Christ. To engage generation X on its own turf is the challenge that the future holds for the parachurch. The organizations able to gain this generation's interest and support will be the key organizations of the twenty-first century.

The Challenge of a Changing Religious Scene

The changing religious scene in which the parachurch is prospering can best be characterized by three factors: (1) the collapse of the traditional church culture, (2) a shift in thinking from ethnocentric concerns to king-dom eyes, and (3) the emergence of the megachurch.

One of the predominant factors fueling the prospering of the para-church is the collapse of the traditional church culture. While there have always been many varied worship traditions in faith, there was a homo-geneity in the Christian culture. Reggie McNeal, director of leadership development for the South Carolina Baptist Convention, characterizes the shift that has occurred from the days when the church was a central part in people's lives. Much of the church culture was—and is—reacting out of fear in the face of this collapse. Some of the obvious evidences of this include a hyper-morality that burns—rather than builds—bridges to the culture. This has opened up an era of growth for parachurch organiza-tions that are more culturally relevant.

Now, though, the church is even less central in many Christians' lives. Some research indicates that even the committed miss an average of four-teen Sundays of attendance per year. Plus, the church does not look the same among most church attendees. Worship wars have broken out, as older and younger worshipers contend for the worship forms and church programs that each finds meaningful.

Parachurch organizations have been able to develop culturally relevant expressions of Christianity that are not tied to church culture, and they have largely sidestepped some of the current tension between the traditional and emerging contemporary church cultures. Parachurch organizations that have taken their Christianity to the streets—in a more first-century style—can serve the church they depend on by providing it with opportunities to engage the culture. But this will take new levels of mutually beneficial strate-gic alliances, as described in the previous chapters.

A second change in the religious scene with which the parachurch must wrestle is the small but growing shift from ethnocentric concern to king-dom eyes. There have been prodigious amounts of smugness in both the local church and the parachurch worlds that "the real kingdom of God action was here—not over there." The local church has been slow to rec-ognize the parachurch's tremendous growth, its impact on the local church, and its role in expressing Christian faith outside the church's walls. One could hardly argue that the proliferation and prospering of the parachurch are not signs of spiritual awakening. It is as if God has led and worked through those who will be responsive to him.

There is a growing willingness (fostered in part by the climatic shift described in the previous chapter) to recognize and join "movements of God." The prayer movement, stimulated by the work of the parachurch called Concerts of Prayers, is bringing parachurch and local churches together. The Willow Creek Association (a parachurch organization serving local churches and born out of a local church, Willow Creek Community Church) is bringing together local churches, denominational leaders, and evangelical-minded parachurch leaders. Mission America is doing the same. There has always been some cooperation between the church and parachurch, as experienced by such denominationally spawned enterprises as Lutheran Social Services or Billy Graham Evangelistic Association.

But this new spirit and emerging climate have a different flavor. The kingdom task is becoming harder and more complex. Pragmatism has set in. Rather than pursue ethnocentric, independent agendas, both the local church and the parachurch see the benefit of a kingdom paradigm. As James F. Engel wrote in *A Clouded Future?* (1996, p. 7), that paradigm is "not a set of abstract propositions to be marketed in a world of competing ideologies." Rather, "it is the story of Jesus Christ authenticated by history and by the ongoing story of the community of the King." This implies more cooperation—cooperation to get behind God wherever he is working and to join together to follow God's lead wherever God leads, even when the evidence of his working is not yet visible to us. Among the baby boomers and Generation Xers, there is a pragmatic willingness to do this—which is hopefully a harbinger of greater kingdom impact for the church.

This kingdom mind-set change is also something of a shift in theology, with a growing emphasis on "the priesthood of the believer." Some characterize it as a second Reformation in which God's work is being returned to the people; the pastor is seen less as the primary kingdom worker and more as the facilitator of kingdom work, which is done through God's people. Church pastors with kingdom eyes are not looking for more church workers, but instead are challenging their people to be agents for Christ, deployed to their world, rather than huddled in the sanctuary of the church. This deployment mind-set has spurred the parachurch onward throughout its history. Prudent parachurch leaders will work hard in the future to have strategic alliances with local churches that are regularly deploying their flocks into the world by providing people with meaningful roles as ministers of the Gospel.

The third significant change in the religious landscape over the last decade has been the emergence of the *megachurch*. Attendance on a single Sunday at one of these churches will number anywhere from one thousand all the way up to over sixteen thousand people—as at Willow Creek Community Church. These megachurches are the fastest growing churches in the United States. Half of the churchgoers in the United States attend the top 12 percent of the nation's churches (Trueheart, 1996, p. 38), which means that a large percentage of Christians attend a megachurch. In the near future an even larger portion of churchgoers will do so. The growing strength of the megachurch raises some questions about the future of the parachurch.

First, we must be clear on why the megachurch is so different. Large churches have been around for centuries. Simply having over a thousand people in attendance does not qualify a church as a megachurch. What is different about these churches is that they have managed to combine the strength of the parachurch with the strength of the small traditional church and have avoided the weaknesses of both. The firmly drawn dividing lines between church and parachurch are partially blurred by the megachurch.

The megachurch resembles a constellation of generalized church ministries and specialized parachurch ministries. For example, within Willow Creek Community Church, all the ministries of the local church can be found—such as worship, evangelism, and ministries for children and youth. But Willow Creek also has extension ministries rarely seen in a single local church—international outreach ministries, urban ministries, a food pantry, crisis pregnancy counseling, addiction recovery, outreach to the homeless and imprisoned, even a ministry that refurbishes donated cars and gives them to needy people. Within most traditional churches, there are too few people to fund and to run such a variety of narrowly focused programs, but once a critical mass of people is reached then it becomes possible to offer highly specialized programs and services that will involve many different people. The ministries that a person could once find only within a parachurch organization are now available at a nearby church.

Even before the phenomenon of the megachurch arrived, Frank Tillapaugh wrote in his book *Unleashing the Church* about the possibility of the church taking on parachurch functions: "Throughout . . . I will be pleading with the local church to get involved in ministries which in recent years have been parachurch domains. . . . The plea is for the local church to get back into the ball game. Not only can we undertake most of the specialized ministries but, because we *are* the church, we have an important advantage. . . . No other organization has the body-dynamic we have" (1982, p. 21). In other words, Tillapaugh saw that the local churches, especially evangelicals, had largely isolated themselves and had focused their efforts on "matters of the soul." The megachurch has expanded the definition of local church ministry to include what was, for decades, the parachurch's work. In addition, it has created an entrepreneurial environment whose "parachurch founders" are often given the freedom to express their vision—within the boundaries of the local church. In essence, the megachurch undoubtedly has and will continue to keep some parachurch ministries from independent operation by incubating and sustaining them within the church's boundaries.

By combining the strengths of both the traditional church and parachurch, the megachurch will pose something of a challenge to parachurch organizations. As was seen in earlier chapters, the parachurch has grown because of inflexibility and an inability to accommodate individual vision on the part of the traditional church. Those who work for a parachurch organization rightly see themselves engaged on the cutting edge of Christian work. Some elements of the megachurch take away these reasons for starting a parachurch organization. A visionary leader might feel restricted in a small church and thus be forced to form a parachurch organization. In a megachurch such as Willow Creek, however, such a leader would find an environment that accepts vision. The unknown here is that if large churches become more friendly to individuals with new ideas, will those talented leaders work within the church instead of taking the risk of starting parachurch organizations?

Another question is whether small to midlevel parachurch organizations will be able to operate successfully in the shadow of the megachurch. Established parachurch organizations with the capability to reach a national audience will hardly be affected by the megachurch. In fact, these large parachurch organizations may be able to partner successfully with a coalition of megachurches. It is likely that many large parachurch organizations will begin to view the megachurch as a worthy partner for ministry. But for more localized parachurch organizations, such as a crisis pregnancy center or an organization dedicated to furthering arts with a Christian worldview, the megachurch will have to be reckoned with. The megachurch is able to provide better facilities and better publicity for a new ministry. As the megachurch movement continues to grow, its sprawling ministries and services are bound to compete with the neighboring smaller parachurch organizations for the hearts, time, and giving of Christians.

Rather than seeing them as competitors, prudent parachurch organizations will see megachurches as worthy partners for more ministry impact. Despite their independence and the huge defenses that most megachurches erect, partnership is possible. It will take an openness on the part of megachurches to see partnership as a way to extend their ministry and to be learners. It will take openness on the part of parachurches to adjust their methodology to accommodate the strengths of megachurches—and to be learners.

Willow Creek Community Church currently partners with World Vision in a variety of programs in the Dominican Republic. Both have had to make adjustments in order to keep the partnership alive for the sake of what they are accomplishing together. More such partnerships will likely emerge as more progressive parachurch organizations and megachurches see strategic alliances as extending their reach.

Prognostication is always a dangerous art. Paths from the present lead off in several different directions, each depending on a number of human and historical variables. Yet it is clear that under each possible scenario the parachurch must account for the megachurch. There are some who predict that the parachurch will enter a decline of influence as the megachurch gains in popularity, yet it should be remembered that the megachurch is still only a local entity—as yet these churches have no interconnected web of ministries and services. Because megachurches generally stand alone in their local areas, they are not able to reach the broad Christian spectrum that a parachurch organization can. For anyone who dreams of extending a ministry beyond a local area, a parachurch organization is still the only choice.

The Challenge of New Leadership

In this book we have seen many parachurch organizations and found that at their heart is the vision of an individual. Here at the conclusion of the book it is fitting to look to the future of parachurch leadership and ask ourselves these questions: Can the parachurch continue to field dynamic leaders? And what steps can the parachurch take to ensure that it can answer yes to the first question?

The cry for leadership goes up from many sources. In the worlds of government and business, there is a constant need for men and women who have leadership abilities. Our complex society makes leadership more essential than ever before, but at the same time increased specialization and individualism make it harder for leaders to develop. The parachurch feels this same pinch for leaders. This pinch will grow increasingly tighter as the present generation of parachurch leadership retires. If individual parachurch organizations are to continue their ministries, they must take steps now to invest in young leaders who can serve with the same vision and energy as the founding leaders. Here are three steps parachurch organizations can take to encourage new leadership.

The first step for the parachurch is to get away from celebrity-driven models of leadership. Modern culture is increasingly centered on celebrity, and it is all too easy for the parachurch to adopt this way of thinking.

When the parachurch is focused on celebrity, image comes to rules over substance, and individual personality over the overall ministry. In some cases the parachurch has come to mimic the secular entertainment world, and an entire organization focuses on promoting a single individual. Nevertheless, the celebrity model has been adopted by parachurch organizations because it works. The U.S. public has come to the place where it is riveted by individual personalities. If a radio or television program is to be a success it is imperative that there be a captivating speaker at the center of the ministry who is able to compete with the high-powered entertainment being offered on other stations. But even though some degree of celebrity may be necessary for ministries, there is the ever-present danger that once the celebrity is gone, the ministry will falter as well. Celebrity-centered ministries tend for this reason to be unstable.

The way to counter this celebrity model of leadership is to learn to nurture and accept leadership at all levels of the organization—even when the founder is alive. In a celebrity-driven organization the tendency is to have one leader, who determines the course of action, while the other senior people in the organization are best described as managers, who try to implement the ideas of the leader. However, a healthy organization does its best to distribute power to a wider base of people, through participation, empowerment, and decentralized decision making. Instead of letting one person dominate, a variety of people are allowed to play important roles, and young people are groomed to take over leadership roles in the future. With this step, a course is set for the parachurch organization to remain strong for many years, not just for the extent of one person's popularity.

A second step for the parachurch that hopes to keep strong leadership is to keep a tight grip on its original values. The temptation is for new leaders to move away from the "outdated" message of the original founders and find a more contemporary message. Sustained success requires continuity with the core mission along with flexibility in forms of execution. Our society thinks of the leader as the person who "creates" strong values—as if these values were nonexistent until the leader made them a necessity.

The Christian must hold onto the fact that it is the values that create the leader, not the other way around. The best example of this is found in the New Testament. The apostle Paul organized the foundations of a religion that would reach the world, and for this he certainly deserves credit as one of the great leaders of the world. But as we read the epistles, we do not find a natural leader. Instead, recall what Paul reports the Corinthian Christians are saying about him: "His letters are weighty and strong, but his bodily presence is weak, and his speech contemptible"

(2 Corinthians 10:10). Evidently it was common for people not to think very highly of Paul's personal presence. It was the message of Christianity that made Paul a great leader. And the early church was powered by people like Paul, who were not important as Roman society judged importance, but who were molded into leaders by the transforming message of Christianity. If a parachurch organization is to remain strong, it must hold onto the values that have empowered it. As the message of the parachurch changes lives, new leaders will arise who, like Paul, become leaders for the sake of the Gospel.

A third important step parachurch organizations can take to maintain leadership is to maintain leaders' integrity. We can think of integrity as the unity between a person's private actions and public persona. The parachurch has been blessed with scores of leaders who place a high value on integrity, but it has also had a few well-publicized cases of leaders who lacked integrity. Billy Graham's ministry is a classic example of a ministry that has been carried on with integrity. From his early days as a traveling evangelist, he and his team made a few resolutions that would last throughout his ministry. These resolutions address the common problems faced by each parachurch organization: mismanagement of money, sexual immorality, failure to partner with the traditional church, and misleading publicity. Throughout his ministry Billy Graham was able to keep a high standard of personal integrity. The success and respect generated by his ministry has been sustained by that integrity.

For the parachurch, integrity of personal values is analogous to Samson's hair. The power of Samson to slay his enemies seemed to come from his tremendous strength. But God had made his long hair the key to his power. Once that hair was clipped, he was powerless before his enemies. With its enormous prosperity the parachurch is tempted to see its success as a product of its own efforts, a simple result of its own technique. From the perspective of the world this may seem like the best explanation. But, as Christians, parachurch leaders know that the source of any success is God, and their message stirs the hearts of listeners only because of the Holy Spirit. And because it is God who gives success, the power of parachurch leaders comes not from inherent ability but personal integrity that flows from the right relationship with God. If evil gets a foothold in the life of a parachurch leader and steals integrity, then the power of the ministry can be expected to disappear as well. Above all else a parachurch organization must watch closely that leaders' personal integrity is maintained.

The Christian community would love to see another Billy Graham arise who can heal divisions and speak a clear message. God will raise this leader up, but we must have minds open enough to see a new kind of leader. The parachurch is moving into a new century with many new challenges, and the new leader will be as different from past leaders as new challenges are from the old ones. Yet two things will not be different: the message and integrity of future leaders will be similar to that preached and lived by Billy Graham and by countless Christians before him.

Conclusion

Even the experts are unable to predict the future. The music that will catch on, the technology breakthroughs, the outward characteristics of future leaders—all these things are veiled to even the most intrepid of future lookers. But amid all the change of this culture, the fundamental human needs remain. In the final analysis the parachurch prospers because it meets the universal need of every culture and person. Almost three thousand years ago the Psalmist cried out, "As a deer longs for flowing streams, so my soul longs for you, O God" (Psalms 42:1). The same passion was expressed by St. Augustine: "You made us for yourself and our hearts find no peace until they rest in you" (1961, p. 21). And this longing to know and experience God has been a constant force in human history. The ubiquitous religious rites and offerings found in every culture give witness to the universal longing for God.

The United States is a nation seeking God. Recent surveys indicate that in 1998, belief in God and miracles reached its highest level in a decade. A full 71 percent of respondents say that they never doubt the existence of God (Aversa, 1997, p. 19). From the beginning of our history, spiritual concerns have been evident. The pilgrims settled in New England so that they could worship as they pleased, and the Spanish and French missionaries carried their Roman Catholic faith to the Southwest and Canada. The reserved Pilgrims and the earnest Catholic missionaries have long disappeared, but the religious longings that drove them to these shores are still with us.

Contemporary spiritual hunger is expressed in the bright colors of a book display: *Finding God on the A Train; Conversations with God; Chicken Soup for the Soul.* And these are just a few of the titles that could be named. It is not only in the United States that this spiritual hunger exists but all over the world. The crowds in every continent that respond to the Billy Graham crusades witness to the universal spiritual need of human beings.

The open road lies ahead. The opening of the next millennium is a time for the parachurch to renew its efforts and envision new types of ministries. Such optimism is based on the solid fact that the spiritual needs of humanity will remain constant. The vacuum of the human heart will continue to long for God. The future bodes well for parachurch organizations as long as they address this fundamental need. At a time when public and private institutions have backed away from spiritual expressions, the parachurch has been and will continue to be a major instrument used by God to reach human hearts. All the other factors for parachurch growth identified in this book pale against this one: God has a commitment to get his redemptive love to people. God's perspective is of his kingdom, and his work is not tied to any human institution. To reach this redemptive goal, God is perfectly willing to enlarge the boundaries of his kingdom.

RESOURCE:
PARACHURCH TAXONOMY

AS PARACHURCH ORGANIZATIONS prosper, little attention is being given to describing the categories of ministry that are their work. The following taxonomy provides a framework with which to describe and organize the many parachurch organizations.

In general, a parachurch organization prospers because it is filling a need that people will support. The *Dictionary of Christianity in America* covers the basics when it defines *parachurch organizations* as "voluntary, not-for-profit associations of Christians working outside denominational control to achieve some specific ministry or social service" (Reid, 1990, p. 863). The prefix *para* suggests that they are "beside" or "beyond" the traditional church. (Chapter Two of this book provides a more detailed definition of the parachurch.)

In developing the taxonomy, information was drawn from three existing systems: the *National Association of Evangelicals 1995–1996 Directory;* the *Evangelical Council for Financial Accountability Member Profile Directory* (January 1997); and the *National Taxonomy of Exempt Entities,* which is used by the Internal Revenue Service to standardize coding between the IRS and the nonprofit community (Hodgkinson and Weitzman, 1996, pp. 277–309). In addition, once the taxonomy was drafted, numerous people in a variety of fields reviewed and edited it with further refinements.

A parachurch taxonomy will provide a useful instrument to facilitate understanding of the parachurch. Obviously this is an initial effort. As the parachurch continues to prosper, the taxonomy will need to be adjusted and refined.

Taxonomy Outline

A   Arts/Culture

B   Associations

C	Audiovisual/Media
D	Camps/Conferences
E	Constituency-Based Ministries
F	Consulting
G	Counseling/Guidance
H	Education
I	Environmental/Agricultural
J	Evangelism
K	Health Care
L	Legal Assistance/Political Action
M	Missions
N	Printed Media
O	Relief and Development
P	Social Services

A Arts/Culture

The arts/culture category is made up of organizations that serve as fellowships for artists, provide Christian-influenced art and cultural activities, and share the gospel through artistic media. Also included are museums that preserve, replicate, and exhibit works of religious art as a means to promote and propagate understanding of the Gospel.

A 10	**Performing arts**
A 11	Dancing/choreography
A 12	Theater/playwriting
A 13	Music
A 20	**Visual arts**
A 21	Painting/drawing
A 22	Photography
A 23	Sculpture/ceramic arts
A 30	**Museums**
A 40	**Art fellowship groups**
A 41	Visual arts

B Associations

Associations serve as a fellowship for persons or organizations sharing a common purpose or interest. Generally, each association has a basic mission statement or statement of faith that its members endorse. In addition, many require that dues be paid. The association offers its members support, information, education, fellowship opportunities, and resources. Often associations hold meetings that allow members to network and support one another. Association members may be organizations, individual persons, or both.

B 10	**Associations serving specific organizations**
B 11	Churches
B 12	Educational institutions
B 13	Fundraising groups
B 14	Gospel rescue missions
B 15	Management organizations
B 16	Newspapers
B 20	**Associations serving individuals—predominantly individuals not necessarily affiliated with a particular agency or organization**
B 21	Christians
B 22	Families
B 23	Ministry workers
B 24	Singles
B 25	Scientists
B 30	**Associations serving specific professions—supporting, training, and encouraging professionals in taking the Gospel into their profession and sharing Christ with co-workers and colleagues; offering support to other believers through Bible studies, conferences, banquets, and so forth**
B 31	Airline industry
B 32	Architects
B 33	Business
B 34	Counseling/social work
B 35	Education

B 36	Legal/law enforcement
B 37	Media
B 38	Medical
B 39	Military

C Audiovisual Media

Audiovisual media organizations produce and disseminate audiovisual materials and programs or provide production facilities for audiovisual materials for the purpose of spreading and communicating the Gospel.

C 10	**Radio broadcasting**
C 11	International stations
C 12	International programs
C 13	Domestic stations—the estimated 1,300 religious radio stations in North America, ranging from part-time to full-time operations (Clark and Virts, 1996, p. ix)
C 14	Consistent domestic programs—programs that air on a regular schedule, at least once a week
C 15	Specialty domestic programs—programs that air only as special engagements
C 20	**Television broadcasting**
C 21	Stations—the estimated 250 religious television stations in the United States (Clark and Virts, 1996, p. ix)
C 22	Consistent programs—programs that air on a regular schedule, at least once a week
C 23	Specialty series programs—programs that air only as special engagements
C 30	**Audio recording, production, and distribution**
C 31	Music
C 32	Training series/instruction
C 40	**Program producers and distributors—organizations that make the programs in the various media, providing the technology to record and distribute**
C 41	Film/TV/video
C 42	Radio

D   Camps/Conferences

Camps, conferences, and retreat centers provide a setting for outdoor ministries and offer Christian hospitality in an organized framework. These facilities and programs serve as meeting places where people of various ages can come together for varying numbers of days to learn about or deepen their relationship with Christ. These programs usually exist for teaching, learning, or renewal purposes.

D 10	**Conference centers**
D 20	**Retreat camps/centers**
D 21	Summer/winter camps
D 22	Day camps
D 23	Youth camps

E   Constituency-Based Ministries

Constituency-based organizations provide services, fellowship, and ministry opportunities to people who are part of a definable group, or constituency.

E 10	**Athletes—organizations that provide opportunity, support, encouragement, and training to Christian athletes in order that they may proclaim Christ to fellow athletes**
E 11	Youth/high school
E 12	College
E 13	Professional
E 20	**Businesspeople**
E 30	**Minorities—organizations that provide support, training, and outreach to those considered members of minorities (by reason of race, religion, socioeconomic level, and so forth)**
E 40	**Handicapped/disabled—organizations that exist in order to reach the physically and mentally disabled in areas and activities that are unique to them in order that they might hear and know the good news of Christ**
E 50	**Church development—organizations that provide support, training, and development to churches' evangelistic outreach**

E 60   Prison/ex-offenders—the estimated 1,600 organizations that seek to reach and proclaim the good news of Christ to men, women, and juveniles currently in prison or to paroled people who have yet to know Christ

E 61   Chaplain/prison worker support

E 70   Senior citizens—organizations that provide support and plan activities that encourage the spread of the Gospel among the elderly population

E 80   Youth—organizations that communicate the word or provide opportunity, support, training, and encouragement to the younger generation

E 90   Gender—organizations that provide support, encouragement, training, and opportunities to men and women for the purpose of effectively communicating the Gospel

E 91   Men

E 92   Women

F   Consulting

Consulting organizations provide a wide variety of technical assistance services, often in support of other parachurch organizations.

F 10   Management—organizations that provide support and assistance to other organizations in the areas of management, networking, marketing, public relations, development, and so forth

F 20   Financial—organizations that provide counseling, encouragement, and consultation mainly to parachurch organizations and their people in the biblical principles of raising and handling money while maintaining high standards of financial integrity and Christian ethics

F 30   Employment—organizations that provide guidance to others on integrating their faith into their work and that perform placements and executive searches and keep track of opportunities in ministry positions both nationally and worldwide

F 40   Conciliation/mediation—organizations that handle Christian dispute resolution

F 50   Media consulting—organizations that purchase airtime and
         produce programming for Christian radio and television
         stations

F 60   Marketing—organizations that provide parachurch
         marketing and advertising consulting and services

F 70   Church growth—organizations that support and assist
         churches in development, training, networking, evangelism,
         discipleship, leadership, and economics in order that they
         might be more effective in communicating the gospel

F 80   Technical support—organizations that provide parachurch
         and similar organizations with education and also technical
         and engineering consulting regarding presentation equipment
         and its operation

G   Counseling/Guidance

Counseling and guidance organizations further the Gospel and glorify
God by providing assistance to those in search of help with physical, spiritual, or emotional needs. These organizations include adoption agencies,
crisis pregnancy care clinics, career counseling programs, and rehabilitation programs.

G 10   Adoption programs

G 20   Crisis pregnancy centers

G 30   Career placement/counseling

G 40   Substance abuse rehabilitation—organizations that assist,
         counsel, and support people in rehabilitation after substance
         abuse by offering retreats, workshops, support groups,
         twelve-step programs, seminars, counseling, and so forth,
         using scripture and prayer and promoting fundamentals
         of Christianity

G 41   Drug rehabilitation

G 42   Alcohol rehabilitation

G 50   Personal

G 51   Family

G 52   Children

G 53   Marriage

G 54   Grief/bereavement

G 55   Homosexuals

H   Education

Educational institutions support and promote the growth of students through education in the context of a Christian worldview; also included in this category are organizations that exist to support and develop educational institutions' effort to provide biblically based education.

H 10   **Colleges/universities—organizations that provide higher education from a Christian worldview perspective**

H 11   Bible colleges—the estimated 600 organizations that specifically prepare and train individuals for ministry, for evangelism, and for church planting, with a curriculum offering at least thirty hours of Bible courses; generally not offering bachelor's degrees but focusing their efforts solely on ministry and the Bible

H 12   Christian colleges/universities—generally, four-year institutions that offer bachelor's degrees and frequently graduate degrees with biblically based classes

H 20   **Seminaries/professional graduate schools—institutions of higher learning that offer postgraduate studies**

H 21   Seminaries—postgraduate schools that offer biblical study in preparation for ministry

H 22   Graduate schools—organizations that offer advanced degrees beyond the bachelor's degree, in a wide variety of specific fields

H 30   **Christian preschools—organizations that provide a biblically based learning environment for children before they enter kindergarten**

H 40   **Christian elementary schools—organizations among the more than 19,000 church-affiliated K–12 schools (according to the National Center for Education) and the American Association of Christian Schools membership of approximately 3,000 (Lockerbie, 1996)**

H 41   Elementary (K–8)

H 42   High school (9–12)

H 50   **Educational support**

H 60   **Special education—organizations that provide biblically based learning opportunities for individuals with learning disabilities or unique learning requirements**

H 70   Training and seminar ministries—organizations that provides training, often through seminars and special training materials, in specific subjects such as ministry and leadership

H 80   Christian apologetics—organizations that provide programs that assist Christians in defending their faith

I   Environmental/Agricultural

Environmental and agricultural organizations and programs acknowledge Christ as Creator of the world and focus on preservation and protection of the environment that he created. Generally, the concerns of these organizations include preserving endangered lands, rescuing endangered species, campus activism, establishment of research and education centers, academic programs, camps, leadership training, and retreats.

I 10   Pollution/waste control

I 20   Wildlife preservation

I 30   Agriculture

I 40   Water conservation

I 50   Conservation

J   Evangelism

In a broad sense all parachurch organizations have some element of evangelism in their mission or purpose statement. However, evangelistic organizations are specifically designed to preach and promote the Gospel to any and all peoples of the world via all media (television, radio, conferences, crusades, seminars, literature, and so forth). These organizations exist primarily for the purpose of winning souls to Christ.

J 10   Individual evangelistic associations—generally organizations that are led by one specific speaker/leader

J 20   General evangelistic associations—generally a pool of speakers and lecturers on which ministries rely

J 30   Evangelical ministries—individuals who use their chosen careers and talents to minister to and evangelize others

K   Health Care

Parachurch health care organizations or programs promote the wellness of individuals, provide general treatment and prevention of diseases, and have biblically based foundations or philosophies.

K 10	**Hospitals—organizations that primarily provide short- or long-term inpatient care**
K 11	Specialty hospitals—hospitals that specialize in one particular area of treatment or study
K 12	General hospitals—hospitals that provide general and routine acute inpatient services
K 20	**Public health/community clinics—organizations that provide basic outpatient wellness checkups, particularly in low-income areas**
K 30	**Long-term care homes—the estimated 6,000 institutions that provide living arrangements or continuous long-term care to elderly or disabled populations**
K 31	Convalescent hospitals—hospitals that provide nursing care and rehabilitation services to elderly, disabled, or terminally ill populations
K 32	Nursing homes—institutions that provide skilled nursing care around the clock
K 33	Retirement homes—institutions that provide accountability, fellowship, and support for active elderly residents who are able to live independently but who also desire community environment with other elderly residents
K 40	**Mental health facilities**
K 41	Inpatient hospitals
K 42	Group homes—homes that offer housing, counseling, and rehabilitation with a biblically based treatment plan to people suffering from a mental illness
K 43	Crisis intervention programs
K 44	Addictive disorders/eating disorders
K 45	Family/friend support—organizations that provide support for family and friends of those suffering with a mental illness
K 50	**Health support services**

K 51	Transport services/blood banks
K 52	Supplies
K 53	Pastoral support
K 54	Support groups—networks that support people who are in similar situations because of the health of a family member
K 55	Funding
K 60	**Medical ministries—organizations that provide medical care as a free ministry to a particular community or population for the purpose of furthering the Gospel**
K 61	Foreign
K 62	Domestic
K 63	Support services

L Legal Assistance/Political Action

Legal assistance and political action organizations do research and lobby and serve as legal advocates and consultants to individuals, families, and special purpose groups on financial, employment, and family issues and on public policies.

L 10	**Legal assistance**
L 11	Financial
L 20	**Political action**
L 21	Family concerns
L 22	Research
L 23	Public policy/lobbying
L 24	International

M Missions

Missions take and spread the word of God to areas both domestic (including the inner city) and international where people have not heard the Christian message. It is estimated that there are over 700 mission organizations whose headquarters are based in North America. In addition, mission support organizations are included in this category; they assist mission organizations in areas such as finance, training, prayer, materials, and transportation.

M 10	**International missions**
M 11	Translators
M 12	Short-term
M 20	**Domestic missions**
M 21	Adult
M 22	Children
M 23	College students
M 30	**Mission support**
M 31	Aviation ministries
M 40	**Inner city**
M 50	**International medical missions**
M 51	Medical/dental
M 60	**Domestic medical missions**
M 61	Medical/dental

N   Print Media

Print media create, compile, produce, and disseminate printed material for the purpose of furthering the Gospel. They also supply other organizations that distribute or sell the material. Also included in this category are literacy programs that encourage learning to read a particular language in order to understand the Gospel.

N 10	**Bible printing agencies**
N 11	International distribution
N 12	Domestic distribution
N 13	Retail distribution
N 20	**Publication and distribution**
N 21	Books
N 22	Music
N 23	Magazines
N 24	Bibles
N 25	Tracts
N 26	Foreign

N 30	**Literacy programs**
N 31	English as a first language
N 32	English as a second language
N 33	Languages other than English

O   Relief and Development

Relief and development organizations provide services and materials such as food, medical supplies, and other critical needs to aid people facing disasters, largely outside the United States, and they also provide help to reestablish and develop the area. These organizations frequently serve as conduits for government aid.

O 10	**International relief and development**
O 11	Food
O 12	Water

P   Social Services

Social service organizations provide a broad range of human services to individuals, families, and communities in an attempt to show Christ's love and to assist people in dealing with the crisis or pain in their lives, restoring them to a higher level of functioning. This category includes services that provide care for children unable to care for themselves independently but whose parents are no longer providing support for various reasons. Gospel missions are also included in this category because they offer a variety of social services.

P 10	**Child support**
P 20	**Family support**
P 21	Family shelters
P 22	Family loan programs
P 30	**Women's support**
P 31	Abuse
P 32	Crisis pregnancy centers
P 40	**Community development**

P 41	Housing
P 42	Safety
P 43	Food
P 44	Technology
P 45	Clothing
P 50	**Child sponsorship—organizations that provide others with opportunities to support a child in need**
P 60	**Gospel rescue missions—the estimated 750 to 1,000 rescue missions founded on a biblical philosophy**
P 61	International
P 62	Domestic

REFERENCES

Adizes, I. *Corporate Lifecycles: How and Why Corporations Grow and Die and What to Do About It.* Upper Saddle River, N.J.: Prentice Hall, 1988.

Andringa, R. C. "Trustees: Their Essential Leadership Function." In W. Willmer (ed.), *Advancing Christian Higher Education.* Washington, D.C.: Coalition for Christian Colleges and Universities, 1996.

Andringa, R. C., and Engstrom, T. *The Nonprofit Board Answer Book: Practical Guidelines for Board Members and Chief Executives.* Washington, D.C.: National Center for Nonprofit Boards, 1997.

Anthony, M. J. *The Effective Church Board.* Grand Rapids, Mich.: Baker, 1994.

Aversa, J. "Survey: More Believe in God." *Orange County Register,* Dec. 22, 1997, p. 19.

Barna, G. *The Power of Vision.* Ventura, Calif.: Regal Books, 1992.

Barna, G. *The Mind of the Donor.* Glendale, Calif.: Barna Research Group, 1994.

Barrett, D. "Annual Statistical Table on Global Mission: 1996." *International Bulletin of Missionary Research,* 1997, *18*(1), 23–24.

Bebbington, D. W. *Evangelism in Modern Britain: A History from the 1730s to the 1980s.* London: Unwin Hyman, 1989.

Bell, P. D. *Fulfilling the Public Trust: Ten Ways to Help Nonprofit Boards Maintain Accountability.* Washington, D.C.: National Center for Nonprofit Boards, 1993.

Benefiel, R. "Transitional Communities and Multi-Congregational Ministry." *Urban Mission,* June 1996, pp. 38–47.

Bennett, W. "Quantifying America's Decline." *Wall Street Journal,* May 1993, Classroom Edition, p. 12.

Biehl, B., and Engstrom, T. *Boardroom Confidence.* Sisters, Oreg.: Questar, 1988.

Billy Graham Evangelistic Association. *Centerline* (Billy Graham Center of Wheaton College, Illinois), summer 1994, p. 3.

Bork, R. *Slouching Towards Gomorrah.* New York: HarperCollins, 1996.

Boskin, O., Aronoff, C., and Lattimore, D. *Public Relations: The Profession and the Practice.* Dubuque, Iowa: Brown and Benchmark, 1997.

Bright, B. *Come Help Change the World.* San Bernardino, Calif.: Here's Life, 1985.

Brown, D. *Understanding Pietism.* Grand Rapids, Mich.: Eerdmans, 1978.

Bryson, J. M. *Strategic Planning for Public and Nonprofit Organizations: A Guide for Strengthening and Sustaining Organizational Achievement.* San Francisco: Jossey-Bass, 1988.

Bunyan, J. *Grace Abounding to the Chief of Sinners.* Grand Rapids, Mich.: Zondervan, 1948. (Originally published 1666.)

Buss, D. *Giving Wings to the Gospel: The Remarkable Story of Mission Aviation Fellowship.* Grand Rapids, Mich.: Baker, 1995.

Calvin, J. *Institutes of the Christian Religion.* Vol. 1. Philadelphia: Westminster Press, 1960.

Carpenter, J. A. "Propagating the Faith Once Delivered: The Fundamentalist Missionary Enterprise, 1920–1945." In J. A. Carpenter and W. Shenk (eds.), *Earthen Vessels: American Evangelicals and Foreign Missions, 1880–1980.* Grand Rapids, Mich.: Eerdmans, 1990.

Carroll, J. W., Johnson, D. W., and Marty, M. E. *Religion in America: 1950 to the Present.* San Francisco: Harper San Francisco, 1979.

Carver, J. *Boards That Make a Difference: A New Design for Leadership in Nonprofit and Public Organizations.* San Francisco: Jossey-Bass, 1990.

Chandler, R. *Racing Toward 2001: The Forces Shaping America's Religious Future.* Grand Rapids, Mich.: Zondervan, 1992.

Christian Management Association. *Christian Ministries Board Survey.* Diamond Bar, Calif.: Christian Management Association, 1986.

Christian Management Association. *Christian Management Report.* Diamond Bar, Calif.: Christian Management Association, Feb. 1997.

Christianity Today, Nov. 6, 1981, cover.

Christian Stewardship Association. "Strategic Planning Discussion Document." Milwaukee, Wis., Sept. 7, 1996.

Clark, D. W., and Virts, P. H. *Changing Channels.* Milwaukee, Wis.: Christian Stewardship Association, 1996.

Clydesdale, T. T. "Soul-Winning and Social Work: Giving and Caring in the Evangelical Tradition." In R. Wuthnow, V. A. Hodgkinson, and Associates (eds.), *Faith and Philanthropy in America: Exploring the Role of Religion in America's Voluntary Sector.* San Francisco: Jossey-Bass, 1990.

Collins, J. C., and Porras, J. I. *Built to Last: Successful Habits of Visionary Companies.* New York: HarperCollins, 1994.

Conway, D. *The Reluctant Steward: A Report and Commentary on the Stewardship and Development Study.* Indianapolis, Ind.: Christian Theological Seminary, 1992.

Co-Operating in World Evangelization: A Handbook on Church/Para-Church Relationships. Lausanne Occasional Papers, no. 24. Lausanne, Switzerland: Lausanne Committee for World Evangelization, 1983.

Covey, S. R. *The Seven Habits of Highly Effective People.* New York: Simon & Schuster, 1989.

Covey, S. R. *First Things First: To Live, to Love, to Learn, to Leave a Legacy.* New York: Simon & Schuster, 1994.

Dobson, J. *Dare to Discipline.* Wheaton, Ill.: Tyndale House, 1970.

Douglas, J. D. (ed.). *Let the Earth Hear His Voice.* Proceedings of the International Congress on World Evangelization, Lausanne, Switzerland. Minneapolis, Minn.: Worldwide, 1974.

Peter F. Drucker Foundation for Nonprofit Management. *The Drucker Foundation Self-Assessment Tool for Nonprofit Organizations. Participant's Workbook: The Five Most Important Questions You Will Ever Ask About Your Organization.* San Francisco: Jossey-Bass, 1993.

Drucker, P. F. *Managing in a Time of Great Change.* New York: Truman Valley Books, 1995.

Engel, J. F. *A Clouded Future? Advancing North American World Missions.* Milwaukee, Wis.: Christian Stewardship Association, 1996.

Evangelical Council for Financial Accountability. *Evangelical Council for Financial Accountability Member Profile Directory.* Washington, D.C.: Evangelical Council for Financial Accountability, 1996.

Findlay, J. F., Jr. *Dwight L. Moody: American Evangelist 1837–1899.* Chicago: University of Chicago Press, 1969.

Focus on the Family. *Who We Are and What We Stand For.* Colorado Springs, Colo.: Focus on the Family, 1997.

Franklin, B. *The Autobiography of Benjamin Franklin.* Mineola, N.Y.: Dover, 1996. (Originally published 1868.)

Fultz, J. "Since CARLA Joined Our Team." *Notes on Translation,* 1995, 9(4), 25–26.

Gerson, M. J. "Do Do-Gooders Do Much Good?" *U.S. News and World Report,* Apr. 28, 1997, p. 34.

Giles, K. *What on Earth Is the Church? An Exploration in New Testament Theology.* Downers Grove, Ill.: InterVarsity Press, 1995.

Gouillart, F. J., and Kelly, J. N. *Transforming the Organization.* New York: McGraw-Hill, 1995.

Graham, B. *Just as I Am: The Autobiography of Billy Graham.* San Francisco: HarperCollins, 1997.

Graves, J. "Plugging the Theological Brain Drain." *Evangelical Missions Quarterly,* Apr. 1992, 26(2), 157–161.

Greeley, A. M., and McManus, W. C. *Catholic Contributions: Sociology and Policy.* Chicago: Thomas More Press, 1987.

Green, J. C. "The 1992 Survey of Religion and Politics." Report to the Pew Charitable Trusts. Akron, Ohio: Survey Research Center, University of Akron, 1992.

Hart, S. "Religious Giving: Patterns and Variations." Paper presented at the annual meeting of the Religious Research Association and the Society for the Scientific Study of Religion, Virginia Beach, Va., Nov. 9, 1990.

Hatch, N. O., and Hamilton, M. S. "Can Evangelicalism Survive Its Own Success?" *Christianity Today,* Oct. 5, 1992, pp. 20–31.

Hayes, E. L. "Effective Boardmanship." *Christian Management Research,* Dec.–Jan. 1987, p. 37.

Hefley, J., and Hefley, M. *Uncle Cam: The Story of William Cameron Townsend, Founder of the Wycliffe Bible Translators and the Summer Institute of Linguistics.* Waco, Tex.: Word, 1974.

Hirsch, D. "Taking the Whole Message to the Whole World." *Together,* July–Sept. 1996, pp. 4–6.

Hodge, C. *Systematic Theology.* Vol. 3. Grand Rapids, Mich.: Eerdmans, 1989.

Hodgins, P. "Program Teaches No Such Thing as Free Lunch." *Orange County Register,* Jan. 19, 1997, p. 6.

Hodgkinson, V. A. "The Future of Individual Giving and Volunteering: The Inseparable Link Between Religious Community and Individual Generosity." In R. Wuthnow, V. A. Hodgkinson, and Associates (eds.), *Faith and Philanthropy in America: Exploring the Role of Religion in America's Voluntary Sector.* San Francisco: Jossey-Bass, 1990.

Hodgkinson, V. A., and Weitzman, M. S. *Giving and Volunteering in the United States.* Findings from a national survey conducted by the Gallup Organization. Washington, D.C.: Independent Sector, 1994.

Hodgkinson, V. A., and Weitzman, M. S. *The Nonprofit Almanac.* San Francisco: Jossey-Bass, 1996.

Hodgkinson, V. A., Weitzman, M. S., and Kirsch, A. D. *From Belief to Commitment: The Activities and Finances of Religious Congregations in the United States.* Washington, D.C.: Independent Sector, 1988.

Hoge, D. R., and Griffin, D. L. *Research on Factors Influencing Giving to Religious Bodies.* Indianapolis, Ind.: Ecumenical Center for Stewardship Studies, 1992.

Hunter, J. D. *Evangelicalism: The Coming Generation.* Chicago: University of Chicago Press, 1987.

Hybels, Bill. *The God You're Looking For.* Waco, Tex.: Word, 1997.

Ingram, R. T. *Ten Basic Responsibilities of Nonprofit Boards.* Washington, D.C.: National Center for Nonprofit Boards, 1996.

InterVarsity. *We're Glad You Asked About InterVarsity Fellowship.* Downers Grove, Ill.: InterVarsity Press (n.d.).

Jeavons, T. H. "Trustees as Stewards: Secular Insights from a Sacred Concept." Paper written for the Symposium on Trusteeship held by the Indiana University Center on Philanthropy, Indianapolis, Nov. 16, 1992.

Kouzes, J. M., and Posner, B. Z. *The Leadership Challenge: How to Keep Getting Extraordinary Things Done in Organizations.* San Francisco: Jossey-Bass, 1995.

Leffel, J., and McCallum, D. "The Postmodern Challenge: Facing the Spirit of the Age." *Christian Research Journal,* fall 1996, pp. 35–40.

Lewis, P. V. *Transformational Leadership.* Nashville, Tenn.: Broadman and Holman, 1996.

Linden, D., and Machan, D. "CEO Profile." *Forbes,* 1997, *59*(10), 152–160.

Lockerbie, B. *From Candy Sales to Committed Donors.* Milwaukee, Wis.: Christian Stewardship Association, 1996.

Malphurs, A. *Developing a Vision for Ministry in the Twenty-First Century.* Grand Rapids, Mich.: Baker, 1992.

Mancuso, A. (ed.). *How to Form a Nonprofit Corporation.* Berkeley, Calif.: Nolo Press, 1996.

Marsden, G. M. *Fundamentalism and American Culture: The Shaping of Twentieth-Century Evangelicalism, 1870–1925.* New York: Oxford University Press, 1980.

Marsden, G. M. *The Soul of the American University: From Protestant Establishment to Established Nonbelief.* New York: Oxford University Press, 1994.

Martin, W. "Mass Communications." In C. Lippy and P. Williams (eds.), *Encyclopedia of the American Religious Experience.* New York: Scribner, 1988.

Maxwell, J. *Developing the Leader Within You.* Nashville, Tenn.: Nelson, 1993.

McKay, P. "The Multiplication Factor." *Stillpoint,* 1997, *12*(2), 18.

Modie, N. "'Lunch Lady, You Save Our Lives!' a Down-and-Outer Says." *Seattle Post-Intelligencer,* Nov. 9, 1997, p. A11.

Nason, J. *Trustee Responsibilities.* Washington, D.C.: Association of Governing Boards of Universities and Colleges, 1989.

"National and International Religion Report." *Current Thoughts and Trends,* May 1994, p. 6.

Neill, S. *A History of Christian Missions.* New York: Penguin Books, 1964.

Newbigen, L. *Sign of the Kingdom.* Grand Rapids, Mich.: Eerdmans, 1980.

Newbigen, L. *The Other Side of 1984: Questions for the Churches.* Geneva: World Council of Churches, 1983.

Noll, M. *A History of Christianity in the United States and Canada.* Grand Rapids, Mich.: Eerdmans, 1992.

Olasky, M. *The Tragedy of American Compassion.* Washington, D.C.: Regnery, 1992.

Patterson, J. T. *Grand Expectations: The United States, 1945–1974.* New York: Oxford University Press, 1996.

Payton, R. L. "God and Money." In D. F. Burlingame (ed.), *The Responsibilities of Wealth.* Bloomington: Indiana University Press, 1992.

Pollard, B. "Serving Where It Makes a Difference." *Boardwise,* May–June 1997, pp. 4–5.

Pollock, J. *Billy Graham: Evangelist to the World.* Minneapolis, Minn.: Worldwide, 1979.

Rabey, S. "John Maxwell's INJOY: Modeling Leadership Principles." *Christian Management Report,* July 1997, pp. 5–6.

Reid, D. (ed.). *Dictionary of Christianity in America.* Downers Grove, Ill.: InterVarsity Press, 1990.

Rice, E. W. *The American Sunday-School Movement and the American Sunday-School Union, 1780–1927.* Philadelphia: Union Press, 1927.

Richards, L. O., and Hoeldtke, C. *A Theology of Church Leadership.* Grand Rapids, Mich.: Zondervan, 1980.

Roberts, W. D., and Siewert, J. A. (eds.). *Mission Handbook.* (14th ed.) Monrovia, Calif.: Missions Advanced Research Communications Center, 1990.

Ronsvalle, J. L., and Ronsvalle, S. *The State of Church Giving Through 1991.* Champaign, Ill.: Empty Tomb, 1992.

Ronsvalle, J. L., and Ronsvalle, S. *Behind the Stained Glass Windows: Money Dynamics in the Church.* Grand Rapids, Mich.: Baker, 1996.

St. Augustine. *Confessions.* New York: Penguin Books, 1961.

Salvation Army. *People: Our Priority.* The Salvation Army, Eastern Territory (n.d.). Nyack, N.Y.

Skinner, B. L. *Daws: The Story of Dawson Trotman.* Grand Rapids, Mich.: Zondervan, 1974.

Smith, D. *All God's Children: A Theology of the Church.* Wheaton, Ill.: Victor Books, 1996.

Snyder, H. A. *The Problem of Wine Skins: Church Structure in a Technological Age.* Downers Grove, Ill.: InterVarsity Press, 1975.

Stafford, T. "His Father's Son." *Christianity Today,* Apr. 22, 1988, pp. 16–22.

Stafford, T. "Anatomy of a Giver." *Christianity Today,* May 19, 1997, 41(6), 20–24.

Stevenson, H. F. (ed.). *The Ministry of Keswick: A Selection from the Bible Readings Delivered at the Keswick Convention.* Grand Rapids, Mich.: Zondervan, 1963.

Stoeffler, F. E. *The Rise of Evangelical Piety.* Leiden, the Netherlands: Brill, 1965.

Stoeffler, F. E. *Continental Pietism and Early Christianity.* Grand Rapids, Mich.: Eerdmans, 1976.

Stout, H. S. *The Divine Dramatist: George Whitefield and the Rise of Modern Evangelicalism.* Grand Rapids, Mich.: Eerdmans, 1991.

Stowell, J. "Re-Engineering the Vision." Speech presented to the Evangelical Foreign Mission Association, Colorado Springs, Colo., Sept. 18, 1995.

Taylor, B. E., Chait, R. P., and Holland, T. P. "The New Work of the Non-Profit Board." *Harvard Business Review,* Sept.–Oct. 1996, pp. 36–46.

Taylor, J., and Wacker, W. *The 500-Year Delta.* New York: HarperCollins, 1997.

Tillapaugh, F. R. *Unleashing the Church: Getting People out of the Fortress and into Ministry.* Ventura, Calif.: Regal Books, 1982.

Tocqueville, A. de. *Democracy in America.* New York: New American Library, 1956. (Originally published 1835.)

Trueheart, C. "Welcome to the Next Church." *Atlantic Monthly,* Aug. 1996, pp. 37–58.

Van Gelder, C. "A Great New Fact of Our Day: America as Mission Field." In G. Hunsberger and C. Van Gelder (eds.), *The Church Between Gospel and Culture: The Emerging Mission in North America.* Grand Rapids, Mich.: Eerdmans, 1996.

Walls, A. F. "The American Dimension in the History of the Missionary Movement." In J. Carpenter and W. Shenk (eds.), *Earthen Vessels: American Evangelicals and Foreign Missions, 1880–1980.* Grand Rapids, Mich.: Eerdmans, 1990.

Weisbord, M. R. *Productive Workplaces: Organizing and Managing for Dignity, Meaning and Community.* San Francisco: Jossey-Bass, 1987.

White, A. H. "Patterns of Giving." In R. Magat (ed.), *Philanthropic Giving: Studies in Varieties and Goals.* New York: Oxford University Press, 1989.

White, J. *The Church and the Parachurch: An Uneasy Marriage.* Portland, Oreg.: Multnomah Press, 1983.

Williams, R., and Miller, M. *Chartered for His Glory: Biola University, 1908–1983.* La Mirada, Calif.: Associated Students of Biola University, 1983.

Willmer, W. K. (ed.). *Money for Ministries.* Wheaton, Ill.: Scripture Press, 1989.

Willmer, W. K. *The Financing of Selected American Protestant Parachurch Religious Institutions.* Final report to the Lilly Endowment, Mar. 29, 1996.

Winter, R. *The Warp and Woof: Organizing for Mission.* Pasadena, Calif.: William Carey Library, 1970.

World Vision International. "World Vision." [http://www.wvi.org]. June 1997.

Wosh, P. *Spreading the Word: The Biblical Business in Nineteenth-Century America.* Ithaca, N.Y.: Cornell University Press, 1994.

Wuthnow, R. *The Restructuring of American Religion: Society and Faith Since World War II.* Princeton, N.J.: Princeton University Press, 1988.

Wuthnow, R. "Pious Materialism: How Americans View Faith and Money." *Christian Century,* Mar. 3, 1993, pp. 238–239.

Wuthnow, R. *God and Mammon in America.* New York: Free Press, 1994a.

Wuthnow, R. "Small Groups: A National Profile." In R. Wuthnow (ed.), *I Come Away Stronger: How Small Groups Are Shaping American Religion.* Grand Rapids, Mich.: Eerdmans, 1994b.

Xenophon. *Conversations of Socrates.* New York: Penguin Books, 1990.

Yankelovich, Skelly, and White, Inc. *The Charitable Behavior of Americans.* Washington, D.C.: Independent Sector, 1986.

Youngren, J. A. "Parachurch Proliferation: The Frontier Spirit Caught in Traffic." *Christianity Today,* Nov. 6, 1981, pp. 39–40.

Zoba, W. M. "Bill Bright's Wonderful Plan for the World." *Christianity Today,* July 14, 1997, pp. 14–27.

INDEX

Jesus Christ, 29, 74, 90, 97, 104, 115, 145, 147
Jews for Jesus, 4
Johnson, D. W., 32
Johnson, L. B., 161, 190
Jonah, story of, 10
Journals (Whitefield), 35
Jungle Aviation and Radio Service, 56

K

Kelly, J. N., 128
Keswick Convention, 172
Killian McCabe and Associates, 160
King, M. L., Jr., 126
Kingdom mind-set, from ethnocentric concerns to, 192–193
Kinsey, A., 49
Kirsch, A. D., 102
Knudson, J., 79
Korean War, 53
Kouzes, J. M., 91

L

Lattimore, D., 62
Lausanne Conference for World Evangelization, 180
Leadership, parachurch: definition of, 89–91; and identification of new leaders, 98–99; and intentional leadership, 91–94; and understanding lack of leadership, 94–98; uniqueness of, 88–89
Leadership style, 70
Leffel, J., 45, 46
Lennon, J., 125–126
Let the Earth Hear His Voice (Douglas), 24
Lewis, P. V., 148
Ligonier Ministries, 26
Lilly Endowment, 68, 134
Lindbergh, C., 56

Linden, D., 108–109
Long Beach Rescue Mission, 25
Los Angeles First Church of the Nazarene, 188, 189
Los Angeles Union Rescue Mission, 7, 75
Luke, Gospel According to, 164
Luther, M., 108

M

Machan, D., 108–109
MAF. *See* Mission Aviation Fellowship
Malachi, Book of, 165, 172
Malphurs, A., 131
Managerial myopia, 122
Managing in a Time of Great Change (Drucker), 18
Mancuso, A., 17
Marriage Servers, 6
Marsden, G. M., 51
Martin, W., 42
Marty, M. E., 32
Mather, F., 157
Mather, J., 157
Matthew, Gospel According to, 29, 90, 106, 108, 163
Maxwell, J., 5, 94
McAllister, D., 129
McCabe, T., 160
McCallum, D., 45, 46
McGee, J. V., 9
McKay, P., 164
McManus, W. C., 103
McNeal, R., 192
McPherson, A. S., 42
Megachurch, 194–196
Message, versus charisma, 88
Methodist denomination, 30
Miller, M., 51, 52
Ministries: and environmental concerns, 6; and evangelism, 5–6; and social work, 6; and specialization, 25–27; variety of, 5–7